MW01251440

Connectionist Modelling in Cognitive Neuropsychology: A Case Study

Connectionist Modelling in Cognitive Neuropsychology: A Case Study

David C. Plaut

Department of Psychology, Carnegie Mellon University, Pittsburgh, USA

Tim Shallice

Department of Psychology, University College London, London, UK

LAWRENCE ERLBAUM ASSOCIATES, PUBLISHERS
Hove (UK) Hillsdale (USA)

Lawrence Erlbaum Associates Ltd., Publishers
27 Palmeira Mansions
Church Road
Hove
East Sussex, BN3 2FA
UK

British Library Cataloguing in Publication Data

A catalogue record for this book is available from the British Library

ISBN 0-86377-336-2
ISSN 0959-4779

Printed and bound in the United Kingdom by BPC Wheatons Ltd., Exeter

CONTENTS

Publisher's Note: Pages 26–153 of this book were first published in *Cognitive Neuropsychology*, 1993, 10(5), 377–500.

INTRODUCTION

Many cognitive abilities can be impaired selectively as a result of brain damage. Among these are object recognition, selective attention, reading, writing, language understanding, speech production, memory, planning, and reasoning. The field of cognitive neuropsychology studies the patterns of impaired and preserved abilities of brain-injured patients, and attempts to relate them to models of normal cognitive functioning. The aim is both to explain the behaviour of the patients in terms of the effects of damage in the model, and to inform the model based on the observed behaviour of patients (Coltheart, 1985; Ellis & Young, 1988; McCarthy & Warrington, 1990; Shallice, 1988).

At first it may seem that little can be learned about the normal operation of an information-processing device as complicated as the brain on the basis of how it behaves under damage. To put it bluntly (Marin, Saffran, & Schwartz, 1976, p. 868), "What can you possibly learn about the way a car works (or a vacuum cleaner, or a computer) by pounding it with a sledgehammer." This extreme objection, however, has real power only if one assumes that symptoms of the damaged system correspond directly to functions within the normal system (Gregory, 1961). Nonetheless, the theoretical difficulties in relating studies of normal and impaired cognitive processes can be substantial (see Shallice, 1988). The current work aims to demonstrate that computational modelling of cognitive processes can play a central role in clarifying the implications of cognitive disorders for our understanding of normal cognition.

Modularity and Dissociations

At its most basic level, the viability of cognitive neuropsychology has rested on what is known as the "modularity hypothesis" (Fodor, 1983; Marr, 1976). On this hypothesis, the functional architecture of the mind is composed of relatively independent subsystems, or modules, that each specialise in carrying out a particular function or in processing a particular type of information. The modules are also held to be neuroanatomically separate, and so can be impaired independently by brain damage. The most straightforward argument in favour of a modular organisation is that it simplifies the design and improvement of the system as a whole (Marr, 1976, p. 485; also see Simon, 1969).

> Any large computation should be split up and implemented as a collection of small sub-parts that are as nearly independent of one another as the overall task allows. If a process is not designed in this way, a small change in one place will have consequences in many other places. This means that the process as a whole becomes extremely difficult to debug or to improve, whether by a human designer or in the course of natural evolution, because

> a small change to improve one part has to be accompanied by many simultaneous compensating changes elsewhere.

Empirical support for modularity comes from the existence of highly specialised cortical areas (Van Essen, 1985), and the relative success of "additive factors" methodology in psychology (Roberts & Sternberg, 1992; Sternberg, 1969). However, the most intuitively compelling, although not the most rigorous, evidence for isolable cognitive subsystems comes from the occurrence of selective cognitive deficits in some neurological patients.

An important methodology in cognitive neuropsychology for isolating cognitive modules involves demonstrating dissociations between the performance of a patient on different tasks. Two tasks are dissociated when the patient performs significantly worse on one than on the other. Ideally, performance on the poor task is much worse than that of normals, whereas performance on the good task is within the normal range.

A single dissociation, however, provides only limited information because it is possible that the poorly performed task is simply much more difficult than the other task, but still well within the abilities of normals. Of particular importance is the demonstration of a double dissociation, in which a second patient is found who also exhibits a dissociation on the same two tasks, but in the *opposite* direction. Under the assumption that the organisation of cognitive processes in the two patients is essentially the same, a double dissociation rules out an explanation based solely on the relative difficulties of the tasks. In this case, the fact that each task can be impaired selectively but still leave the other unaffected provides strong evidence that the two tasks are carried out by separable cognitive mechanisms. However, it should be kept in mind that the logic of making inferences from single and double dissociation is, in general, far more uncomplicated than described here, particularly when a patient's performance on the "unimpaired" task is not within normal limits (see Shallice, 1988, Chapter 10).

Rather more problematic, but still informative, are associations among symptoms exhibited by patients, particularly if the association is based on quantitative data (see Caramazza & McCloskey, 1991; Shallice, 1991, for discussion). If a patient is impaired on both of two tasks, it suggests that they are subserved by the same mechanism, which is now impaired. However, it is also possible that they are subserved by separate mechanisms that just happen to be affected by the same brain lesion because they are neuroanatomically close or related, or even that the patient has suffered multiple lesions. The argument for a common mechanism is strengthened somewhat if all or most of a large number of similar patients exhibit the same association, but neuroanatomical proximity remains a possible, if perhaps unpalatable, explanation.

In the current work, we focus on the difficult empirical puzzle posed by remarkable consistency in the association of a large, diverse set of symptoms exhibited by virtually all patients with a particular type of acquired reading disorder known as deep dyslexia. We show how this symptom-complex can be understood as a natural consequence of damage in a reading system that operates according to certain basic computational principles.

Information Processing Models

Models based on the modularity hypothesis and its subsidiary assumptions have flourished in cognitive neuropsychology (see, e.g., Caramazza, 1984; 1986; Coltheart, 1985; Coltheart, Sartori, & Job, 1987; Patterson, Coltheart, & Marshall, 1985). These models are typically cast as information-processing flow diagrams, otherwise known as "box-and-arrow" models. It is assumed that brain damage can impair or eliminate particular components in a model selectively, while the remaining components continue to operate normally. Giving an account of the deficits of a particular patient involves specifying a functional architecture, together with a set of "lesions" to the architecture, such that the resulting system "exhibits" the same pattern of impaired and preserved behaviour as does the patient. Figure 1 illustrates this approach for deep dyslexia (Morton & Patterson, 1980).

The fact that "exhibits" must be scare-quoted in the preceding paragraph reveals a major limitation in the way this methodology has typically been applied. Specifically, most effort has focused on identifying and fractionating the components of the functional architecture, whereas relatively little effort has gone into specifying the representations and computations within each component—exactly how the boxes work (although see Caramazza & Miceli, 1990; McCloskey, Badecker, Goodman-Schulman, & Aliminosa, 1994, for exceptions). In this way, conventional theorising in cognitive neuropsychology (Shallice, 1988, but see McCloskey & Caramazza, 1991) subscribes implicitly to the philosophy that it is possible to characterise a computation independently of the precise details of how that computation is implemented (Marr, 1982). It has been argued that, as a result, it is difficult to derive predictions of the behaviour of the model without more specific claims about the nature of the representations and computations that actually produce the behaviour (Seidenberg, 1988).

Computational Modelling

Typically, predictions of the behaviour of an information-processing model, both in normal operation and under damage, have consisted of descriptions based on fairly general notions about how the various modules

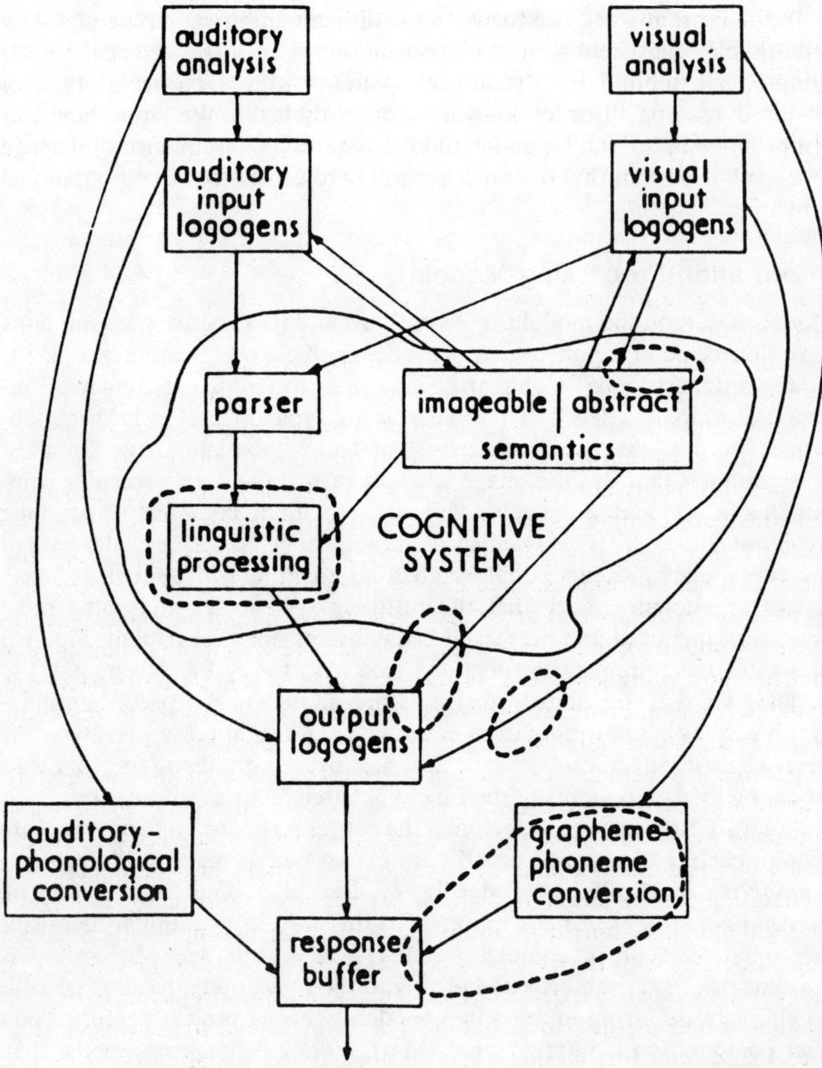

FIG. 1 An explanation for deep dyslexia in terms of lesions (enclosed by dotted lines) to a functional architecture for understanding and pronouncing written and spoken words. A written word is presented as a stimulus to the upper-right "visual analysis" component, and its pronunciation is read out of the "response buffer" at the bottom. (From Morton & Patterson, 1980, p. 115.)

would operate and interact. Although these types of predictions may suffice for capturing the more general characteristics of normal and impaired cognitive functioning, they become increasingly unreliable as the model is elaborated to account for more detailed phenomena. Computational modelling makes it possible to demonstrate that the underlying theory is sufficient to account for the phenomena by making the behaviour of a detailed cognitive model explicit. A working simulation is a stringent test of the underlying theory, guaranteeing that it is neither vague nor internally inconsistent. Furthermore, the behaviour of the simulation can be used to generate specific predictions of the theory. However, building a working simulation involves making design decisions that introduce theoretically irrelevant details. It is often difficult to identify what aspects of a model are responsible for its success, and the degree to which these aspects are theoretically motivated (see McCloskey, 1991; Seidenberg, 1993, for discussion specific to connectionist modelling). The most comprehensive approach involves an interplay between computational and empirical work, in which simulations focus experimentation on particular issues, and empirical results constrain the development of the computational model.

There are many alternative computational formalisms within which we can develop computational models of neuropsychological disorders. Perhaps the most straightforward modelling approach holds that the specific choice of formalism is unimportant. In this way, it retains the perspective of most box-and-arrow theorising, that the identity and function of each component in the model can be abstracted from the details of how that function is implemented. A clear example of this style of research is found in Kosslyn, Flynn, Amsterdam, and Wang's (1990) work in modelling object recognition and visuospatial processing in high-level vision.

Although a detailed description of the operation of the model falls outside our current concerns, a consideration of the general form and approach of the model is instructive. The model is cast within a conventional box-and-arrow framework (see Fig. 2). There are components for recognising objects based on features derived from information in a visual buffer that falls within an attentional window. Other components associate object identity with the identities and positions of parts of the object, and carry out the spatial transformations that relate the predicted parts with what is found in the visual buffer. The model aims to reproduce, and thereby account for, a wide range of normal and impaired behaviour in high-level vision.

A guiding principle in the design of the model is the "hierarchical decomposition constraint," which requires that elaboration of the model must only involve subdividing existing components rather than introducing components that cut across existing boundaries. The underlying assumption is that consideration of implementation details is germane only *after* the overall organisation of the system is determined. Accordingly, Kosslyn et al. (1990) provide very few details of the implementation of the model, stating (p. 243): "we are interested in the ways subsystems interact, not in

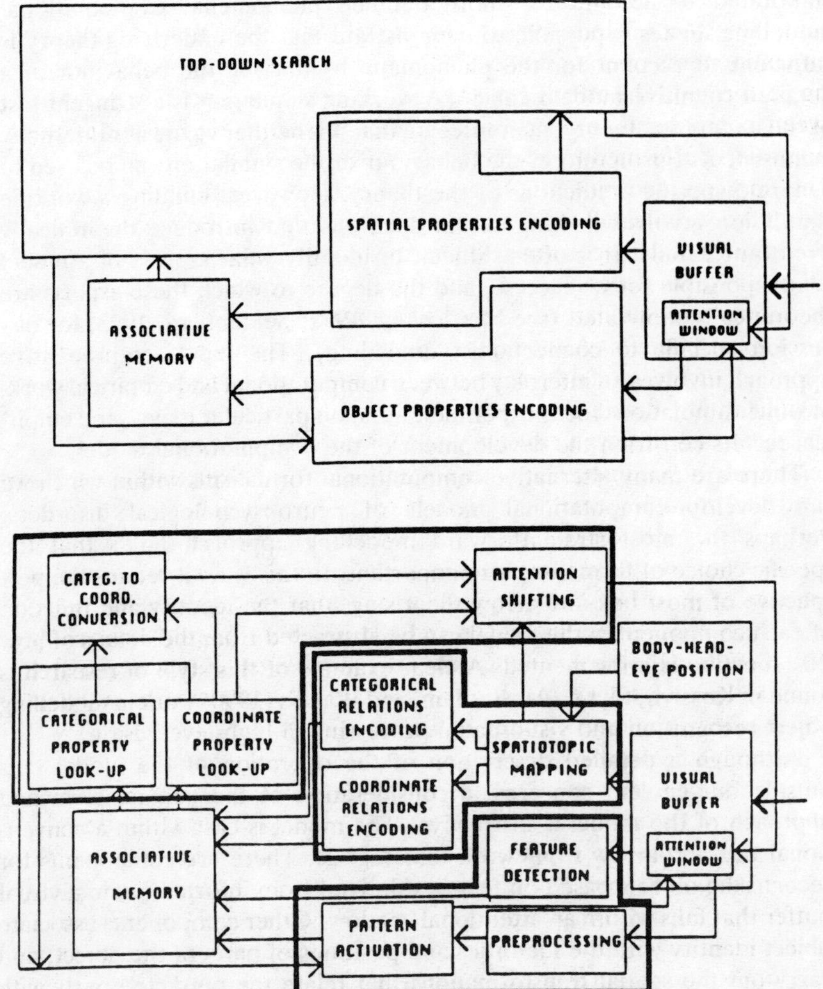

FIG. 2 Kosslyn, Flynn, Amsterdam, and Wang's (1990) model of high-level vision. The top figure (p. 214) presents the major subsystems of the model; the bottom figure (p. 237) presents the decomposition of these subsystems into specific functional components.

how they actually process input." Nonetheless, some aspects of the implementation can be inferred from descriptions in the text and from personal communication with S. Kosslyn (June, 1988).

The model is implemented as a conventional program, in which each component is a subroutine that manipulates data structures such as lists and arrays. Components can operate in parallel; however, each component must complete its computation before it generates output to other components (cf. McClelland, 1988). The control structure that determines when components operate is specified externally based on the task that is being performed. The effects of "damage" to each component, or pathway between components, are explicitly defined based on the nature of the computation performed by the component.

The implemented model performs a range of recognition and discrimination tasks on a small set of schematic, hand-segmented inputs. When the definitions of damage are applied to the model, it fails to perform some or all of the tasks depending on the nature of the damage. Some of these impairments are similar to the basic characteristics of some neuropsychological patients. Although many types of patients are discussed in the context of the model, no attempt is made actually to replicate their behaviour in any detail.

In evaluating this type of work, it is important to determine how the development of a computational model contributes to our understanding beyond the unimplemented description of the theory. The implemented model certainly demonstrates that the underlying theoretical claims are internally consistent and can give rise to the behaviour they are intended to explain. The role of computational modelling is less interesting, however, if it merely verifies the coherence of the theory. Ideally, modelling should contribute to the development of the theory per se. In fact, Kosslyn and his colleagues (1990, footnote p. 241) identify a number of ways in which the development of the model from earlier work (Kosslyn, 1987) was shaped by the process of developing a working implementation. Unfortunately, the possible opportunities for this type of interaction between modelling and theorising are limited significantly by the lack of attention paid to implementation details. In essence, the computational formalism of conventional programming is too unconstrained—it provides little bias towards carrying out computations in one way vs. another. Computational modelling can have a much more profound impact on theorising when the nature of the formalism strongly influences the organisation of the representations and computations in the model.

CONNECTIONIST MODELS

Computational modelling is most interesting when the formalism contributes significantly to a natural explanation for empirical phenomena that are counterintuitive when viewed within other formalisms. For this reason, connectionist networks are becoming increasingly influential in a number of areas of psychology as a methodology for developing computational models of cognitive processes. These networks compute via the parallel co-operative and competitive interactions of a large number of simple neuron-like processing units (see Fig. 3). Typically, each unit has an associated activity level, or *state*, typically ranging between 0 and 1. Positive or negative real-valued *weights* on connections between units modulate how the units interact. In most formulations, the total input to a unit is simply the weighted sum of the states of units from which it received connections; its own state is a smooth, nonlinear function of this total input. All of the long-term knowledge of the system is encoded in the weights; learning involves modifying the weights to improve performance on some task.

In performing a task, input is presented to the network by setting the states of some designated *input* units. The remaining units then update their states to be maximally consistent with each other, and with the input, given the knowledge encoded in the weights. The resulting pattern of activity across all of the units constitutes the network's interpretation of

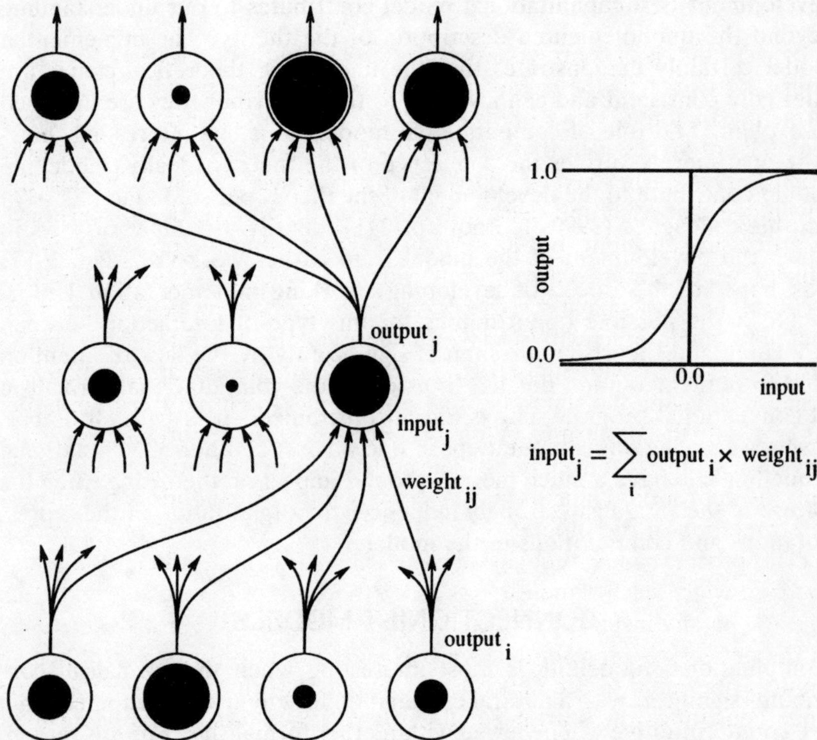

FIG. 3 A generic connectionist network, composed of layers of units (circles) that communicate via weighted connections (arrows). The output (state) of each unit, depicted by the size of the black circle within it, is a smooth, nonlinear function of its total input, which is a weighted sum of the outputs of other units.

the input. The states of designated *output* units represent the response of the network to the input. The input and output units are called *visible* because their correct states are determined by the environment external to the network; any remaining units are thus *hidden*. As the environment does not specify the states of hidden units, the learning procedure must develop internal representations over those units that are useful for solving the task.

Connectionist networks have been applied successfully to problems in a wide range of cognitive domains, such as high-level vision and attention, learning and memory, reading and language, speech recognition and production, and sequential reasoning (see Quinlan, 1991; McClelland, Rumelhart, & the PDP research group, 1986). For more details on the operation of connectionist networks, see Rumelhart, McClelland, and the PDP research group (1986b) and Hertz, Krogh, and Palmer (1991).

Attractors and Damage

A concept that is of central importance in relating the operation of connectionist networks to the behaviour of neurological patients is that of an attractor. In some connectionist networks, the units are organised into a sequence of layers such that units in later layers receive connections only from units in earlier layers. This type of *feedforward* architecture has the advantage that each unit need only compute its state (activity level) once in processing an input, but has the disadvantage that the possible ways in which units can interact are severely restricted. In contrast, more complex, *recurrent* networks have no restrictions on how units can be connected, so that units can interact within a layer and provide feedback to earlier layers. When presented with input, units must update their states repeatedly, because changing the state of a unit may change the input to earlier units. As a result, the pattern of activity over the entire network changes over time in response to a fixed input. The network must learn to settle gradually into the appropriate final pattern of activity that corresponds to the correct interpretation of the input.

This process can be thought of as movement in a multi-dimensional *state space* in which each dimension encodes the state of a particular unit (see Fig. 4). At any instant, the current pattern of activity over all of the units in the network is represented as a particular point in this space. When an input is presented to the network, the initial pattern of states of all of the units constitutes the starting point in state space. As units update their states, the overall pattern of activity changes over time, eventually settling into some final pattern representing the network's interpretation of the input. In state space, this settling process corresponds to movement of the initial point, eventually arriving at the point representing the final pattern.

FIG. 4 A depiction of attractors in state space (top), and a demonstration of their ability to clean-up or complete corrupted patterns (bottom). State space has a dimension for each unit in the network, although only two dimensions are shown here. Points *A* and *B* correspond to two possible initial (input) patterns. The arrows show the movement of points in state space towards one of the three attractor patterns. The dotted lines show the boundaries between the basins of the attractors. (From Hertz et al., 1991, pp. 12–13.)

Another input might settle to a different activity pattern, corresponding to a different final point. Each such final pattern is called an *attractor* in state space. In an attractor network, there is a region in state space around each attractor, called its *basin* of attraction, such that, if the activity of the network falls anywhere within this region, it will move towards the attractor during settling. In this way, attractor patterns are stable and similar patterns get pulled towards them. The shapes and positions of the attractor basins in state space depend on the ways that units interact, which in turn depend on the connection weights. Learning in a recurrent network amounts to building and shaping the attractor basins so that the network settles to the appropriate attractor when started at the initial pattern of activity corresponding to each input.

The usefulness of attractors becomes apparent when we consider how a recurrent network with a given set of weights maps initial activity patterns onto final activity patterns. All of the patterns within a particular basin of attraction map to the same attractor pattern. Since points that are nearby each other in state space represent similar patterns of activity, the operation of the attractor can be thought of as a kind of similarity-based categorisation. The fundamental property of attractors is that they carve up the large, typically continuous space of all possible activity patterns into a much smaller discrete set of (attractor) patterns on the basis of similarity.

The ability of attractors to give the same output to similar inputs is useful in many situations. For example, consider a network with attractors for particular input patterns. Suppose we present the network with a noisy or incomplete version of one of these patterns. As long as the corrupted pattern is more similar to the original than to any other (i.e. falls within the appropriate attractor basin), the operation of the network in settling will "clean-up" or "complete" the pattern. If each pattern is composed of separate types of information to be associated, such as a name with a face, then the ability of the network to reconstruct one part given another can be used to implement associative or content-addressable memory (Hinton & Anderson, 1981). The network can also be thought of as generalising to novel inputs that fall within the basin of attraction of a familiar input. Whether this generalisation is appropriate will depend on the definition of the task and on details of the layout of attractor basins.

In addition to giving the same interpretation to similar inputs, attractors are also useful when similar inputs require very *different* interpretations (points *A* and *B* in Fig. 4). An example of this is in understanding written words, in which it is common that visually similar words (e.g. CAR and CAP) must produce completely different meanings. This is difficult for connectionist networks in which the representation of an entity is distributed over a number of units (Hinton, McClelland, & Rumelhart, 1986). The reason is that other units are influenced by the input on the basis of a simple weighted sum of unit activities. Since similar inputs are represented by similar patterns of activity, they produce similar summed input to other units. In a feedforward network, this bias to give similar interpretations to similar inputs can be overcome either by introducing many layers of nonlinear units between the input and output, or by having very large weights between units. Unfortunately, both of these approaches require very long learning times. In a recurrent network, the nonlinear units recompute their states at every time step. As a result, state differences that are initially small can be magnified into quite large ones as the network settles. In essence, the network can learn to position the boundaries between attractor basins to "pull apart" similar initial patterns of activity so they settle to possibly quite distant final patterns. Thus, even though CAR and CAP may generate similar initial patterns, the network can ultimately settle on very different interpretations.

The nature of attractors is particularly important in understanding the effects of damage on the behaviour of a network. Damaging a connectionist network typically involves removing some of the units and/or connections, or adding random noise to the weights (although see Small, 1991, for a discussion of other possibilities). Attractors make a network more robust to damage in the same way as they clean-up noisy or incomplete input. In fact, corrupted input can be interpreted as damage to the input layer of the network. This damage changes the initial pattern of activity, moving the starting point of the network in state space. As long as this point still falls within the appropriate basin of attraction, the network behaves normally. However, if the noise or damage moves the starting point outside the basin of the correct attractor, the operation of the network will clean-up the initial pattern into the final pattern corresponding to some other attractor. This can be seen in Fig. 4 by imagining that the point *A* moves to the other side of the dotted line between *A* and *B* (representing a boundary between two attractor basins). The new final pattern for *A* may correspond to another familiar attractor, or it may correspond to an unfamiliar, "spurious" attractor. In either case, the network has misinterpreted the input and will generate an incorrect response. These incorrect responses are analogous to the errors made by some patients with brain damage in performing certain cognitive tasks.

The effects of damage to units and connections internal to the network turn out to be more complex than for damage to input units. If the damaged units and connections are involved in the interactions that implement the attractors, then damaging them corrupts the layout of the attractors themselves (the dotted lines in Fig. 4). Some attractors may disappear, others may be created, and the boundaries between existing attractors may move. These modifications can also cause an input to fall within the basin of attraction of an inappropriate attractor.

Connectionist Neuropsychology

Beyond their computational properties, a major attraction of using connectionist networks to model cognitive processes is that their abstract similarity to neurobiology suggests that the nature of computation in these networks may provide insight into how cognitive processes are implemented in the brain (Sejnowski, Koch, & Churchland, 1989). Evidence that is often put forward in support of this claim is that, like brains, connectionist networks degrade gracefully under damage. That is, with partial damage, the network's performance on a task is only partially impaired rather than being completely lost. However, most demonstrations of this property have considered the effects of damage only on very general measures of performance, such as the total number of errors on a task (e.g. Sejnowski & Rosenberg, 1987). The relevance of connectionist modelling to the neural implementation of cognitive processes would be far better established if it were shown that the *detailed* pattern of breakdown and recovery of behaviour in damaged connectionist networks resembles that of patients with cognitive impairments due to neurological damage. To this end, a number of researchers have begun to explore the correspondence of the behaviour of damaged connectionist networks and patient behaviour in a wide range of domains. Each of these studies shows how particular computational properties of connectionist networks can contribute to our understanding of complex, often counterintuitive, neuropsychological phenomena (also see Farah, 1994).

Early work by McClelland and Rumelhart (1986) showed how the patterns of retrograde and anterograde memory deficits, frequently claimed to occur in amnesic patients (e.g. Milner, 1966; Squire, 1987; but see Warrington & McCarthy, 1988), are also found in a network in which the consolidation of weight changes during learning has been degraded. More recently, Levine and colleagues (Bapi & Levine, 1990; Levine, 1986; Levine & Prueitt, 1989) modelled the tendency of patients with frontal lobe damage to repeat previous responses and be overly distracted by novel stimuli (e.g. Milner, 1963) by disrupting the interactions between sensory and reinforcement representations (also see Dehaene & Changeux, 1989; 1991). In other work concerning frontal lobe functioning, Cohen and Servan-Schreiber (1992) reproduced the characteristics of the abnormal use of context in schizophrenics by adjusting the sensitivity of units to their inputs in a way that corresponded to the influence on individual neurons of the abnormal levels of excitory neurotransmitters in these patients.

In the domain of semantic memory, Farah and McClelland (1991) reproduced a selective deficit in recognising and recalling functional information about living vs. nonliving things (Warrington & Shallice, 1984) by introducing damage to visual semantics, under the hypothesis that the representations of living things rely more heavily on visual than on functional information. In other work addressing visual comprehension, Plaut and Shallice (1993) reproduced the mixture of perseverative and semantic influences on the errors that optic aphasic patients make in naming visually presented objects (e.g. Lhermitte & Beauvois, 1973) by lesioning a network trained to generate semantics from high-level visual representations.

Connectionist models have also been applied to disorders of high-level vision and attention. Cohen, Romero, Servan-Schreiber, and Farah (in press) mimicked the apparent difficulty that some patients with parietal damage have in "disengaging" attention from an ipsilesional location to attend to a contralesional stimuli (Posner, Walker, Friedrich, & Rafal, 1984) by unilaterally damaging a competitive mechanism for allocating attention. Burton et al. (1991) and Farah, O'Reilly, and Vecera (1993) have shown that partial damage within a connectionist face recognition system can impair overt recognition and naming of faces severely despite leaving performance on more "covert" tasks, like priming or name relearning, relatively intact, as has been observed in prosopagnosic patients (e.g. De Haan, Young, & Newcombe, 1987). Also recently, Humphreys, Freeman, and Müller (1992) replicated the pattern of impaired feature grouping observed in a visual agnosic patient (Humphreys & Riddoch, 1987)

Finally, in the domain of rehabilitation, Plaut (1992, in press) demonstrated that the recovery of treated items and generalisation to untreated items documented in a therapy study with an acquired dyslexic patient (Coltheart & Byng, 1989) also occurs when retraining a damaged network that derives the meanings of words from their orthography (also see Hinton & Plaut, 1987; Hinton & Sejnowski, 1986).

ACQUIRED DYSLEXIA

Perhaps the most detailed attempts at relating the behaviour of damaged connectionist networks to that of brain-injured patients has been in the domain of acquired reading disorders (Hinton & Shallice, 1991; Mozer & Behrmann, 1990; Patterson, Seidenberg, & McClelland, 1990). This is in part because investigations of reading in both cognitive psychology and neuropsychology (Coltheart, 1987) have produced a rich, and often counterintuitive, set of empirical findings. In addition, reading is appealing as a domain for computational modelling because the surface forms (i.e. strings of letters and phonemes) are fairly simple. Furthermore, reading is a particularly appropriate domain in which to use relatively unstructured connectionist models (cf. Feldman, Fanty, & Goddard, 1988; Sejnowski et al., 1989) to study the neural implementation of cognitive processes as it is unlikely that the brain relies on specialised neural circuitry to accomplish such an evolutionary recent skill. Nonetheless, separate neuroanatomical *areas* may become specialised for particular reading processes as a result of experience during reading acquisition, and thus be independently susceptible to brain damage (see Farah, 1990, for similar arguments, and Howard et al., 1992; Petersen et al., 1988, for relevant empirical data).

Prior to the late 1960s, the major distinction among acquired dyslexic patients was simply whether the reading deficit was accompanied by a deficit in writing—"alexia with agraphia"—or whether it occurred in isolation—"alexia without agraphia," or "pure alexia" (Déjerine, 1892). Little attempt was made to distinguish between different types of reading deficits until Marshall and Newcombe (1966; 1973) identified three separate types of acquired dyslexia based on the typical patterns of errors that patients made in reading aloud. *Surface* dyslexia involved phonological confusions in the procedure by which words are sounded-out based on typical spelling-sound correspondences (e.g. INSECT → "insist"; hard to soft *c*). *Deep* dyslexia involved semantic confusions, in which words were often misread as semantically related words (e.g. DINNER → "food"). The third type of dyslexia that Marshall and Newcombe identified, involving visual confusions between words, has not been as widely recognised by researchers as has either surface or deep dyslexia.

A particularly notable aspect of Marshall and Newcombe's (1973) work that laid the groundwork for future information processing models of neuropsychological disorders was that they explained the existence of these distinct types of dyslexia in terms of damage to a "dual-route" model of normal reading. In their model, written words can be pronounced through either of two mechanisms. The first is a phonological system that translates from spelling to sound—for instance, by the use of grapheme-phoneme correspondence (GPC) rules. This system enables people to read word-like nonsense letter strings (e.g. MAVE) as well as words with *regular* pronunciations that obey standard spelling-sound correspondences (e.g. GAVE). The second mechanism for pronouncing words is by the use of a semantic system that recognises and assigns them meaning. The specific pronunciation of a word can then be accessed directly from its meaning. This semantic route enables people to read *exception* words that violate the standard GPC rules (e.g. HAVE). According to Marshall and Newcombe, surface dyslexic patients have damage to the semantic route and thus read only by the phonological route, whereas deep dyslexic patients read only via the semantic route because of damage to the phonological route. The errors produced by these patients reflects the imperfect operation of the remaining undamaged route in isolation. The third type of dyslexia was thought to involve damage to visual processes prior to the phonological and semantic routes—in more recent terminology it would be termed a *peripheral* dyslexia, in contrast to surface and deep dyslexia, which are *central* (Shallice & Warrington, 1980).

Further research has examined the characteristics of both surface and deep dyslexia in more detail. Some of this research has prompted a division of surface dyslexia into two separate types (Shallice & McCarthy, 1985). *Fluent* patients (e.g. MP: Bub, Cancelliere, & Kertesz, 1985; KT:

McCarthy & Warrington, 1986; HTR: Shallice, Warrington, & McCarthy, 1983) exhibit generally normal latencies and correct performance in reading of words with regular spelling-to-sound correspondences, even though word comprehension is severely impaired. These patients can also pronounce nonwords appropriately. However, they often misread exception words, usually by giving a more regular pronunciation (e.g. PINT mispronounced to rhyme with MINT). This type of *regularisation* error occurs predominantly on exception words that occur infrequently—typically, high-frequency exception words can be read almost as well as regular words. Thus, there is an interaction between the effects of frequency and of regularity. *Nonfluent* surface dyslexic patients (e.g. JC, ST: Marshall & Newcombe, 1973; ROG: Shallice & Warrington, 1980) are also better at reading regular words than exception words. However, compared with fluent patients, they read more slowly with many corrections, make more errors on regular words and nonwords, produce a lower proportion of regularisations of exception words, and have better comprehension. In fact, Shallice and McCarthy (1985) argued that nonfluent surface dyslexia is caused by a more peripheral visual disturbance, and that only the fluent type truly reflects the isolated operation of the phonological route. For a more comrehensive discussion of surface dyslexia, see Patterson et al. (1985).

In contrast to patients with surface dyslexia, patients with deep dyslexia cannot read nonwords, and their ability to read a word is unaffected by the nature of its spelling-sound correspondences (Coltheart, Patterson, & Marshall, 1980). In addition to semantic errors, they also make visual errors (e.g. SCANDAL → "sandals"), derivational or morphological errors (e.g. HIRE → "hired"), and function word substitutions (e.g. AND → "of"). They also find content words much easier to read than function words, and concrete words much easier to read than abstract words. The behaviour of deep dyslexic patients is described in more detail later. Most researchers assume that, in addition to severe impairment of the phonological route, deep dyslexic patients also have partial damage to the semantic route (see Shallice, 1988, for discussion).

In addition to surface and deep dyslexia, a third type of central dyslexia, known as *phonological* dyslexia, was identified by Beauvois and Derouesné (1979; also see Funnell, 1983; Patterson, 1982; Shallice & Warrington, 1980). Similar to deep dyslexic patients, patients with phonological dyslexia are severely impaired at reading nonwords aloud, although they have no problem pronouncing them in repetition. However, unlike deep dyslexic patients, phonological dyslexic patients have relatively intact word reading, and they show little if any effect of concreteness or part-of-speech, with the possible exception of some difficulty on function words. Phonological dyslexia is typically thought to involve an impairment to the phonological route, or phonology itself, with little or no impairment to the semantic route. In fact, Glosser and Friedman (1990) have argued that deep and phonological dyslexia fall on a continuum, with deep dyslexia arising from more extensive damage.

In attempting to account for phonological dyslexia, some researchers (e.g. Coltheart, 1985; Coltheart, Curtis, Atkins, & Haller, 1993; Morton & Patterson, 1980; Sartori, Masterson, & Job, 1987; Schwartz, Saffran, & Marin, 1980) claim that it is necessary to introduce a third route, separate from both the phonlogical and semantic routes, that applies only to whole words. Others (e.g. Seidenberg & McClelland, 1989; Shallice & McCarthy, 1985; Van Orden, Pennington, & Stone, 1990) propose a single, broad phonological route that maps between orthography and phonology at different levels of structure (individual graphemes-phonemes to whole words). However, interpretation of phonological dyslexia in terms of reading models needs to proceed with caution as, with rare exceptions (e.g. Derouesné & Beauvois, 1985), phonological dyslexic patients have difficulty in purely phonological operations, such as blending phonemes to produce a word (Patterson & Marcel, 1992). Thus, their particular difficulty in reading nonwords may arise, at least in part, from impairments outside the reading system per se.

Before turning to a detailed case study of connectionist neuropsychology as applied to deep dyslexia, we describe in some detail existing implemented models of other types of acquired dyslexia.

Neglect and Attentional Dyslexias

Neglect dyslexia is a peripheral reading disorder, typically following right parietal damage, in which patients often ignore the leftmost portion of written material even when it falls entirely within the intact portions of their visual fields (Bisiach & Vallar, 1988; Kinsbourne & Warrington, 1962; Riddoch, 1991; Sieroff, Pollatsek, & Posner, 1988). In left neglect dyslexia, the more common form, the accuracy of reading a string of letters is better when the stimulus is presented further to the right (Behrmann, Moscovitch, Black, & Mozer, 1990; Ellis, Flude, & Young, 1987), or when it forms a word (Behrmann et al., 1990; Brunn & Farah, 1991; Sieroff et al., 1988). Incorrect responses typically consist of words in which the leftmost letters of the stimulus are omitted (e.g. CHAIR → "hair"), augmented (e.g. LOVE → "glove"), or, most commonly, replaced (e.g. HOUSE → "mouse"). When two letter strings are presented (e.g. SUN FLY), the left one is often ignored (Sieroff et al., 1988), but this occurs less frequently when they combine to form a compound word (e.g. COW BOY; Behrmann et al., 1990). Thus, the severity of the deficit is influenced both by peripheral (sensory) and central (lexical) manipulations. Neglect dyslexia often accompanies more generalised hemispatial neglect (Bisiach & Vallar, 1988; Friedland & Weinstein, 1977) but has been dissociated from it in at least some patients (Costello & Warrington, 1987). It is traditionally interpreted as a deficit in allocating spatial attention to contralesional stimuli (Posner et al., 1984). In fact, explicit instructions or cueing manipulations that bias attention towards the left can often alleviate the deficit (Karnath, 1988; Riddoch & Humphreys, 1983; Riddoch, Humphreys, Cleton, & Fery, 1990), and neglect-like attentional manipulations in normals can elicit analogous lexical effects (Behrmann, Moscovitch, & Mozer, 1991).

Mozer and Behrmann (1990) reproduced these characteristics of neglect dyslexia in a pre-existing connectionist model of word recognition, known as MORSEL (for *M*ultiple *O*bject *R*ecognition and *SEL*ective attention; Mozer, 1991; see Fig. 5). Retinotopic letter features are combined into letters, and then into letter clusters, by the operation of a hierarchically organised subnetwork called BLIRNET (for *B*uilds *L*ocation *I*nvariant *R*epresentations). Letter clusters are context-dependent triples of letters that represent spaces explicitly (designated by "_") and can span across an intermediate position (designated by "*"). For example, the letter clusters for the isolated word CAT are __C, _CA, CAT, AT_, T__, __*A, _*AT, _C*T, C*T_, CA*_, and A*__. Letter clusters provide a unique representation for most words (but see Pinker & Prince, 1988, for a discussion of their limitations). The scheme is loosely modelled after that of Wickelgren (1969).

The input of letter features to BLIRNET is partially gated by an Attentional Mechanism (AM) that attempts to form a spatially contiguous "spotlight" of activity on the basis of where letter features occur. The letter cluster activity produced by BLIRNET is cleaned-up into the pattern for a particular word under the top-down influence of lexical/semantic units within a Pull-Out network.

Mozer and Behrmann (1990) modelled the attentional impairment in neglect dyslexia by introducing a monotonic gradient of damage to the connections from the letter features to the AM, with damage most severe on the left and least on the right. This damage biases the AM towards forming an inaccurate spotlight that includes only the rightmost letters of a single input string, or the rightmost of two input strings. Letter features that fall outside the spotlight are transmitted to BLIRNET with much lower probability, so that the resulting letter cluster activity is inaccurate in representing the left-hand side of the input. The clean-up of the Pull-Out network can often reconstruct the correct pattern of activity for the letter string from this corrupted activity, particularly when the entire input forms a word (corresponding to some of the lexical/semantic units). However, when clean-up within the Pull-Out network fails, the result is often the pattern for another word that differs from the presented word only on the

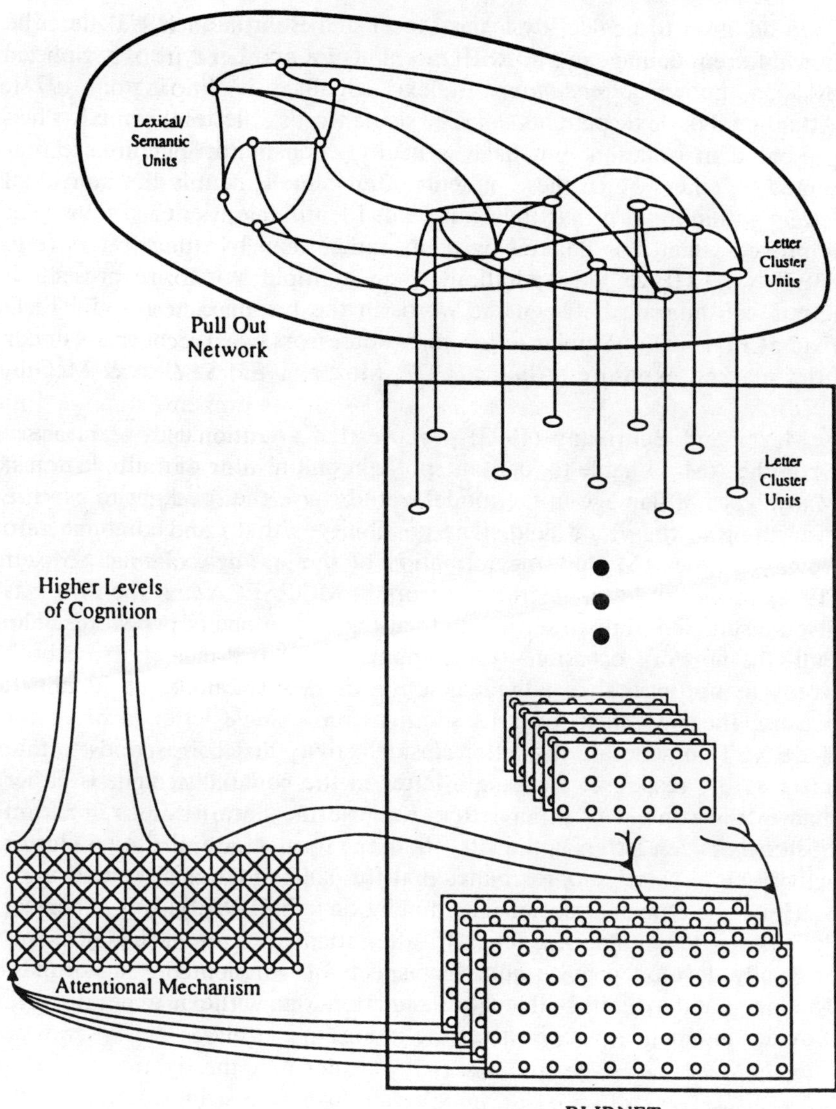

FIG. 5 The main components of MORSEL. (From Mozer & Behrmann, 1990, p. 98.)

left. Reading accuracy is better if the letter string is presented further to the right because the damage from these positions to the AM is less severe. Similarly, accuracy is improved by cueing in the model through the unimpaired top-down input to the AM from so-called "Higher Levels of Cognition" (see Fig. 5). In this way, the damaged model reproduces the main characteristics of neglect dyslexia.

In addition to neglect dyslexia, Mozer and Behrmann (1993) describe how different damage in MORSEL accounts for another type of peripheral dyslexia, known as *attentional* dyslexia (Shallice & Warrington, 1977). Attentional dyslexic patients can read single words or letters correctly when presented in isolation, but have difficulty when multiple items are presented together. Thus, these patients often cannot identify the individual letters within a word that they can read. Identifying a letter is somewhat improved when it is flanked by digits rather than by other letters (e.g. 83B40 vs. LHBMC). In addition, when multiple words are presented, letters can migrate between the words in the response (e.g. WIN FED read as FIN FED). Similar letter migration errors occur in normals under brief masked exposure (Allport, 1977; Mozer, 1983; Shallice & McGill, 1978).

Mozer and Behrmann (1993) propose that attentional dyslexia arises when the AM is unable to focus its spotlight on only one of multiple items. Many types of damage in the model would cause the spotlight to capture everything in the visual field. One possibility is that reduced connection weights in the AM slow the formation of the spotlight. In fact, Mozer (1991) produced letter migration errors in MORSEL when the AM was given insufficient time to settle into focusing on just one of two words. The Pull-Out network occasionally recombines the letter clusters from both words inappropriately. Individual letters in words cannot be identified because the AM must focus its spotlight on a single letter in order for BLIRNET to generate the letter cluster activity that corresponds to that letter as the response. Reading a letter in the context of digits is easier than in the context of other letters because the network does not form clusters between letters and digits, so, in the former case, the letter cluster activity more closely approximates that for isolated letter presentation.

Thus, one type of attentional manipulation in MORSEL leads to neglect dyslexia, whereas another leads to attentional dyslexia. MORSEL was originally developed to account for aspects of word reading in normals. The fact that it exhibits both neglect and attentional dyslexia under damage provides independent support for the model.

Surface Dyslexia

As described earlier, surface dyslexic patients can pronounce correctly regular words and nonwords, but often regularise exception words, particularly if they are low in frequency (e.g. YACHT → "yatched"). Thus, they would appear to be reading entirely by a phonological route that sounds out words based on spelling-to-sound correspondences. Patterson et al. (1990) attempted to reproduce similar effects by damaging a model of word pronunciation that had previously been shown to account for a wide range of effects in normal reading (Seidenberg & McClelland, 1989; see Fig. 6). The model takes the form of a connectionist network that maps orthographic representations of the written forms of words onto phonological representations of their pronunciations. It is closely related to Sejnowski and Rosenberg's (1987) NETtalk model in this respect. Orthographic representations in the Seidenberg and McClelland model are roughly similar to the letter clusters in MORSEL, except that each of the 400

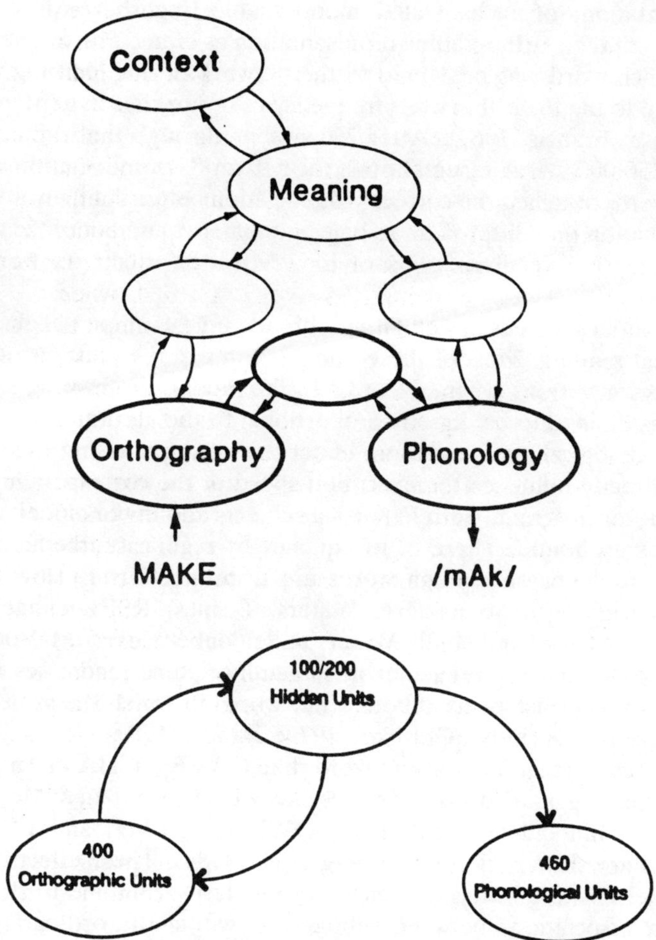

FIG. 6 Seidenberg and McClelland's (1989) general framework for lexical processing (top, p. 526), and the structure of the portion of this framework that was implemented (bottom, p. 527).

orthographic units is involved in representing a number of related letter clusters instead of just one. Phonological representations, composed of triples of phonemic features, are distributed in a similar fashion over 460 phonological units (see Rumelhart & McClelland, 1986, for details). In the network, 200 hidden units receive connections from each orthographic unit and send connections back to these units as well as to each phonological unit.

The network was trained with back-propagation (Rumelhart, Hinton, & Williams, 1986a) to generate both the orthographic and phonological representations of each of 2897 monosyllabic English words when presented with their orthographic representation as input. The frequency with which each word was presented to the network during learning was proportional to the logarithm of its frequency of occurrence in written English (Kuçera & Francis, 1967). After 250 sweeps through the training corpus (about 150,000 word presentations), the network's pronunciation of 97.3% of the words matched the correct pronunciation better than any alternative pronunciation that differed by a single phoneme. A number of the incorrect responses were regularisations of low-frequency exception words (e.g. SOOT → "suit").

The model succeeds in simulating a broad range of empirical phenomena in normal reading. Most of these findings concern the patterns of naming latencies for various types of words. In the model, the naming latency of a word is defined to be directly proportional to the accuracy of the generated phonological representation, under the assumption that this accuracy would directly influence the execution speed of the corresponding articulatory motor program. Both in normal subjects and in the model, a variety of effects are found. There is a frequency-by-regularity interaction, such that low-frequency exception words are disproportionally slow to name (Seidenberg, 1985; Seidenberg, Waters, Barnes, & Tanenhaus, 1984; Taraban & McClelland, 1987; Waters & Seidenberg, 1985). Furthermore, among low-frequency regular words, naming latency increases with the number of inconsistent neighbours (i.e. words in which the same body is pronounced differently; Glushko, 1979; Jared, McRae, & Seidenberg, 1990). Thus, regular inconsistent words like GAVE (cf. HAVE) are slower to name than regular consistent words like MUST (Taraban & McClelland, 1987), and ambiguous words like TOWN (cf. OWN) and LOVE (cf. STOVE) are slower still (Seidenberg et al., 1984). These effects occur in the model because both frequency and regularity combine to strengthen common associations between subpatterns within the orthographic and phonological representations.

The model shows analogous effects of consistency in nonword naming latency—in particular, nonwords derived from regular consistent words (e.g. NUST) are faster to name than nonwords derived from exception words (e.g. MAVE from HAVE; Glushko, 1979; Taraban & McClelland, 1987). However, the model's *accuracy* at pronouncing nonwords is much worse than that of skilled readers. Besner, Twilley, McCann, and Seergobin (1990) reported that, on nonword lists from Glushko (1979) and from McCann and Besner (1987), the model is only 59% and 51% correct, whereas skilled readers are 94% and 89% correct, respectively. Although Seidenberg and McClelland (1990) pointed out that the scoring criteria used for the network was more strict than that used for the subjects, the network's performance is still much worse even taking this into account.

The model also replicates the effects of frequency and consistency in lexical decision (Waters & Seidenberg, 1985) when responses are based on the accuracy with which the network can regenerate the input orthographic representation. Again, however, the model is not as accurate at lexical decision under some conditions as are normal subjects (Besner et al., 1990; Fera & Besner, 1992).

Despite these limitations, the Seidenberg and McClelland model would seem well suited for addressing surface dyslexia as neither it nor the patients (at least those of the fluent type) can rely on semantic mediation in reading. Accordingly, Patterson et al. (1990) lesioned the model by removing different proportions of units or connections, and compared its performance on different classes of words with that of surface dyslexic patients. The pronunciation generated by the damaged network to a given word was compared with the correct pronunciation as well as a plausible alternative—for exception words, the alternative consisted of the regularised pronunciation. After damage, regular and exception words are read equally well, and there is no effect of frequency in reading exception words. Exception words are much more likely than regular words to produce the alternative (regularised) pronunciation, but a comparison of the phonemic features in errors revealed that the network shows no greater tendency to produce regularisations than other errors that differ from the correct pronunciation by the same number of features. This pattern of results is unlike that of surface dyslexic patients, who read regular words much better than exception words, are worse at reading exception words with low frequency, and are particularly prone to regularisation errors.

Using a more detailed procedure for analysing responses, Patterson (1990) found that removing 20% of the hidden units produces better performance on regular vs. exception words and a (nonsignificant) trend towards a frequency-by-regularity interaction. Thus, on frequency-matched regular and exception words (Taraban & McClelland, 1987), both high- and low-frequency regular words are read well (93% correct on each), high-frequency exception words are also read reasonably well (86%), but low-frequency exception words are more impaired (78%). This pattern of performance is similar to a relatively mild surface dyslexic patient, MP, on the same set of words (high-frequency regulars: 95%; low-frequency regulars: 98%; high-frequency exceptions: 93%; low-frequency exceptions: 73%; Bub et al., 1985). More severe damage to the model, however, fails to simulate the more dramatic effects exhibited by patient KT (high-frequency regulars: 100%; low-frequency regulars: 89%; high-frequency exceptions: 47%; low-frequency exceptions: 26%; McCarthy & Warrington, 1986). Instead, performance on regular words declines considerably, producing a pattern that is more similar to nonfluent surface dyslexia. In addition, with the less severe damage, only about half of the network's errors to exception words are regularisations, whereas both MP and KT produce regularisation rates of around 85%. Finally, both of these patients show near-normal performance in reading nonwords, whereas the *undamaged* model already shows abnormally poor performance. Overall, the attempts to account for surface dyslexia by damaging the Seidenberg and McClelland model have been less than satisfactory (see Behrmann & Bub, 1992; Coltheart et al., 1993, for further criticisms).

In more recent simulation work, Plaut and McClelland (1993, see also Plaut, McClelland, Seidenberg, & Patterson, Note 10) explored the use of alternative orthographic and phonological representations that make the regularities between written and spoken words more explicit. An attractor network using the new representations learned to pronounce correctly 99.7% of the Seidenberg and McClelland (1989) corpus (augmented with 101 additional words), including the low-frequency exception words, and yet was also able to read pronounceable nonwords as well as skilled readers. In particular, when using the same scoring criteria as were applied to subjects, the model correctly pronounces 96.5% of Glushko's (1979) nonwords and 88.8% of McCann and Besner's (1987) nonwords. These findings refute dual-route claims that multiple mechanisms are necessary to read both exception words and nonwords, thereby opening up the range of possible architectures that might plausibly underlie human word reading.

Damaging the Plaut and McClelland (1993) model produces results qualitatively similar to those of Patterson (1990), although the regularisation rates and nonword reading performance are somewhat higher. This pattern of behaviour is similar to nonfluent surface dyslexia. By contrast, a much better match to fluent surface dyslexia is found in the behaviour of the *undamaged* network earlier in learning, before it has mastered the entire training corpus (Plaut, Behrmann, Patterson, & McClelland, 1993). Specifically, after 700 sweeps through the training data, the network reads all of the Taraban and McClelland (1987) regular words correctly and 91.7% of the high-frequency exceptions, but only 62.5% of the low-frequency exceptions. The network pronounces 97.7% of Glushko's (1979) nonwords correctly, and 90.9% of the errors on exception words are regularisations. This pattern of performance closely matches that of MP. Furthermore, the performance of the network after only 400 sweeps closely matches that of KT (high-frequency regulars: 100%; low-frequency regulars: 95.8%; high-frequency exceptions: 50.0%; low-frequency exceptions: 33.3%; Glushko nonwords: 98.8%; regularisation rate: 89.3%). This correspondence suggests that, in normal readers, some exception words (particularly those of low frequency) are never mastered by the phonological route, and that fluent surface dyslexia arises when this intact route operates in isolation due to semantic damage. Empirical support for this interpretation comes from recent findings that, in patients with progressive deterioration of lexical semantics, there is a close relationship between the extent of semantic impairment on individual exception words and their tendency to be regularised (Graham, Hodges, & Patterson, 1994; Patterson & Hodges, 1992).

The relative success of attempts to model neglect dyslexia and, more recently, surface dyslexia by lesioning connectionist models of normal word reading suggests that these models can capture important aspects of cognitive processes and their underlying neurological implementation. However, there is little understanding of what principles of operation in these models are responsible for their successes and limitations (McCloskey, 1991). In the current work, we focus on the detailed pattern of symptoms exhibited by patients with deep dyslexia. Based on previous preliminary simulations (Hinton & Shallice, 1991), we undertake a systematic exploration of the relevance of the major design decisions that enter into developing a connectionist model of deep dyslexia. The enterprise serves as a "case study" of the application of connectionist modelling in cognitive neuropsychology. We find that what appears to be a rather perplexing combination of symptoms is, in fact, a natural consequence of damage to systems that embody particular computational principles. The occurrence of the deep dyslexia symptom-complex in brain-injured patients thus provides striking evidence in favour of the possibility that the human reading system also operates according to these principles. In this way, the work demonstrates how connectionist modelling can provide insight into the detailed nature of cognitive processes and their breakdown following brain damage that might well be difficult to obtain through the use of empirical methodologies alone. As a result, a close interplay between empirical and computational investigations may be the most fruitful research strategy for cognitive neuropsychologists to adopt in future work.

Deep Dyslexia

Despite its familiarity as a concept in cognitive neuropsychology, deep dyslexia remains controversial. It was first suggested as a symptom-complex by Marshall and Newcombe (1973), who described two patients, GR and KU. These patients both made semantic errors in attempting to read aloud and also made visual and derivational errors. Coltheart (1980a) was able to add another 15 cases. Kremin (1982) added another 8 and over 10 more are referred to by Coltheart, Patterson, and Marshall (1987).

Beginning with the semantic errors, Coltheart (1980a) also extended the list of common properties to 12 (examples of errors are from DE, Patterson & Marcel, 1977):

1. Semantic errors (e.g. BLOWING → "wind," VIEW → "scene," NIGHT → "sleep," GONE → "lost").
2. Visual errors (e.g. WHILE → "white," SCANDAL → "sandals," POLITE → "politics," BADGE → "bandage").
3. Function-word substitutions (e.g. WAS → "and," ME → "my," OFF → "from," THEY → "the").
4. Derivational errors (e.g., CLASSIFY → "class," FACT → "facts," MARRIAGE → "married," BUY → "bought").
5. Nonlexical derivation of phonology from print is impossible (e.g. pronouncing nonwords, judging if two nonwords rhyme).
6. Lexical derivation of phonology from print is impaired (e.g. judging if two words rhyme).
7. Words with low imageability/concreteness (e.g. JUSTICE) are harder to read than words with high imageability/concreteness (e.g. TABLE).
8. Verbs are harder than adjectives, which are harder than nouns, in reading aloud;
9. Functions words are more difficult than content words in reading aloud.
10. Writing is impaired (spontaneous or to dictation).
11. Auditory-verbal short-term memory is impaired.
12. Whether a word can be read at all depends on its sentence context (e.g. FLY as a noun is easier than FLY as a verb).

Given the uniformity of the patients' symptoms, Coltheart characterised the symptom-complex as a syndrome.

In the conclusion of their review article, "Deep dyslexia since 1980," Coltheart et al. (1987) argue that deep dyslexia presents cognitive neuropsychology with a major challenge. They raise two main issues specific to the domain of reading. First, they argue that standard "box-and-arrow" information-processing accounts of deep dyslexia (e.g. Morton & Patterson, 1980) provide no explanation for the observed combination of symptoms. If a patient makes semantic errors in reading aloud, why are many other types of behaviour virtually always observed? Second, they point out that the standard explanations for semantic errors and for effects of concreteness involve *different* impairments along the semantic route (Coltheart et al., 1987, pp. 421–422).

> The loss of semantic information for abstract words that explained visual errors in oral reading cannot readily explain semantic errors in oral reading, since semantic errors typically occur on moderately concrete words. . . . The deficit in the semantic routine that gives a pretty account of semantic errors is, rather, an abnormal sloppiness in the procedure of addressing a phonological output code from a set of semantic features. . . . Must we now postulate several different semantic-routine impairments in deep dyslexia, and if so, why do we not observe patients who have one but not the other: in particular, patients who make semantic errors but do not have difficulty with abstract words?

Recently, Hinton and Shallice (1991) have put forward a connectionist approach to deep dyslexia that addresses the first of these points. They reproduced the co-occurrence of semantic, visual, and mixed visual-and-semantic errors by lesioning a connectionist network that develops attractors for word meanings. Although the success of their simulations is encouraging, there is little understanding of what underlying principles are responsible for them. In this book, we evaluate and, where possible, improve on the most important design decisions made by Hinton and Shallice. First, we demonstrate the robustness of the account by examining network architectures different from the original model. We also improve on the rather arbitrary way that the model realised an explicit response by extending it to generate phonological output from semantics. Next, we evaluate the significance of the particular learning procedure used to train the original model by re-implementing it in a more plausible connectionist formalism. Finally, we investigate whether the remaining characteristics of deep dyslexia—in particular, Coltheart, Patterson, and Marshall's third issue relating to effects of concreteness—can be explained by the same account proposed for the co-occurrence of error types. The remainder of this section presents a brief discussion of additional aspects of deep dyslexia, motivations for a connectionist account, a summary and evaluation of the Hinton and Shallice results, and a general overview of the remainder of the book.

One problematic aspect of characterising deep dyslexia as a syndrome is that, in fact, not all of the 12 properties given earlier are always observed when an acquired dyslexic patient makes semantic errors in reading. Thus, patient AR (Warrington & Shallice, 1979) did not show the content word effects (7 and 9), and had relatively intact writing and auditory short-term memory (10 and 11). Three other patients have been described who make semantic errors in reading aloud (and do so also when any other speech responses are required) and yet make few if any visual errors (Caramazza & Hillis, 1990; Hillis, Rapp, Romani, & Caramazza, 1990).[1] The lack of complete consistency across patients has led to criticisms of the attempt to characterise the symptom-complex as directly reflecting an impairment to some specific processing component. Some of these arguments are specific to deep dyslexia. For example, Shallice and Warrington (1980) held that deep dyslexia was not a "pure syndrome." Others, though, have made more general critiques. Morton and Patterson (1980) and Caramazza (1984; 1986) denied the theoretical utility of generalising over patients for extrapolation to normal function, and Shallice (1988a) claimed more specifically that error patterns did not provide an appropriate basis for this purpose.

Despite these objections to the theoretical utility of the deep dyslexia symptom-complex, Coltheart et al. (1987) stress that work since 1980 reinforces the virtually complete uniformity of symptom pattern found across a large number of patients. This means that to dismiss deep dyslexia as theoretically irrelevant would be at least as dangerous as to accept it uncritically as the manifestation of some specific impairment. For the present we will leave consideration of these methodological criticisms until the General Discussion and will assume provisionally that deep dyslexia is a valid theoretical concept.

Many other properties of the reading of individual deep dyslexic patients have been recorded. In this book we will be particularly concerned with four:

1. *Additional types of reading errors.* Mixed visual-and-semantic (e.g. SHIRT → "skirt") were recorded in all of the patients reviewed by Colt-

[1]One could argue that two of these patients at least are hardly "acquired dyslexics" since their problem is held to be at the phonological output lexicon. This, though, presupposes that one can make a clear distinction between reading impairments and other difficulties. Yet, although it remains generally accepted that nonsemantic phonological reading procedures are grossly impaired in deep dyslexic patients (see, e.g., Marshall & Newcombe, 1973), it has been argued that there are additional deficits in the semantic reading route, and that these can differ in their location, with some patients even being *output* deep dyslexics (Friedman & Perlman, 1982; Shallice & Warrington, 1980). Thus, the "clear distinction" between reading and nonreading difficulties is absent from the literature.

heart (1980a) on whom there is adequate data; in KF (Shallice & McGill, 1978) and PS (Shallice & Coughlan, 1980) they were also shown to occur at a higher rate than one would expect if they were all arising as visual errors or as semantic errors independently. Another error type, observed even earlier by Marshall and Newcombe (1966), is that of *visual-then-semantic* errors (e.g. SYMPATHY → "orchestra," presumably via *symphony*, by GR), described in eight of the patients reviewed by Coltheart (1980a).

2. *Influences of semantic variables on visual errors.* In general, the abstract/concrete dimension does not just relate to the issue of how successfully different types of words are read. The stimuli producing visual errors tend to be more abstract than the responses, and more abstract than the stimuli producing other types of responses (see, e.g., Shallice & Warrington, 1980).

3. *Confidence in errors.* The confidence with which errors are produced has been studied in three patients. PW and DE (Patterson, 1978) were much more likely to be sure that they were correct for visual errors than for semantic errors, but GR gave equally high confidence ratings for both visual and semantic errors and for correct responses (Barry & Richardson, 1988).

4. *Lexical decision.* Deep dyslexic patients can often distinguish words from orthographically regular nonwords, even when they are quite poor at reading the words explicitly (Patterson, 1979). Lexical decision was "surprisingly good" for 9 of the 11 cases listed by Coltheart (1980a) for which there was data.

Turning to theoretical accounts of the symptom-complex, we will follow Marshall and Newcombe (1973), and many others, by presuming that phonological reading procedures are grossly impaired in these patients, and that this can account for characteristics 5, 6, and presumably 11 (see discussions in Coltheart, 1980a; 1980c; Coltheart et al., 1987). However, if it is held that the complete cluster of properties have a common functional origin, what can it be? The most prosaic possibility is that the syndrome arises from a set of functionally independent deficits that co-occur for anatomical reasons (e.g. Morton & Patterson, 1980; Shallice, 1988a; Shallice & Warrington, 1980). If, however, the impairments are only specified in terms of damage to hypothetical subcomponents or transmission routes, many questions remain to be answered. Why do visual and derivational errors so often co-occur with semantic ones? Why do mixed visual-and-semantic and visual-then-semantic errors occur? If the general advantage for concrete words results from impaired access to abstract semantics per se, why has only one patient (CAV, Warrington, 1981) been observed with superior reading performance on *abstract* words? How does one account for the effects of concreteness on visual errors? Ad hoc explanations have been given for some of these points (see Morton & Patterson, 1980; Shallice & Warrington, 1980), but nothing resembling a well-developed theory along these lines exists.

An interesting version of the "anatomical coincidence" explanation is the claim that deep dyslexic reading reflects reading by the right hemisphere (Coltheart, 1980b; 1983; Saffran, Bogyo, Schwartz, & Marin, 1980). The attraction of this hypothesis is the similarities that have been demonstrated between reading in deep dyslexia and in patients reading with an isolated right hemisphere (e.g. Patterson, Vargha-Khadem, & Polkey, 1989; Zaidel & Peters, 1981). However, these analogies have been criticised (see, e.g., Patterson & Besner, 1984a; Shallice, 1988a) and at least one patient with many deep dyslexic characteristics has been described whose reading was abolished after a second *left* hemisphere stroke (Roeltgen, 1987). Overall, whereas the theory is based on empirical analogues for certain aspects of deep dyslexia (e.g. the nature of right hemisphere semantics by which it might produce the symptom-complex), it is principally an attempt to localise rather than to provide a mechanistic account. Since no mechanistic account exists for many aspects of any other neuropsychological syndrome except for neglect dyslexia (Mozer & Behrmann, 1990), this is hardly a strong criticism of the theory from present-day perspectives. However, an explanation oriented towards this more complex goal remains a major target for understanding deep dyslexia.

Motivation of a Connectionist Account

Connectionist modelling offers a promising approach to producing a mechanistic account of deep dyslexia. Connectionist networks are becoming increasingly influential in a number of areas of psychology as a methodology for developing computational models of cognitive processes. In contrast to conventional programs that compute by the sequential application of stored commands, these networks compute via the massively parallel co-operative and competitive interactions of a large number of simple neuron-like processing units. Networks of this form have been applied to problems in a wide range of cognitive domains, such as high-level vision and attention, learning and memory, language, speech recognition and production, and sequential reasoning (see McClelland, Rumelhart, & the PDP research group, 1986; Quinlan, 1991; and recent Cognitive Science Society conference proceedings).

In addition to their usefulness in modelling normal cognitive functioning, a number of general characteristics of connectionist networks suggest that they may be particularly well-suited for modelling neuropsychological phenomena (Allport, 1985). Modular theories of cognitive processes can be expressed naturally by dedicating separate groups of units to represent different types of information. In this way the approach can be viewed as an elaboration of, rather than an alternative to, more traditional "box-and-arrow" theorising within cognitive neuropsychology (cf. Seidenberg, 1988). Also, partial lesions of neurological areas and pathways can be modelled in a straightforward, relatively atheoretical manner by removing a proportion of units in a group and/or connections between groups. In contrast, simulations of neuropsychological findings within more traditional computational formalisms (e.g. Kosslyn, Flynn, Amsterdam, & Wang, 1990) must typically make more specific assumptions about how damage affects particular components of the system. Furthermore, since knowledge and processing in a connectionist network is distributed across a large number of units and connections, performance degrades gracefully under partial damage (Hinton & Sejnowski, 1986). This means that a range of intermediate states between perfect performance and total impairment can occur. Together with the richness of the computational formalism, this allows behaviour more detailed than the simple presence or absence of abilities to be investigated (Patterson, 1990).

A number of authors have attempted to explain patient behaviour based on intuitions about how connectionist networks or other cascaded systems (McClelland, 1979) would behave under damage, without actually carrying out the simulations (e.g. Miller & Ellis, 1987; Riddoch & Humphreys, 1987; Shallice & McGill, 1978; Stemberger, 1985). However, the highly distributed and dynamic nature of these networks makes such unverified predictions somewhat suspect. More recently, a few researchers have begun to explore the correspondence of the behaviour of damaged connectionist networks and patient behaviour, primarily in the domain of acquired dyslexia. Mozer and Behrmann (1990) reproduced aspects of neglect dyslexia in a pre-existing connectionist model of word recognition (Mozer, 1990) by disrupting its attentional mechanism. Patterson, Seidenberg, and McClelland (1990) attempted to model a form of surface dyslexia by damaging a network model of word pronunciation that previously had been demonstrated to account for a wide range of effects in normal reading (Seidenberg & McClelland, 1989). In addition, a number of other investigations are under way in other domains (e.g. Burton, Young, Bruce, Johnston, & Ellis, 1991; Cohen & Servan-Schreiber, 1992; Dehaene & Changeux, 1991; Farah & McClelland, 1991; Levine & Prueitt, 1989; Plaut, 1992; Plaut & Shallice, 1993). Although the successes of these initial demonstrations are certainly limited, they are sufficiently encouraging to warrant an attempt to understand, in a more general way, the strengths and limitations of connectionist neuropsychology.

Much of the initial motivation for pursuing a connectionist account of deep dyslexia comes out of preliminary work by Hinton and Sejnowski

(1986) on the effects of damage in networks. They were not primarily concerned with modelling deep dyslexia, but rather with investigating how distributed representations can mediate in mapping between arbitrarily related domains (Hinton, McClelland, & Rumelhart, 1986). They trained a network with the Boltzmann Machine learning procedure (Ackley, Hinton, & Sejnowski, 1985) to activate a specific subset of 30 semantic features via 20 intermediate units when presented with the graphemes of each of 20 3-letter words. The undamaged network performed the task almost perfectly, but when single intermediate units were removed, 1.4% of the responses of the network were incorrect. Interestingly, 59% of these incorrect responses were the exact semantics of an alternative word, and these word errors were more semantically and/or visually similar to the correct word than would be expected by chance. Although the demonstration was highly simplified, it showed that damage to a network that maps orthography to semantics can produce a pattern of errors with some similarity to that made by deep dyslexic patients.

A Preliminary Connectionist Model of Deep Dyslexia

Based on Hinton and Sejnowski's initial work, Hinton and Shallice (1991, hereafter H&S) undertook to model the error pattern of deep dyslexia more thoroughly. Developing the model involved making four sets of design decisions that apply to the development of any connectionist simulation:

1. *The task*: What input/output pairs is the network trained on and how are they represented as patterns of activity over groups of input and output units?
2. *The network architecture*: What type of unit is used, how are the units organised into groups, and in what manner are the groups connected?
3. *The training procedure*: How are examples presented to the network, what procedure is used to adjust the weights to accomplish the task, and what is the criterion for halting training?
4. *The testing procedure*: How is the performance of the network evaluated—specifically, how are lesions carried out and how is the behaviour of the damaged network interpreted in terms of overt responses that can be compared with those of patients?

The following four subsections describe the characteristics of the model in terms of each of these issues. The adequacy and limitations of these decisions are then discussed and serve to motivate the simulations presented in this book.

The Task

H&S defined a version of the task of mapping orthography to semantics that is somewhat more sophisticated than that used by Hinton and Sejnowski, although still far from realistic. Orthography was represented in terms of groups of position-specific letter units (McClelland & Rumelhart, 1981). In order to keep the task simple, 40 3- or 4-letter words were chosen with restrictions on what letters could occur in each position, resulting in a total of 28 possible graphemes (see Table 1).

Rather than assign a completely arbitrary semantics to each word, H&S designed a set of 68 semantic features intended to capture intuitive semantic distinctions (see Table 2). On average, about 15 of the 68 features are present in the semantic representation of a word. The words were chosen to fall within 5 concrete semantic categories: indoor objects, animals, body parts, foods, and outdoor objects. The assignment of semantic features to words has the property that words in the same category tend to be more similar (i.e. share more features) than words in different categories (see Fig. 7). However, H&S did not demonstrate directly that their semantic categories faithfully reflect the actual semantic similarity among words. Figure 7 conveys some sense of the similarity within and between categories, but a more direct impression can be obtained from a

TABLE 1
The Words Used by Hinton and Shallice

(a) Letters Allowed in Each Position

Pos.	*Letters*
1	B C D G H L M N P R T
2	A E I O U
3	B C D G K M P R T W
4	E K

(b) Words in Each Category

Indoor Objects	*Animals*	*Body Parts*	*Foods*	*Outdoor Objects*
BED	BUG	BACK	BUN	BOG
CAN	CAT	BONE	HAM	DEW
COT	COW	GUT	HOCK	DUNE
CUP	DOG	HIP	LIME	LOG
GEM	HAWK	LEG	NUT	MUD
MAT	PIG	LIP	POP	PARK
MUG	RAM	PORE	PORK	ROCK
PAN	RAT	RIB	RUM	TOR

TABLE 2
Semantic Features Used by Hinton and Shallice

1 max-size-less-foot	21 indoors	46 made-of-metal
2 max-size-foot-to-two-yards	22 in-kitchen	47 made-of-wood
3 max-size-greater-two-yards	23 in-bedroom	48 made-of-liquid
	24 in-livingroom	49 made-of-other-nonliving
4 main-shape-1D	25 on-ground	50 got-from-plants
5 main-shape-2D	26 on-surface	51 got-from-animals
	27 otherwise-supported	
6 cross-section-rectangular	28 in-country	52 pleasant
7 cross-section-circular	29 found-woods	53 unpleasant
	30 found-near-sea	
8 has-legs	31 found-near-streams	54 man-made
	32 found-mountains	55 container
9 white	33 found-on-farms	56 for-cooking
10 brown		57 for-eating-drinking
11 green	34 part-of-limb	58 for-other
12 colour-other-strong	35 surface-of-body	59 used-alone
13 varied-colours	36 interior-of-body	60 for-breakfast
14 transparent	37 above-waist	61 for-lunch-dinner
15 dark		62 for-snack
	38 mammal	63 for-drink
16 hard	39 wild	
17 soft	40 fierce	64 particularly-assoc-child
	41 does-fly	65 particularly-assoc-adult
18 sweet	42 does-swim	
19 tastes-strong	43 does-run	66 used-for-recreation
	44 living	
20 moves	45 carnivore	67 human
		68 component

Features within a block were considered "closely related" for the purposes of interconnecting semantic units.

full display of the similarity (i.e. proximity in semantic space) of each pair of words, shown in Fig. 8. Because the words are ordered by category in the figure, the extent and uniformity of the similarity within each category is reflected by an 8-by-8 block along the diagonal of the matrix, whereas between-category similarity is reflected in off-diagonal blocks. A number of interesting characteristics are apparent from the similarity matrix. Words for body parts are quite similar to each other, and quite different from words in other categories. In contrast, indoor objects are not uniformly similar to each other, and many are quite similar to foods, particularly those that are used with food (i.e. CUP, CAN, MUG, PAN). Outdoor objects also vary considerably in their similarities with each other, and are often also similar to animals (which are also found outdoors). However,

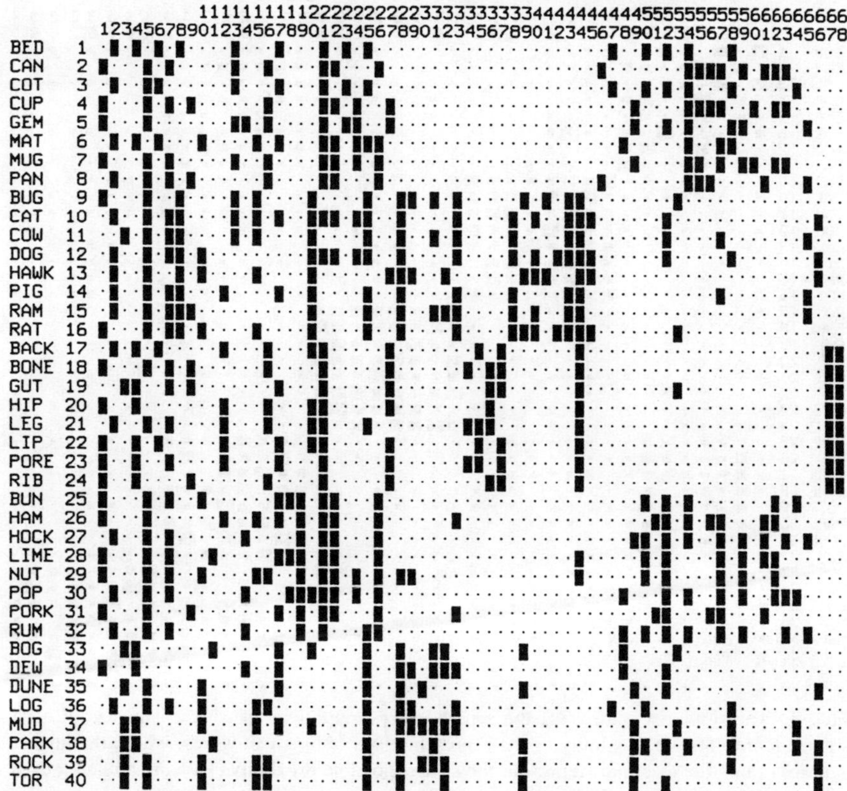

FIG. 7 The assignment of semantic features to words used by H&S. A black rectangle indicates that the semantic representation of the word listed on the left contains the feature whose number (from Table 2) is listed at the top.

the overall strength of the five on-diagonal blocks supports the use of category membership as a general measure of semantic similarity.

A further requirement of a satisfactory approximation of the task of mapping orthography to semantics that H&S did not verify for their representations is that the relationship between the visual and semantic representations of a word is arbitrary. In other words, the visual similarity of two words provides no information about their semantic similarity, and vice versa. One way to test the independence of visual and semantic similarity is that the probability of a randomly selected word pair being both visually and semantically similar, m, should be approximately equal to the product of the independent probabilities of visual similarity, v, and semantic similarity, s. Based on the definitions of visual and semantic similarity used by H&S and described later, among all possible nonidentical word pairs in the set, $m = 0.062$, $v = 0.36$, and $s = 0.18$, so $vs = 0.065$ is roughly equal

FIG. 8 The similarity matrix for the semantic representations of words. The size of each square represents the proximity of the representations of a pair of words, where the largest squares (along the diagonal) represent the closest possible proximity (1.0) and a blank quare represents the farthest possible proximity (0.0).

to *m*. Thus, visual and semantic similarity are approximately independent in the H&S word set.

Even taking these considerations into account, there is no question that the representations used by H&S fail to reflect the full range of orthographic and semantic structure in word reading. The use of position-specific letter units, the selection of semantic features, and their assignment to words, were based more on computational than empirical grounds. In fact, it is not particularly plausible that the semantic representations of a word in the human cognitive system is based on individual feature units at the level of *found-on-farms* and *used-for-recreation*. However, these representations exhibit the characteristics that are essential for demonstrating the influences of both visual and semantic similarity on deep dyslexic reading: (a) visually similar words (i.e. with overlapping letters) have similar orthographic representations, (b) words with similar meanings (i.e. in the same category) have similar semantic representations, and (c) there is no systematic relationship between the orthographic and semantic representations of a word.

The Network

Figure 9 depicts the network used by H&S. The 28 *grapheme* units were connected to a group of 40 *intermediate* units, which in turn were connected to the 68 *sememe* units (the "direct" pathway). In order to allow the sememe units to interact, H&S introduced connections at the semantic level in two ways. First, they added direct connections between sememe units, but rather than include all possible 4624 such connections, they only connected sememe units that represent closely related features (as defined in Table 2). Although these direct connections help the network ensure that sememes are locally consistent, not all relationships among semantic features can be encoded by pairwise interactions alone. In order to allow *combinations* of sememes to influence each other directly, H&S also introduced a fourth group of 60 *clean-up* units that receive connections from, and send connections to, the sememe units. This pathway can enforce more global consistency among semantic features. In order to reduce the total number of connections, only a random 25% of the possible connections between any 2 layers were included, resulting in about 3300 connections for the entire network.

Each unit in the network had a real-valued activity level, or *state*, ranging between 0 and 1, computed by a smooth, nonlinear function of the summed input received from other units.

The Training Procedure

The network was trained in the following way. The states of the grapheme units were set to the appropriate input pattern for a word, and the states of all other units were set to 0.2. The network was then run for 7 iterations, in which each unit updated its state once per iteration, generating a pattern of activity over the sememe units. The network was initialised to have small random weights, so that at the beginning of training

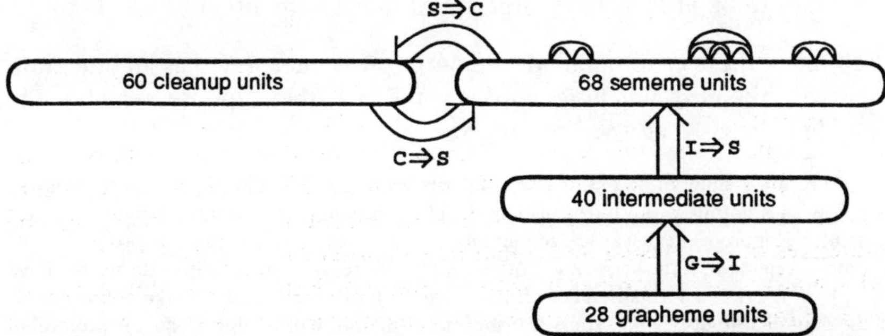

FIG. 9 The network used by H&S. Notice that sets of connections are named with the initials of the names of the source and destination unit groups (e.g. G → I for grapheme-to-intermediate connections).

the pattern of semantic activity produced by the word was quite different from its correct semantics. An iterative version of the back-propagation learning procedure, known as *back-propagation through time* (Rumelhart, Hinton, & Williams, 1986a; 1986b; Williams & Peng, 1990), was used to compute the way that each weight in the network should change so as to reduce this difference for the last 3 iterations. These weight changes were calculated for each word in turn, at which point the accumulated weight changes were carried out and the procedure was repeated. After about 1000 sweeps through the 40 words, when the network was presented with each word, the activity of each sememe unit was within 0.1 of its correct value for that word, at which point training was considered complete.

The Effects of Lesions

After training, the intact network produced the correct semantics of each word when presented with its orthography. The network was then lesioned by removing either a random subset of the units in a layer or the connections between two layers, or by adding random noise to the weights. Under damage, the semantics produced by a word typically differed somewhat from the exact correct semantics. Yet even though the corrupted semantics would fail the training criteria, it might still suffice for the purposes of naming. H&S defined two criteria that had to be satisfied in order for the damaged network to be considered to have made a response:

1. A *proximity* criterion ensured that the corrupted semantics was sufficiently close to the correct semantics of some word. Specifically, the cosine of the angle (i.e. normalised dot product) between the semantic vector produced by the network and the actual semantic vector of some word (in the 68-dimensional space of sememes) had to be greater than 0.8.[2]
2. A *gap* criterion ensured that no other word matched nearly as well. Specifically, the proximity to the generated semantics of the best matching word had to be at least 0.05 larger than that of any other word.

If either of these criteria failed, the output was interpreted as an omission; otherwise the best matching word was taken as the response, which could be either the correct word or an error.

---

[2]There are a number of reasonable similarity metrics that could be used for comparing the network's output with known responses. The normalised dot product (angle cosine) is particularly appropriate because the summed input to each unit is the dot product of its incoming weights with the activities of other units. As a result, two activity patterns that have high *proximity* (i.e. a normalised dot product near 1.0) will tend to make similar contributions to the summed input to other units. Furthermore, the normalised dot product is preferable to the more familiar euclidean distance metric because not all types of difference between two semantic patterns would be equally disruptive to an output system. In particular, differences in direction (e.g. towards another meaning) are more significant than differences in magnitude (which maintain the *relative* levels of unit activity).

In order to compare the behaviour of the network under damage with that of patients, H&S systematically lesioned sets of units or connections over a range of severity. For 10 instances of each lesion type, all 40 words were presented to the network, and omission, correct, and error responses were accumulated. As an approximation to the standard error classification used for patients (cf. Morton & Patterson, 1980), an error was defined to be visually similar to the input word if the two words overlapped in at least one letter, and semantically similar if the two words belonged to the same category. Based on these definitions, errors were classified into four types:

1. *Visual* (V): responses that are visually (but not semantically) similar to the stimulus (e.g. CAT → "cot").
2. *Semantic* (S): responses that are semantically (but not visually) similar to the stimulus (e.g. CAT → "dog").
3. *Mixed visual-and-semantic* (V&S): responses that are both visually and semantically similar to the stimulus (e.g. CAT → "rat").
4. *Other* (O): responses that are unrelated to the stimulus (e.g. CAT → "mug").

Applied to all possible pairs of words, these definitions give rise to the chance rates v, s, and m used earlier to demonstrate that visual and semantic similarity are approximately independent.

The most important result was that all lesions produced semantic, mixed visual-and-semantic, and visual errors at rates higher than would be expected by chance (with the sole exception of lesions of the sememe-to-cleanup (S → C) connections—the lesion type most resistance to damage). Here, "chance" is determined by comparing the ratio of each error rate to that of *other* errors with the predicted ratio, under the assumption that error responses are generated randomly from the word set. This is because a random pattern of responding would match the chance distribution of errors and not simply the chance rate for a particular error type.

It should be pointed out that mixed visual-and-semantic errors might arise simply from the chance rate of semantic similarity among visual errors, and the chance rate of visual similarity among semantic errors, rather than reflecting an additional influence on errors. The expected rate of mixed errors, M, can be calculated from the observed rates of visual errors, V, and semantic errors, S, under the assumption that visual and semantic errors result from two independent processes (Shallice & McGill, 1978):

$$M \leqslant V \frac{s}{1-s} + S \frac{v}{1-v}$$

where v, s, and m are as defined earlier. However, for all but one lesion type—removing intermediate-to-sememe (I → S) connections—the number of mixed visual-and-semantic errors was greater than would be expected if visual and semantic similarity were caused independently. Furthermore, the network showed a greater tendency to produce visual errors with early damage (closer to the graphemes) and semantic errors with later damage (closer to the sememes), although even damage completely within the semantic clean-up system produced an above-chance rate of visual errors. Thus, lesions throughout the network resulted in the basic co-occurrence of error types found in deep dyslexia.

H&S also demonstrated that, even when the semantics produced by the system were insufficient to drive a response system plausibly, enough information was often available to make between- and within-category discriminations. For instance, removing all of the connections from the sememe to clean-up units (S → C) reduced explicit correct performance to 40%. However, of the 60% remaining trials producing an omission, 91.7% of these resulted in semantics that were closer to the centroid of the correct category than to that of any other category (chance is 20%), and 87.5% were closer to the semantics of the correct word in that category than to that of any other word in the category (chance is 12.5%). The effect was weaker with earlier damage: Removing 30% of the grapheme-to-intermediate connections (G → I) produced 35.3% correct performance with 48.3% between-category and 49.0% within-category discrimination on omission trials.

Finally, a peculiar and interesting effect emerged when the connections from the clean-up to sememe units (C → S) were lesioned. The network showed a significant selective preservation of words in the foods category (75% correct) relative to those in other categories (next best, 34% correct).[3] The effect was quite specific; it did not occur for other lesions in the network, nor for the same lesion in a second version of the network trained with different initial random weights.

Attractors

An important concept in understanding H&S's results is that of an *attractor*. The sememe units in the network change their states over time in response to a particular orthographic input. The initial pattern of semantic activity generated by the direct pathway may be quite different from the exact semantics of the word. Interactions among sememe units, either directly via intra-sememe connections or indirectly via the clean-up units, serve gradually to modify and clean-up the initial pattern into the final correct pattern. This process can be conceptualised in terms of movement in the 68-dimensional space of possible semantic representations, in which the state of each sememe unit is represented along a separate dimension. At

[3]This effect was significant at the 0.01 level and not at the 0.1 level, as incorrectly stated in Hinton and Shallice (1991).

any instant in processing a word, the entire pattern of activity over the sememe units correspond to a single point in semantic space. The exact meanings of familiar words correspond to particular alternative points in the space. The states of sememe units change over time in such a way that the point representing the current pattern of semantic activity moves to the point representing the nearest familiar meaning. In other words, the pattern corresponding to each known word meaning becomes an attractor in the space of semantic representations: Patterns for nearby but unfamiliar meanings move towards the exact pattern of the nearest known meaning. The region in semantic space corresponding to the set of initial patterns that move to a given attractor is called its *basin* of attraction. The shapes and positions of the basins depend on the ways that units interact, which in turn depend on the connection weights. Hence, we speak of a network as developing or building attractors over the course of learning.

H&S offer an intuitive explanation for co-occurrence of visual and semantic influences on errors in terms of the effects of damage in a network that builds attractors in mapping between two arbitrarily related domains. Connectionist networks have difficulty learning to produce quite different ouputs from very similar inputs, yet visually similar words (e.g. CAT and COT) often have quite different meanings. One effective way a network can accomplish this mapping is to construct large basins of attraction around each familiar meaning, such that any initial semantic pattern within the basin will move to that meaning (see Fig. 10).

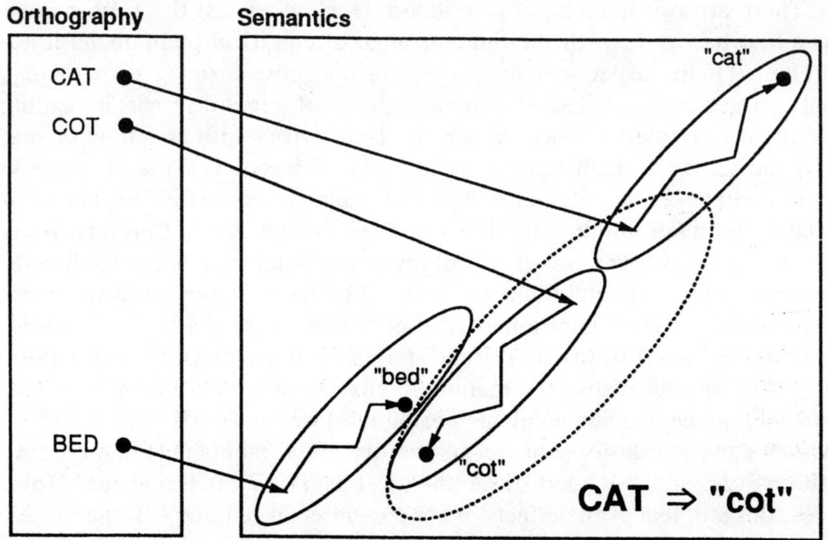

FIG. 10 How damage to semantic attractors can cause visual errors. The solid ovals depict the normal basins of attraction; the dotted one depicts a basin after semantic damage.

Visually similar words are then free to generate fairly similar initial semantic patterns as long as they each manage to fall somewhere within their appropriate basin of attraction. In this way the network learns to shape and position the basins so as to "pull apart" visually similar words into their final distinct semantics. Damage to the semantic clean-up distorts these basins, occasionally causing the normal initial semantic pattern of a word to be captured within the basin of a visually similar word. Essentially, the layout of attractor basins must be sensitive to both visual and semantic similarity, and so these metrics are reflected in the types of errors that occur as a result of damage.

Evaluation of the Model

The aim of H&S's work was to provide a unified account of the nature and co-occurrence of semantic, visual, and mixed reading errors in deep dyslexia. Most previous explanations of why virtually all patients who make semantic errors also make visual errors (e.g. Gordon, Goodman-Schulman, & Caramazza, Note 3; Morton & Patterson, 1980) have had to resort to proposing lesions at multiple locations along the semantic route. Shallice and Warrington (1980) speculated that an inability to access part of the semantic system adequately might give rise to the co-occurrence of errors. However, H&S actually demonstrated that all of these error types arise naturally from single lesions anywhere in a connectionist network that builds attractors in mapping orthography to semantics. Only the quantitative distribution of error types varied systematically with lesion location.

There are two main types of criticism levelled against the H&S model. The first has to do with the limited range of empirical phenomena it addresses. Of the aspects of deep dyslexia that pose problems for theory, only three were modelled—the very existence of semantic errors in reading aloud, the frequent co-occurrence of visual errors with semantic errors, and the relatively high rates of occurrence of mixed visual-and-semantic errors. However, an adequate theory of deep dyslexia would also need to account for a fair number of other aspects of the syndrome. Certain aspects (5, 6, and 10, as listed earlier, p. 26) involve difficulties in mapping directly between print and sound and are covered by the assumption of the gross impairment in the operation of the nonsemantic route(s). Two others, function word substitutions (3) and derivational errors (4), can be interpreted as special cases of semantic or mixed visual-and-semantic errors, and so can be explained in an analogous fashion (see Funnell, 1987). Another two, auditory short-term memory impairments (11) and context effects (12), are dismissed by Coltheart et al. (1987) as too vague. However, this still leaves the effects of concreteness on reading (7), the effects of part-of-speech (8 and 9), and also a number of the additional effects: the interactions between the abstract/concrete dimension and visual errors, confidence ratings, lexical decision, and the visual-then-semantic errors. These phenomena will all be considered directly in this book. One final effect, impaired writing, will be addressed in the General Discussion.

The second type of criticism of the H&S model relates to its generality. H&S argue that the co-occurrence of different error types obtained in deep dyslexia is a natural consequence of lesioning a connectionist network that maps orthography to semantics using attractors. However, their conclusions were essentially based on a single type of network that had many specific features. This is an inevitable consequence of the fact that the design decisions that went into developing the model reflect a tradeoff between (at least) three types of constraint: (a) empirical data from cognitive psychology and neuropsychology, (b) principles of what connectionist networks find easy, difficult, or impossible to do, and (c) limitations of the computational resources available for running simulations. Although H&S attempt to motivate and justify many of their choices, it was only an assumption that the specific features of the resulting model did not significantly contribute to its overall behaviour under damage. Although it is clearly impossible to evaluate every possible aspect of the model, a major focus of this book is to identify those aspects which are critical to reproducing the deep dyslexic error pattern, and those which are less central.

Overview

Most attempts to model acquired dyslexia by lesioning connectionist networks (Mozer & Behrmann, 1990; Patterson, Seidenberg, & McCelland, 1990) have been based on pre-existing models of word reading in normals (Mozer, 1990; Seidenberg & McClelland, 1989). These studies have primarily aimed to provide independent validation of the properties of the normal models that enable them to reproduce phenomena they were not initially designed to address. The work of H&S is rather different in nature in that they were less concerned with supporting a specific model of normal word comprehension than with investigating the effects of damage in a fairly general type of network in the domain of reading via meaning. To the extent that the behaviour of the damaged network mimicked that of deep dyslexic patients, the principles that underly the network's behaviour may provide insight into the cognitive mechanisms of reading in normals, and their breakdown in patients. In this way, the relevance of H&S's simulations to cognitive neuropsychology depends on identifying and evaluating those aspects of the model responsible for its ability to reproduce patient behaviour. In this book, we attempt to provide such an analysis. The three main technical sections, concerning the relevance of network architecture, training procedure, and scope of the task domain, are summarised next.

The Relevance of Network Architecture

H&S provide only a general justification for the network architecture they chose. Hidden units are needed because the problem of mapping orthography to semantics is not linearly separable. Recurrent connections are required to allow the network to develop semantic attractors, whose existence constitutes the major theoretical claim of the work. The choices of numbers of intermediate and clean-up units, restrictions on intra-sememe connections, and connectivity density were an attempt to give the network sufficient flexibility to solve the task and build strong semantic attractors, while keeping the size of the network manageable. Some aspects of the design, particularly the selective use of intra-sememe connections, were rather inelegant and ad hoc. A section entitled "The Relevance of Network Architecture" describes simulations involving a range of network architectures that attempt to evaluate directly the impact of architectural distinctions on the pattern of errors produced under damage. The results demonstrate that the qualitative error pattern after damage is surprisingly insensitive to architectural deatils, as long as attractors continue to operate downstream from the lesion.

Following the architectural comparisons, we investigate more detailed aspects of the pattern of correct and impaired performance shown to varying degrees by all of the networks. These considerations serve both to verify the generality of the results, and to extend the range of phenomena in deep dyslexia accounted for by the modelling approach.

Generating Phonological Responses. A serious limitation of H&S's work involves the use of proximity and gap criteria in determining the response produced by the network under damage. These criteria were intended to approximate the requirements of a system that would actually generate responses based on semantic activity. H&S provided evidence that the main qualitative effects obtained do not depend on specific values for these criteria, but their adequacy as an approximation to an output system was left unverified. To this end, we develop an *output* network that generates explicit phonological responses on the basis of semantic activity. When combined with each of the previously developed *input* networks, the resulting complete implementations of the semantic route replicate the co-occurrence of error types, thereby verifying the generality of the original results based on response criteria. In addition, lesions to the output network itself also produce the deep dyslexic error pattern, thus providng an account of the similarity among subvarieties of the syndrome.

Item- and Category-specific Effects. The small size of the H&S word set raises the possibility that many of the effects arise from idiosyncratic characteristics of the word set itself, and not to any real systematic relationship between orthography and semantics. We verify that the effects we have demonstrated are distributed across the entire word set. We also discuss peculiar selective preservation or impairment of performance for particular categories after some types of lesions.

Definitions of Visual and Semantic Similarity. H&S used definitions of visual and semantic similarity, in terms of letter overlap and category membership, that are analogous to those used for patients. However, these definitions only approximate the actual similarity structure of the visual and semantic representations of words. We demonstrate that a distribution of error types occurs when errors are classified using criteria based on the orthographic and semantic proximity of words, indicating that the use of the original definitions for visual and semantic similarity does not significantly bias the results.

Visual-then-semantic Errors. Visual-then-semantic errors are generally assumed to arise from the combined effects of two separate lesions, producing a visual error followed by a semantic error. We demonstrate that they occur after single lesions in our networks, when the damaged input network fails to clean-up a visual error completely, which is then misinterpreted as a semantically related word by the intact output network.

Effects of Lesion Severity. Most of our results, as well as those of H&S, are based on averaging the effects of lesions resulting in moderate correct performance. We investigate the effect of lesion severity on error pattern, demonstrating higher overall error rates and a higher proportion of unrelated errors with increasing lesion severity.

Error Patterns for Individual Lesions. Some issues in deep dyslexia, involving the relationship of performance on individual words for the same lesion, cannot be addressed if data are averaged across lesions. We show that peculiar error combinations, such as reversals like THUNDER → "storm" and STORM → "thunder" by GR (Marshall & Newcombe, 1966), also occur in our networks.

The Relevance of Training Procedure

H&S justify the use of an admittedly implausible learning procedure in two ways. The first is to emphasise that they were not directly concerned with simulating aspects of the acquisition of reading, but only its breakdown in mature, skilled readers. Thus, the learning procedure can be viewed solely as a programming technique for determining a set of weights that is effective for performing the task. The second justification they use is to point out that back-propagation is only one of a number of ways of performing gradient descent learning in connectionist networks. Other more plausible gradient descent procedures, such as contrastive Hebbian learning in deterministic Boltzmann Machines (Hinton, 1989b; Peterson & Anderson, 1987), are more computationally intensive than back-propagation but typically develop similar representations.

In a section entitled "The Relevance of Training Procedure," we present simulations that replicate and extend the H&S results using a deterministic Boltzmann Machine (DBM). Specifically, lesions throughout a DBM that maps orthography to phonology via semantics produce qualitatively the same error pattern as was found with the back-propagation networks. In addition, the DBM has interesting computational characteristics that are useful for understanding two additional aspects of deep dyslexic reading behaviour: greater confidence in visual vs. semantic errors, and preserved lexical decision with impaired naming.

Confidence in Visual vs. Semantic Errors. Some deep dyslexic patients are more confident that their visual error responses are correct as compared with their semantic error responses. Two analogues for confidence are developed in the DBM: the speed of settling, and the quality of the resulting representations. Using both measures, visual errors are produced with more confidence than semantic errors after damage.

Lexical Decision. Deep dyslexic patients can often distinguish non-words from words they cannot read. Similarly, the DBM continues to show good lexical decision performance after damage when *yes* responses to a letter string are based on the degree to which the string can be re-created on the basis of orthographic and semantic knowledge.

Extending the Task Domain

A rather severe limitation of the H&S model is that it was trained on only 40 words, allowing only a very coarse approximation to the range of visual and semantic similarity among words in a patient's vocabulary. In particular, important variables known to affect patients' reading behaviour, such as word length, frequency, syntactic class, and imageability/concreteness, were not manipulated. Simulations presented in a section entitled "Extending the Task Domain: Effects of Concreteness" extend the H&S approach to account for effects of concreteness in deep dyslexic reading performance.

Following Jones (1985) and others, we develop a semantic representation in which concrete words have "richer" representations, in terms of number of active features, than do abstract words. A back-propagation network is developed that maps orthography to phonology via these representations. Because abstract words have far fewer features, they are less able to engage the semantic clean-up mechanism effectively, and must rely more heavily on the direct pathway. As a result, lesions to the direct pathway of the input network reproduce the effects of concreteness/imageability and their interaction with visual errors found in deep dyslexia: better correct performance for concrete over abstract words, a tendency for error responses to be more concrete than stimuli, and a higher proportion of visual errors in response to abstract compared with concrete words. By contrast, severe lesions to the clean-up pathway produce the reverse advantage for abstract words, similar to the concrete word dyslexic patient, CAV (Warrington, 1981).

The book concludes with a General Discussion in which we focus on the principles that underly the ability of networks to reproduce the characteristics of deep dyslexia, and their degree of generality. We then evaluate the degree to which these computational principles account for the full range of patient behaviour. The relationship between the current approach and other theoretical accounts of deep dyslexia is considered next. We conclude by considering more general issues regarding the impact of connectionist modelling in neuropsychology.

THE RELEVANCE OF NETWORK ARCHITECTURE

Perhaps the most perplexing aspect of connectionist modelling is the design of network architecture, by which we mean choices of numbers of units and their connectivity. One reason the choices in network design often appear rather arbitrary is that they are influenced both by general connectionist principles and by the specific nature of the task at hand. Unfortunately, the general principles are rarely made explicit, and the effect of particular architectural decisions on different aspects of network behaviour in a specific task is often ill-understood. H&S attempt to make explicit both the general and specific considerations that went into developing their model. The general considerations involve a tradeoff between ensuring that the network has sufficient capacity to solve the task, while keeping the network as small as possible to stay within available computational resources. The specific considerations centre around attempting to facilitate the ability of the network to map between two domains, orthography and semantics, which are arbitrarily related. These two types of concerns influence the number, size, and interconnectivity of unit layers.

The simplest architecture would be to connect input units directly to output units, but such networks have severe computational limitations that prevent them from learning arbitrary associations (Minsky & Papert, 1969). In general, to accomplish such tasks it is necessary to add at least one layer of nonlinear *hidden* units between the input and output layers (Ackley et al., 1985). Because these layers are not part of the input or output, the representations they use must be determined by a general learning procedure. Typically only one hidden layer is used because most learning procedures slow down exponentially with the number of intervening hidden layers (see, e.g., Plaut & Hinton, 1987). Such three-layer networks are ubiquitous in connectionist modelling because they can learn any boolean function with enough hidden units (an exponential number in the worst case, but only a polynomial number for most "reasonable" functions; Denker et al., 1987).

In considering how units are connected, a major architectural distinction is between *feed-forward* and *recurrent* networks. In a feed-forward network, unit layers can be ordered such that units receive connections only from earlier layers. For a given input pattern, this restriction allows the final state of each unit to be computed in a single pass through the network, from input to output. However, for this very reason the extent to which units in a feed-forward network can interact is extremely limited. In particular, feed-forward networks cannot develop attractors because each unit in the network only updates its state once—the network cannot reapply the unit nonlinearities to clean up a pattern of activity over time. By contrast, recurrent networks have no restrictions on how units are connected, enabling interactions between units within a layer, and from later to earlier layers. When presented with input, units must repeatedly recompute their states, because changing the state of a unit may change the input to earlier units. In this way, recurrent networks can gradually settle into a stable set of unit states, called a *fixedpoint* or an *attractor*, in which unit inputs and outputs remain constant.[4] Recurrent networks are particularly appropriate for temporal domains, such as language processing (Elman, 1990) and motor control (Jordan, 1986). They are also more effective at learning arbitrary associations because the reapplication of unit nonlinearities at every iteration can magnify initially small state differences into quite large ones. Feed-forward networks require very large weights and, hence, very long training time to map similar inputs to quite different outputs. Unit interactions in a recurrent network can fill out and clean up initially noisy or incomplete patterns, producing behaviour in which the initial pattern of activity moves towards the nearest attractor state.

The existence of attractors for word meanings forms the basis for H&S's explanation of the co-occurrence of visual and semantic errors in deep dyslexia. In order to allow such attractors to develop, H&S introduced direct connections among closely related sememe units. However, these connections only allow pairwise interactions—there is no way for *combinations* of sememes to have direct influences. For example, only the conjunc-

[4]In addition to *point* attractors, recurrent networks can be trained to settle into *limit cycle* (Pearlmutter, 1989) and *chaotic* attractors (Skarda & Freeman, 1987), but this type of behaviour is not directly relevant for our purposes.

tion of *green* and *found-woods* implies *living*—neither feature alone does. These higher-order semantic *micro-inferences* (Hinton, 1981) strengthen the attractors for words (i.e. increase the sizes and depth of their basins of attraction) by filling out the initially incomplete semantics generated bottom-up and with only pairwise interactions. In order to implement them there must be hidden units that receive connections from some sememe units and send connections to others. Although H&S could have used the intermediate units for this purpose by introducing feedback connections to them from semantics, they chose instead to introduce a second set of hidden (clean-up) units as an approximation to the influences of other parts of the cognitive system on lexical semantics—these might be thought of as including aspects of meaning with less direct influence on naming (e.g. the visual semantics of objects; Beauvois, 1982; Shallice, 1987; 1988b). In addition, separating the groups of hidden units allows them to specialise differently: One group can mediate directly between orthography and semantics; the other can make inferences among semantic features.

A final consideration in architecture design is the pattern of connectivity between layers of units. The capacity of a network is largely determined by its number of connections, since the weights on these connections encode the long-term knowledge used to solve the task. For a given number of connections, there is a trade-off between using many sparsely connected units versus using fewer densely connected units. Using many units results in a higher-dimensional representation in a layer, allowing easier discrimination between similar patterns in earlier layers. However, because each unit is only sparsely connected to layers providing input, the complexity of the distinctions it can learn is limited. In particular, as connectivity density is reduced it becomes harder for individual units to be sensitive to higher-order structure in earlier layers and enforce higher-order coherence in later layers.

Most connectionist networks use complete connectivity between layers, but this can result in a large number of connections for networks with even a moderate number of units. Full connectivity between layers in the H&S network would have resulted in almost 17,000 connections. Networks with far more capacity than is required to learn a task tend to approximate a table-lookup strategy without capturing any interesting structure in the task. Accordingly, H&S chose to include only a random 25% of the possible connections between layers, and intra-sememe connections only among related semantic features, in order to reduce the network to a computationally reasonable size of about 3300 connections. In addition, reduced connectivity makes the bottom-up input from orthography to semantics relatively impoverished, particularly because the usefulness of individual intermediate units is limited by the absence of individual $G \rightarrow I$ connections when input letters are represented by single grapheme units.

H&S argued that impoverished bottom-up input to sememe units encouraged reliance on clean-up interactions, resulting in stronger semantic attractors.

Even among recurrent networks with hidden units that build strong attractors with a minimum number of connections, there are a vast number of possible network architectures. H&S chose one and demonstrated that its behaviour under damage had interesting similarities with the reading behaviour of deep dyslexic patients. For computational reasons it is clearly not feasible to implement every alternative architecture in order to investigate the generality of the H&S results. However, it is important to gain a better understanding of the relevance of the particular aspects of their design. In this section, we develop five alternative architectures that differ from the H&S model in terms of numbers of hidden units, connectivity density, existence of intra-sememe connections, location of clean-up pathway, and separation of intermediate and clean-up units. We then systematically lesion each of these networks and compare the effects, in order better to understand the impact of architectural differences on behaviour under damage. Following this, we take up a number of separate issues concerning aspects of the pattern of performance shown to varying degrees by all of these networks. These considerations serve both to verify the generality of the results, and to extend the range of phenomena in deep dyslexia accounted for by the modelling approach.

Alternative Architectures

Figure 11 depicts each of the five alternative architectures for mapping orthography to semantics. The networks, and the main issues they are intended to address, are the following:

40–60 *Intra-sememe connections*. This network most closely approximates the original H&S network, with 40 intermediate units, 60 clean-up units, and 25% connectivity density. However, it lacks any direct connections among sememe units, so it will allow us to investigate the importance of such connections. The network has 3252 connections.

10–15d *Connectivity density*. Rather than using 25% connectivity density, the *10–15d* network has complete connectivity between layers. Lesions to this network will allow us to evaluate the impact of connectivity density (hence the *d* in the name). In order to keep the number of connections approximately the same as the other networks, only 10 intermediate units and 15 clean-up units were used. The resulting network has 3134 connections.,

40–80i *Location of clean-up*. This network has clean-up prior to semantics, at the level of the intermediate units (hence the *i*), rather than within semantics. We can thus evaluate the importance of the location of

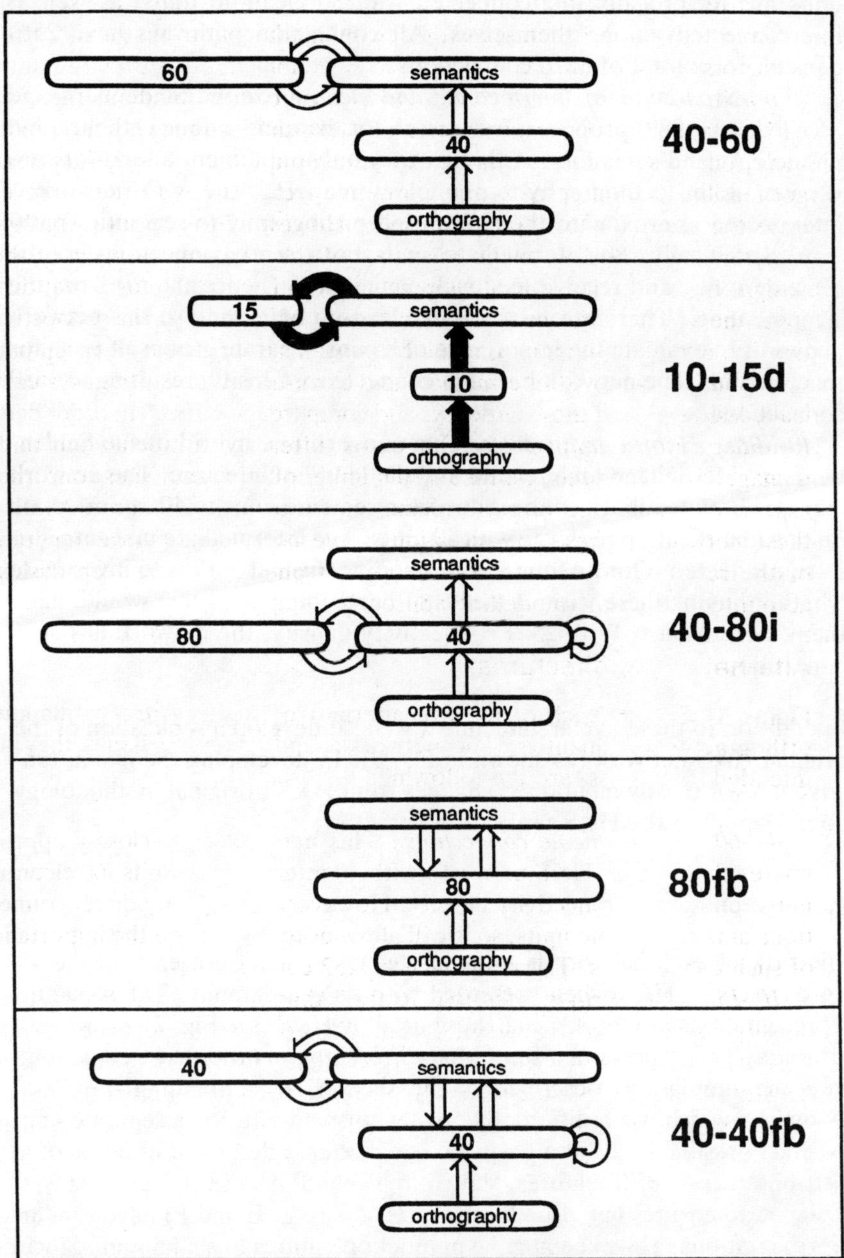

FIG. 11 Five alternative network architectures for mapping orthography to semantics.

clean-up on behaviour under damage, and whether the attractors must be *semantic* in order to produce the H&S results. Specifically, the intermediate units are reciprocally interconnected with 80 clean-up units, as well as interconnected among themselves. All connection pathways have 25% density, for a total of 3226 connections.

80fb Separation of intermediate and clean-up units. Seidenberg and McClelland (1989) propose a framework for mapping among orthography, phonology, and semantics. Although they only implement a feed-forward version of the orthography-to-phonology mapping, the *80fb* network is intended to approximate their proposed orthography-to-semantics pathway. Specifically, 80 intermediate units both send connections to the sememe units, and receive feedback connections (hence the *fb*) from the sememe units. There are no separate clean-up units, and so this network allows us to evaluate the importance of having separate groups of units for this function. The network has 25% connectivity density, resulting in 3550 connections.

40–40fb Hybrid architecture. This network is a hybrid of the Seidenberg and McClelland architecture and the H&S architecture. The network includes both feedback connections from sememe units to 40 intermediate units and a clean-up pathway with 40 units. The intermediate units are also intra-connected. Our intention in developing this network is to investigate whether having these various means of developing attractors would make them more robust. With 25% connectivity density, the network has 3626 connections.

In addition to these five architectures, we also develop a replication of the original H&S network (as shown in Fig. 9). In developing the five alternative networks, any mentioned changes from H&S's original methodology do not apply to the H&S replication network.

The Task

The task of each network is to generate the semantics of each of the 40 words used by H&S when presented with its orthography. The semantic representations are the same as those used by H&S (see Fig. 7). However, orthography is represented somewhat differently, in order to be consistent with the simulations described in the section on "Extending the Task Domain," which use a different word set. Instead of using a separate unit for each possible letter at a position, each letter is described in terms of a distributed code of 8 features, shown in Table 3. The set of features was designed to ensure that visually similar letters (e.g. E and F) have similar representations, while keeping the number of features to a minimum. Since the H&S word set has some 4-letter words, a total of 32 *orthographic*

TABLE 3
The Assignment of Features to Letters for the Distributed Orthographic Code

A	01010110	J	11100000	S	00100001
B	10111001	K	10001011	T	11000100
C	00101000	L	11000001	U	10100100
D	10111000	M	10000111	V	00000110
E	11001000	N	10000010	W	00000111
F	11000000	O	00111100	X	00001110
G	01100001	P	10110000	Y	10000110
H	11001101	Q	00110010	Z	01000011
I	11001100	R	10110011		

The meaning of the features are roughly (1) contains a vertical stroke; (2) contains a horizontal stroke; (3) contains a curved stroke; (4) contains a closed part; (5) horizontally symmetric; (6) vertically symmetric; (7) contains diagonal stroke; (8) discriminator between otherwise identical letters.

units—in contrast to letter-specific grapheme units—will serve as the input layer of each network.

The Training Procedure

Each network was trained in the same way as the H&S network, with two differences. The first is that the network was allowed to run for eight instead of seven iterations to allow information about the input to cycle through the clean-up loop and influence the semantic units an extra time. The second difference is that the orthographic input presented to each network was corrupted by independent gaussian noise with mean 0.0 and standard deviation 0.1. Training on noisy input amounts to enforcing a particular kind of generalisation: Inputs that are *near* known patterns must give identical responses. Thus, each word's attractor must be strong enough to attract the range of initial semantic patterns that are generated from the noisy versions of its orthography.

Training continued until each network could activate semantic features for each word to within 0.1 of its correct value. For each network, the following number of sweeps through the set of words was required, in increasing order: H&S replication: 333; *40–60*: 2640; *10–15d*: 3625; *40–40fb*: 4083; *80fb*: 7302; and *40–80i*: 14,008. First notice that, although training with noisy input should encourage stronger attractors, it takes an order of magnitude more training to do so. For the networks trained with noise, training required a few thousand sweeps for all but the *40–80i* network. The reason that this latter network took so much longer is that it lacks any interactions among sememe units, so these units cannot clean themselves up into binary responses. They must rely on the clean-up at the intermediate level to eliminate the influences of noise and to drive them appropriately. Driving units into binary responses using only feed-forward connections typically involves traversing down the bottom of a long shallow ravine in weight space, which requires many sweeps through the training set (see Plaut & Hinton, 1987).

The Effects of Lesions

Twenty instances of lesions of a range of severity were applied to the main sets of connections in each network. A wide range of severities were investigated: 0.05, 0.1, 0.15, 0.2, 0.25, 0.3, 0.4, 0.5, and 0.7. Using a proximity of 0.8 and a gap of 0.05 as the criteria for a response, correct, omission, and error responses were accumulated. Each error response was then categorised in terms of its visual and semantic similarity to the stimulus. The percentages of overall correct responses and distributions of error types were determined for each network. For reasons of space we present here only a small selection of the results—for more details, see Plaut (Note 9). In particular, the basic analyses of the type carried out by H&S are given for two networks only, namely the *40–60* network (Fig. 12) and the *40–80i* network (Fig. 13). Results are averaged over lesion severities that produce overall correct performance between 15–85%. The number of lesion severities falling within this range is indicated in parentheses below the label for each lesion location in the error distribution graphs. In addition, "Chance" is the distribution of error types if responses were chosen randomly from the word set. Its absolute height is set arbitrarily—only the relative rates are informative.

Summary of Architecture Comparisons

Generality of the Hinton and Shallice Findings

There are a number of general conclusions that can be drawn from the properties of this set of networks. The overall pattern of results with respect to correct performance and explicit error rates after lesioning is shown in Table 4. Two results are clearly apparent. First, as in the original H&S simulations, lesions to the clean-up pathway are less deleterious than those to the direct pathway. However, another aspect of the H&S findings does not generalise. For some networks, I → S lesions are more damaging than O → I lesions, but for others the opposite effect holds.

As was true of the H&S network, the rates of explicit errors are relatively low, with the highest being just above 30% after O → I lesions in the *10–15d* network. Although the error rates of deep dyslexic patients vary considerably, in general they are much higher than after most lesions in the network. Weakening the response criteria would increase the overall explicit response rate, including errors, but this would also presumably

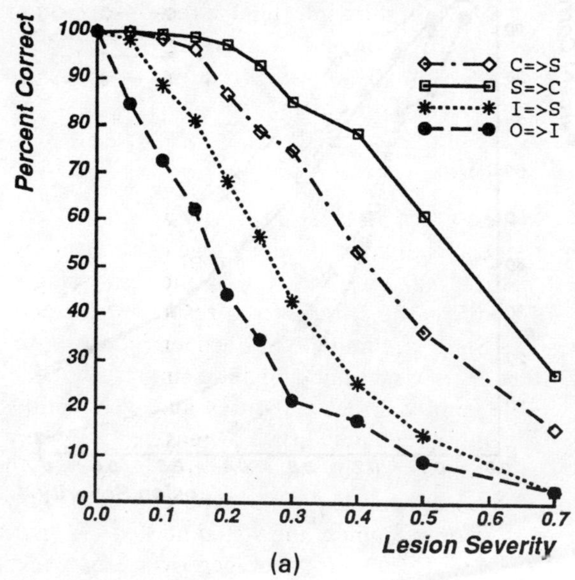

(a)

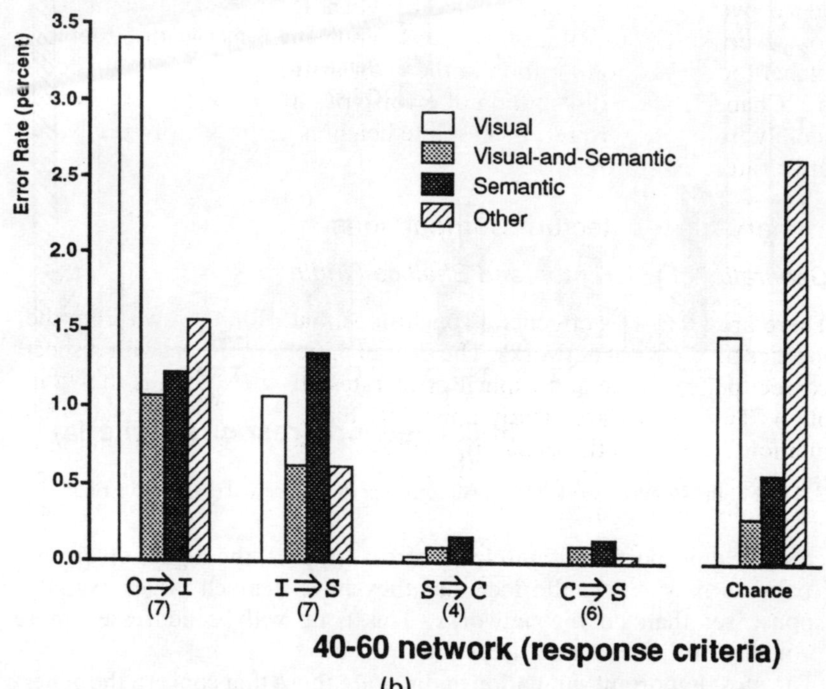

(b)

FIG. 12 For the *40–60* network, (a) overall correct performance and (b) error distributions.

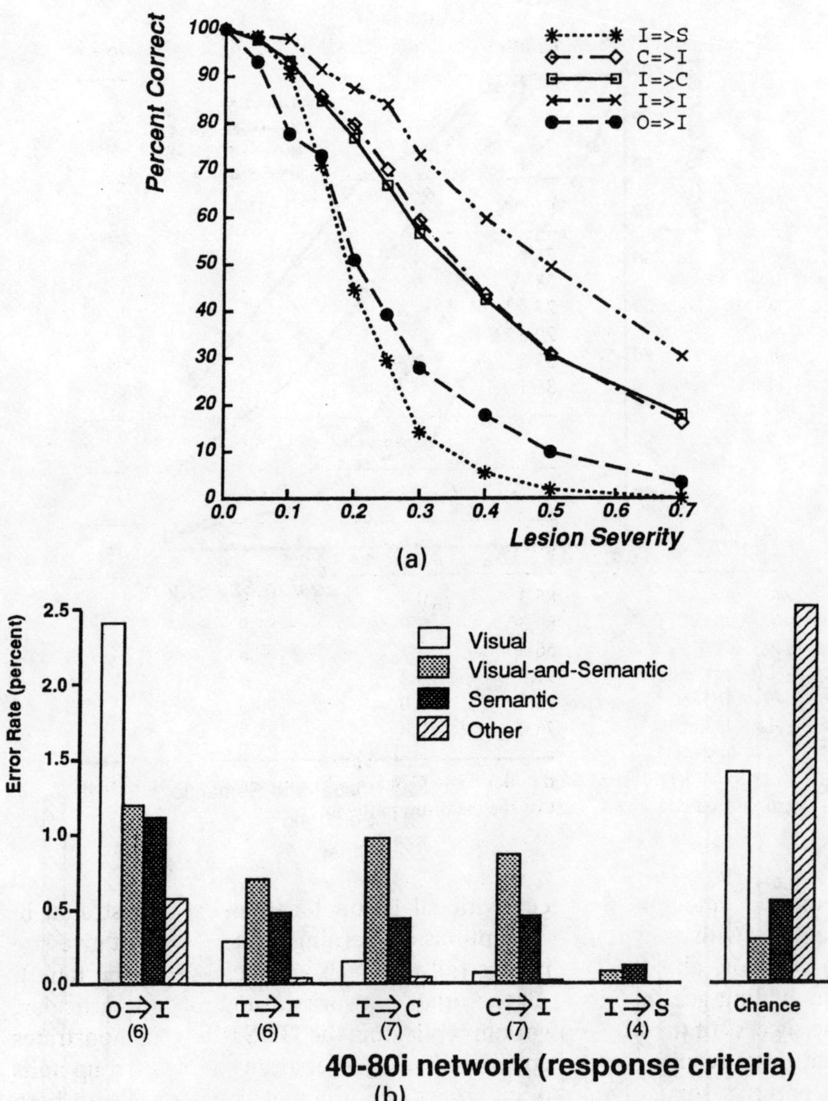

FIG. 13 For the *40–80i* network, (a) overall correct performance and (b) error distributions.

increase the proportion of unrelated errors. In part, the higher error rates of patients may reflect the fact that they have a much larger available response set than do the networks. This issue will be addressed more thoroughly in the General Discussion.

The most important simulation findings are those that concern the generality of the theoretically critical results obtained by H&S. These fall into two parts. H&S's main conclusion was that all types of error—visual,

TABLE 4
Correct and Error Rates after Lesions of Severity 0.3 in Each Network

	Direct Pathway Lesions			
	O → I		*I → S*	
Network	*Correct*	*Errors*	*Correct*	*Errors*
40–60	21.9	11.8	42.9	4.1
10–15d	38.1	31.5	50.1	8.6
40–80i[a]	27.9	7.1	14.1	0.0
80fb	29.4	13.3	9.6	1.4
40–40fb	31.5	14.0	46.9	2.5
H&S replication	38.1	5.0	8.4	2.8
	Clean-up Pathway Lesions			
	S → C or I → C		*C → S or C → I*	
Network	*Correct*	*Errors*	*Correct*	*Errors*
40–60	85.3	0.4	74.9	0.4
10–15d	80.3	3.0	81.9	1.4
40–80i[a]	56.5	2.5	59.3	2.3
80fb	91.0	0.3	—	—
40–40fb	96.0	0.0	90.3	0.3
H&S replication	76.0	0.3	25.9	1.4

[a]S → I lesions are listed under "S → C or I → C," and the I → S connections should be considered part of the clean-up pathway.

semantic, and mixed—occur with all lesion locations. As illustrated in Table 5, with a few minor exceptions concerning lesion sites that give rise to very low absolute error rates (all of which are included in the table), this finding generalises to all the other networks examined. In particular, the success of the *80fb* network in replicating the H&S results demonstrates that those results do not depend on having a separate set of clean-up units to perform semantic micro-inferences. Intermediate units can learn both to convey information about orthography and to interact with semantics to form attractors for word meanings. However, using intermediate units in this way has implications for the distribution of error types—in particular, the rates of mixed visual-and-semantic errors. A second finding of H&S was that mixed visual-and-semantic errors occur more frequently than one would expect given the independent rates of visual errors and of semantic errors. This finding appears to be less general than the simple co-occurrence of error types. The replication of the H&S network, using the original input representation and trained without noise, also exhibits

TABLE 5
Error Distributions Produced by Representative Lesions in Each Network

	Overall Error Rates			Conditional Probabilities				
Network	*Lesion*	*n*	*Rate*	*Vis*	*V&S*[a]	*Sem*	*Other*	*V/S Ratio*
	O→I	7	7.3	46.7	14.9	16.9	21.5	2.76
40–60	I→S	7	3.7	29.8	16.8	36.5	16.8	0.82
	C→S	6	0.3	—	35.7	50.0	14.3	0.00
	O→I	8	25.0	53.4	14.4	10.3	21.9	5.18
10–15d	S→C	6	3.6	35.1	32.2	27.0	5.7	1.30
	C→S	6	0.5	—	60.0	36.0	4.0	0.00
	O→I	6	5.3	45.3	22.8	21.3	10.6	2.13
40–80i	I→Ci	7	1.6	9.0	61.8	27.0	2.2	0.33
	I→S	4	0.2	—	40.0	60.0	—	0.00
	O→I	6	8.1	43.7	21.3	15.2	19.8	2.88
80fb	I→S	4	1.8	11.9	45.8	33.9	8.5	0.35
	S→I	3	0.7	—	68.8	18.8	12.5	0.00
	O→I	6	9.6	45.0	17.4	18.7	18.9	2.41
40–40fb	I→S	5	1.7	12.1	31.8	50.0	6.1	0.24
	C→S	5	0.7	—	28.6	71.4	—	0.00
	O→I	7	3.8	30.3	36.5	24.6	8.5	1.23
H&S replication	I→S	5	2.2	8.1	46.5	41.9	3.5	0.19
	C→S	6	1.0	6.1	61.2	32.7	—	0.19
Chance Distribution				29.9	6.2	11.8	52.2	2.47

Data are from lesions that resulted in 15–85% correct performance in each network. "*n*" refers to the number of lesion severities producing performance falling within the 15–85% range, and "Rate" is the average percentage of word presentations producing explicit error responses for these lesions.

[a]V&S = visual and semantic.

higher than expected mixed rates. However, among networks using the distributed letter representations and trained with noise, the effect is only found when the intermediate units are directly involved in developing attractors—the *40–80i*, *80fb*, and *40–40fb* networks, but not the *40–60* and *10–15d* networks (compare Figs. 12b and 13b).

Why might these differing patterns of effects occur? One possibility is that the *40–60* and *10–15d* networks form strong semantic attractors using the clean-up pathway, so that maximum visual similarity effects occur at a considerably earlier stage of processing than maximum semantic similarity effects. Thus, the transformation from visual to semantic similarity is realised through separable stages. The replication of the H&S network, trained without noise, forms weaker semantic attractors using the clean-up units, so that more of the work of mapping visual to semantic similarity is carried out by the direct pathway. This compresses the stages over which visual and semantic similarity operate, and therefore makes interactions between them in the stimulus set—the potential for mixed errors—more critical. This is also true of the networks in which intermediate units are involved in implementing attractors. In these networks, the attractors lie at a stage where visual and semantic influences cannot be separated.

It should be pointed out that this account is somewhat speculative—the main point is that the mixed error findings of H&S, although narrowly robust, do not generalise to all lesion sites of all connectionist networks. It is a consequence of particular characteristics of some network architectures.

The Strength of Attractors

At a more general theoretical level, the argument that H&S put forward, of the importance of attractors in the generation of errors, is borne out. The robustness of a network to lesions of a set of connections, measured by the rate of correct performance, increases with the strength of the attractors at levels after the locus of damage. At the same time, the rates of explicit errors from lesions to these connections also rise. In essence, the attractors serve to clean-up both correct and incorrect responses, reducing the number of omissions caused by damage. In contrast, lesions at or beyond the level of the last attractors in a network produce a very low rate of overt responses, both correct and incorrect.

This effect can be seen by comparing the *40–60* network with the *10–15d* network (see Table 4). Both networks use the same input and output representations, were trained identically, and develop attractors at the semantic level. However, the overall correct performance and explicit error rates for the *10–15d* network are higher than for the *40–60* network for both O → I and I → S lesions. The *10–15d* network develops stronger attractors because its full connectivity between layers makes it more effective than the *40–60* network at implementing semantic micro-inferences that depend on the interaction of two or more semantic features on a third. The probability that the semantic features involved will be appropriately connected to some clean-up unit is 1.0 in the *10–15d* network but quite small ($0.25^3 \simeq 0.016$) in the *40–60* network due to its 25% connectivity density. The replication of the H&S network, which it was argued has weaker semantic attractors than the *40–60* network, is less robust overall to lesions of the direct pathway (although the balance between O → I and I → S is reversed) and has lower explicit error rates.

For the *40–80i* and *80fb* networks, correct and error rates are comparable to those of the *40–60* network for O → I lesions, which are located before the level at which their attractors operate. A different pattern is obtained from lesions to I → S connections, which are post-attractor for the *40–80i* network, within-attractor for the *80fb* network, and pre-attractor for the *40–60* network. Both the correct and error rates are much lower for the first two networks than for the *40–60* network (e.g. I → S [0.3], correct: *40–80i*: 14.1% and *80fb*: 9.6% vs. *40–60*: 42.9%; errors: *40–80i*: 0.2% and *80fb*: 1.8% vs. *40–60*: 3.7%).[5] The very low error rate for the post-attractor I → S lesions in the *40-80i* network reinforces the arguments presented earlier, that the occurrence of explicit errors depends on damaged input being cleaned-up into an incorrect attractor.

Quantitative Variation in Error Pattern

For all networks, error rates are much higher for O → I lesions than for I → S lesions, presumably because the output of the undamaged I → S connections will be more likely to be closer to a word representation than will their damaged output. In addition, for the networks that have attractors only at the semantic level (H&S replication, *40–60*, *10–15d*), both the absolute and relative rates of visual errors drop sharply between O → I and I → S lesions, and the absolute and relative rates of semantic errors climb (although the absolute rise is a modest one). This general trend is shown directly in the ratio of visual errors to semantic errors for lesions closer to orthography compared with lesions closer to semantics (see the right-hand column of Table 5). These findings are similar to those obtained by H&S and indicate that such networks can give rise to the quantitative differences in the distribution of error types found across deep dyslexic patients.

We now turn to a number of separate issues that concern more detailed aspects of the pattern of correct and impaired performance shown to varying degrees by all of these networks. These considerations serve both to verify that the general effects produced by the networks are not due to idiosyncratic characteristics of the word set or interpretation procedure, and also to demonstrate that the networks behave like deep dyslexic patients in terms of the pattern of responses after individual lesions.

Generating Phonological Responses

Most data on deep dyslexic reading comes from tasks in which the patient produces a verbal response to a visually presented word. Since the output of each network we have considered thus far consists of a pattern of semantic activity, some external procedure is needed to convert this pattern

[5] Not surprisingly, the hybrid *40–40fb* network shows hybrid characteristics.

into an explicit response so that it can be compared with the oral reading responses of deep dyslexic patients. Following H&S, the procedure we have used compares the semantic activity produced by the network with the correct semantics of all known words, selecting the closest-matching word as long as the match is sufficiently good (the *proximity* criterion) and sufficiently better than any other match (the *gap* criterion). The rationale for these criteria is that semantic activity that is too unfamiliar or ambiguous would be unable to drive an output system effectively. However, satisfying the criteria only coarsely approximates the requirements of an actual output system. In particular, although it may be reasonable that semantic activity failing the criteria could not drive a response system, no evidence was given that semantic activity satisfying the criteria could succeed in generating a response. Also, the criteria are insensitive to the relative semantic and phonological discriminability of words and so may inadvertently be biased towards producing certain effects. Finally, at a more general level, if too much of the difficulty of a problem is pushed off into the assumed mechanisms for generating the input or interpreting the output, the role of the network itself becomes less interesting (Lachter & Bever, 1988; Pinker & Prince, 1988).

For these reasons, it would be a significant advance over the use of response criteria to extend the networks to derive explicit phonological responses on the basis of semantic activity. Implementing a full version of the semantic route would ensure that the occurrence of the deep dyslexic error pattern under damage is due to properties of the network and not to those of an interpretation procedure external to the network. Furthermore, a number of additional issues can be addressed in a model that maps orthography to phonology via semantics that cannot be addressed in a network that only derives semantics. Specifically, H&S could consider only the *input* and *central* forms of deep dyslexia (Shallice & Warrington, 1980). Furthermore, they had to assume that the specific nature of the output system plays no role in these patients' reading errors, contrary to many theories of deep dyslexia (e.g. Coltheart et al., 1987; Marshall & Newcombe, 1966). With a full semantic route, it becomes possible to investigate directly impairments in deriving phonology from semantics by lesioning connections in the phonological output system. In addition, without having to apply criteria to semantics, we can investigate the effects of lesions to the semantic units themselves.

Accordingly, we develop an *output* network analogous to the *input* networks described earlier, but which takes as input the semantic representation of a word and produces a phonological representation. This network is then combined with each input network that maps from orthography to semantics, resulting in much larger networks that map from orthography to phonology via semantics.

The Task

The input to the output network consists of the 40 semantic representations that served as the output of the input networks. A phonological representation was defined in terms of 33 position-specific *phoneme* units (see Table 6). For each word, exactly 1 unit in each of 3 positions is active, possibly including a unit in the third position that explicitly represents the absence of a third phoneme. This representation allows the units that represent alternative phonemes in the same position to compete in a "winner-take-all" fashion.

Because damage will impair the ability of the network to derive the

TABLE 6
Phonological Representations of the Hinton and Shallice Words

(a) Phonemes Allowed in Each Position

Pos.	*Phonemes*
1	b d dy g h j k l m n p r t
2	a ar aw e ew i ie o oa ow u
3	b d g k n m p t –

(b) Assignment of Phonemes to Words

Indoor Objects		*Animals*		*Body Parts*	
BED	/b e d/	BUG	/b u g/	BACK	/b a k/
CAN	/k a n/	CAT	/k a t/	BONE	/b oa n/
COT	/k o t/	COW	/k ow –/	GUT	/g u t/
CUP	/k u p/	DOG	/d o g/	HIP	/h i p/
GEM	/j e m/	HAWK	/h aw k/	LEG	/l e g/
MAT	/m a t/	PIG	/p i g/	LIP	/l i p/
MUG	/m u g/	RAM	/r a m/	PORE	/p aw –/
PAN	/p a n/	RAT	/r a t/	RIB	/r i b/

Foods		*Outdoor Objects*	
BUN	/b u n/	BOG	/b o g/
HAM	/h a m/	DEW	/dy ew –/
HOCK	/h o k/	DUNE	/dy ew n/
LIME	/l ie m/	LOG	/l o g/
NUT	/n u t/	MUD	/m u d/
POP	/p o p/	PARK	/p ar k/
PORK	/p aw k/	ROCK	/r o k/
RUM	/r u m/	TOR	/t aw –/

The letter(s) used to represent phonemes are not from a standard phonemic alphabet but rather are intended to have more intuitive pronunciations. Also, the definitions are based on British pronunciations (e.g. HAWK and PORK rhyme).

correct pronunciations of words, we need some way of deciding whether corrupted phonological activity constitutes a well-formed pronunciation. Given our phonological representation, a natural criterion is to require that exactly 1 phoneme unit be active in each of the 3 positions in order to produce a response. However, since units have real-valued outputs which are rarely 0 or 1, we need a more precise definition of "active" and "inactive." The criterion we use is that the most active phoneme at each position is included in the response if its likelihood, relative to the competing phonemes at that position, exceeds a *phonological response criterion* of 0.6.[6] If, at each position, exactly one phoneme satisfies this criterion, the concatenation of these phonemes is produced as the response; otherwise, the phonological activity produced by the network is considered ill formed and it fails to respond.

It is important to point out that this type of criterion is quite different from the H&S criteria, which ensure that an output is semantically *familiar*. The criterion we employ does not rely on any knowledge of the particular words the network has been trained on—it considers only the *form* of the output representation. Also notice that, under this procedure, there are a large number of legal responses other than those the network is trained to produce. We call such responses *blends* because they typically involve a phonological blend of known responses (i.e. a literal paraphasia). The architecture and training procedure for the output network were designed specifically to discourage the production of blends under damage, rather than to simulate the development or detailed operation of the human speech production system (see Plaut & Shallice, Note 9, for futher relevant simulation results and discussion).

The Network Architecture

Figure 14 depicts the architecture of a complete network that maps orthography via semantics to phonology, using the *40–60* input network. The output network forms the top half of this complete network, with the semantic units (without a clean-up circuit) constituting its input layer. It consists of a direct pathway from semantics to phonology via 40 intermediate units, and a phonological clean-up pathway involving an additional 20 clean-up units. Only a random 25% of the possible connections in the direct pathway are included, but all possible connections in the clean-up

[6]More formally, if y_i is the output of phoneme unit i, and d_i is its smallest difference from 0 or 1 (i.e. $d_i = y_i$ if $y_i \leqslant 0.5$ and $1 - y_i$ otherwise), then the network produces a response if, for every position p, $\Pi_{i \epsilon p} d_i > 0.6$ and exactly one $y_i > 0.5$. The product is the probability of the most likely binary output vector at the position when the states of the phoneme units are interpreted as independent probabilities. Thus, the response procedure is closely related to the maximum-likelihood interpretation of the cross-entropy error function used to train the network (Hinton, 1989a).

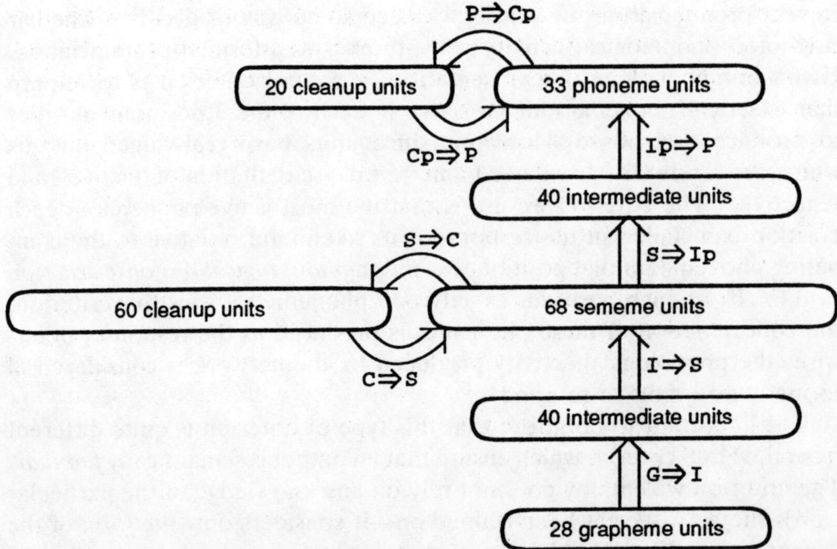

FIG. 14 The architecture for mapping orthography to phonology via semantics. Notice that the names of sets of connections involving the intermediate and clean-up units in the phonological output network are subscripted with a *p* to differentiate them from the corresponding sets of connections in the input network.

pathway are included. This full connectivity density allows the output network to develop strong phonological attractors, much like the semantic attractors of the *10–15d* network.[7] The output network has a total of 2745 connections.

The Training Procedure

Our training strategy will be to develop the output network incrementally. Training parts of the network separately at the outset encourages each part to accomplish as much of the task as possible, without relying on the strengths of the other parts. It should be mentioned that, although the approach of developing phonological attractors independent of semantics is primarily computationally motivated, it is not unreasonable on empirical grounds that attractors for word pronunciations might develop as part of the process of learning to speak before these attractors would become available in reading.

The phonological clean-up pathway of the output network was trained to produce the correct phonemes of each word during the last 3 of 6

[7]A second output network architecture, which included additional connections among phoneme units within each position, was also investigated, and produced qualitatively similar results as the output network described here (see Plaut, Note 8).

iterations when presented with these phonemes corrupted by gaussian noise with a standard deviation of 0.25. Because the phoneme units are both the input and output units for this stage of training, the phonemes cannot be presented by clamping the states of these units. Rather, these units were given an external input throughout the 6 iterations which, in the absence of other inputs, would produce a specified corrupted activity level. This technique is known as *soft clamping*. The direct pathway was trained to produce the phonemes of each word from the semantics of each word, corrupted by gaussian noise with standard deviation 0.1. The input units were clamped in the normal way. Each pathway was trained to activate the phoneme units to within 0.2 of their correct values for a given input. After very extensive training they accomplished this in general, but the amount of noise added to their inputs made it impossible to guarantee this performance on any given trial. For this reason, training was halted when each pathway met the stopping criteria over 10 successive sweeps through the training set.

The separately trained clean-up and direct pathways were then combined into a single, complete output network. This is straightforward because the two pathways have non-overlapping sets of connections, except for the biases of the phoneme units. For these, the biases from the clean-up pathway were used. The network was then given additional training with noisy input, during which only the weights in the direct pathway were allowed to change. In this way the direct pathway adjusted its mapping to use the fixed phonological clean-up more effectively in generating correct word pronunciations.

Finally, separate copies of the output network were attached to each input network and given a final tuning to ensure that the output network operated appropriately when its input was generated over time by an actual input network, rather than being clamped. The weights of the input networks were not allowed to change, so that they continued to derive the correct semantics for each word. After this final training, which took at most a few hundred additional training sweeps, each complete network would derive the semantics and phonology of each word correctly from its orthography.

The Effects of Lesions

Twenty instances of lesions of the standard range of severity were applied to the main sets of connections, as well as to the semantic units, in each extended network. Correct, omission, and error responses were accumulated using phonological response criteria of 0.6, as described earlier. The percentages of overall correct responses and distributions of error types were then determined for each network. Again, in the interest of space and for ease of comparison, we present detailed analyses only when the output network is attached to the *40–60* input network.

Figure 15 presents the overall correct rates of performance after lesions throughoput the extended *40–60* network. Compared with the use of response criteria (see Fig. 12a), the output network makes the *40–60* net-

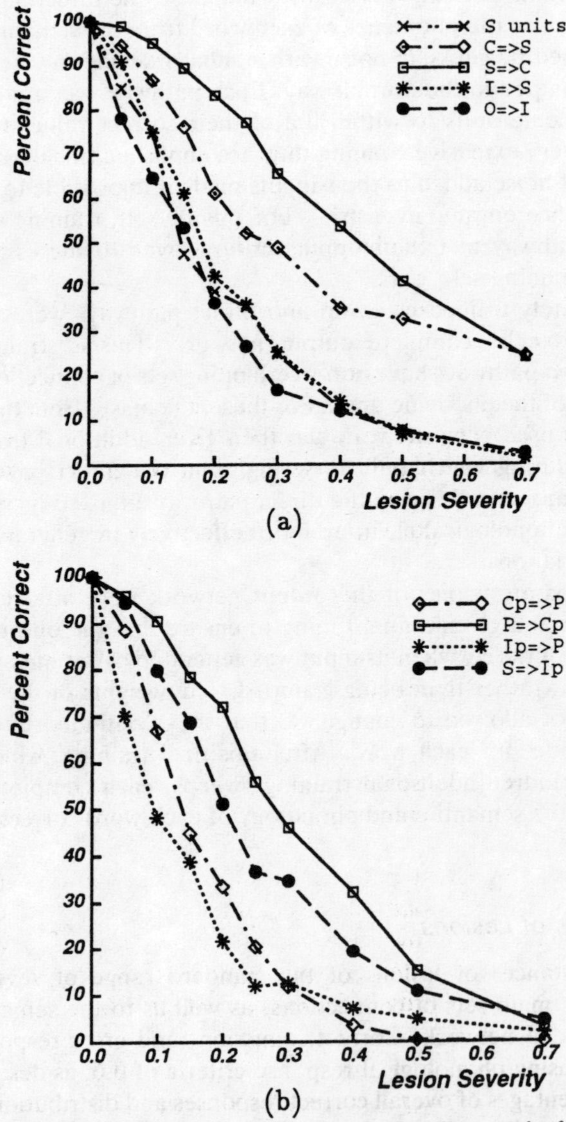

FIG. 15 Overall correct performance of the extended *40–60* network after (a) input and central lesions, and (b) output lesions.

work somewhat more sensitive to lesions—on average, correct performance is 14.2% lower. However, the relative levels of impairment for different input lesion locations remains the same, with O → I lesions producing the greatest impairment and S → C lesions producing the least. Also, lesions to the semantic units are far more debilitating than lesions to the connections in the clean-up pathway. Output lesions reduce correct performance by 12.2% more, on average, than the corresponding input lesions. The impairment after Cp → P lesions is far worse than the corresponding C → S lesions. However, compared with O → I lesions, S → Ip lesions are less detrimental.

Figure 16 shows the distribution of error rates for all lesions of the extended *40–60* network. In addition to visual and semantic similarity, errors can now be phonologically similar—that is, have overlapping phonemes. Since visual and phonological similarity typically co-occur, we considered an error to be phonological only if it was more phonologically than visually similar (e.g. HAWK /h aw k/ and PORK /p aw k/). In addition, some potential errors are appropriately categorised as phonological-and-semantic under this definition (e.g. DEW /dy ew -/ and DUNE /dy ew n/). It should be pointed out that errors categorised as visual or mixed visual-and-semantic may actually result from phonological rather than visual influences—the current word set does not contain enough words that dissociate visual and phonological similarity to investigate the relative contribution of these two influences. We will take up the issue of distinguishing the influences of visual and phonological similarity on errors in the General Discussion.

Compared with the corresponding data using the response criteria (see Fig. 12b), the extended *40–60* network shows a somewhat lower rate of semantically related and unrelated errors with early lesions (O → I and I → S), but in general the error patterns are rather similar. Semantic clean-up lesions now produce significant error rates because of the attractors provided by the output network. The distributions of these errors are roughly similar to the distributions for earlier lesions. By contrast, lesions to the semantic units themselves leads to a stronger bias towards semantic similarity in errors.

Lesions to the direct pathway of the output network (S → Ip and Ip → P) produce error patterns much like input lesions, although there is a slightly greater bias towards semantic errors relative to visual/phonological errors. These latter errors almost certainly reflect phonological rather than visual similarity.[8] However, most striking is the extremely low

[8]It is still possible that errors produced by damage after semantics would show influences of visual similarity. The output network receives input from semantics before its activity has settled correctly, and the initial semantic patterns are influenced by visual similarity (see Fig. 10). However, this effect on errors due to damage in the output network is likely to be small relative to the effect of phonological similarity.

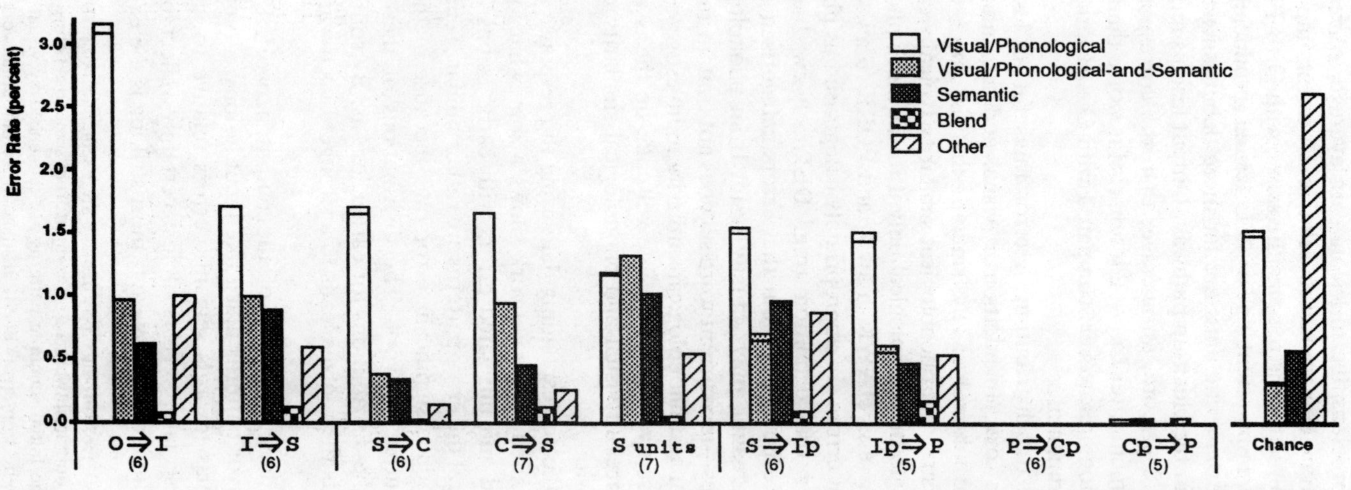

FIG. 16 Error distributions for the extended *40–60* network. Phonological errors are shown as an extra bar over visual errors, and phonological-and-semantic errors are shown as an extra bar over visual-and-semantic errors.

error rate for lesions within the phonological clean-up pathway (P → Cp and Cp → P). Although many words can still be read correctly with impaired clean-up—average correct performance after these lesions is 50.3%—it is very rare that phonology will be cleaned up into a well-formed pronunciation. In this way, phonological clean-up lesions produce behaviour much like semantic clean-up lesions in networks with no phonological output system—in both cases, lesions to connections that implement the last level of attractors result in very low rates of explicit errors. This result provides direct support for H&S's claim that attractors are critical for producing error responses.

Except for phonological clean-up lesions, the rates of visual, mixed visual-and-semantic, and semantic errors, relative to the rates of *other* errors, is greater than predicted by chance for all lesion locations. Thus, lesions anywhere along a pathway from orthography to phonology via semantics produce qualitatively similar patterns of errors. In this way, the implication from H&S's results, that the mere occurrence of particular error types is insufficient to determine a patient's lesion location, appears to generalise to lesions all along the semantic route. In addition, the fact that lesions to a full implementation of the semantic route produce qualitatively similar error patterns as when responses are based on criteria applied to semantics provides support for the validity of our architectural comparisons based on networks that only map orthography to semantics.

Item- and Category-specific Effects

The small size of the H&S word set raises the possibility that many of the effects arise from idiosyncratic characteristics of the word set itself, and not to any real systematic relationship between orthography and semantics. In particular, it is possible that only a handful of words account for most of the errors. In this section we address the extent to which the effects we have demonstrated are distributed across the entire word set.

Considering correct performance first, although there is a reasonable amount of variability among words, it is not the case that some words are always impaired or intact regardless of the type of damage. Thus, for the *40–60* network using the response criteria, overall correct rates per word vary between 34.6% (LOG) and 81.5% (CAT). The pattern of overall correct performance depends somewhat on how output is generated, although the correlation between the correct rates using the response criteria and those using the output network is moderate but significant (0.47, $P < 0.005$).

There are also some systematic differences in correct performance across categories. In fact, particular lesions in some networks can produce quite dramatic category effects that are even more pronounced than those observed by H&S. For example, C → S(0.7) lesions in the *10–15d* network produce a striking selective preservation of animals (78% correct) and selective impairment of body parts (3% correct) relative to other categories (35% average correct), as well as relative to other lesions yielding similar overall correct performance, such as I → S(0.4) (32% average correct). Interestingly, the *40–40fb* network also shows a selective preservation of animals after C → S(0.7) lesions (96% correct), but now foods and outdoor objects (31% and 26% correct), rather than body parts (56% correct), are selectively impaired. The nature of the selective deficits observed after damage appears to have as much to do with the particular characteristics of individual networks as with the relationship among semantic representations. In fact, the selective preservation of foods found by H&S did not arise in a second network that only differed from the first in its initial random weights—a type of variation typically not considered important (but see Kolen & Pollack, 1991). Clearly more research is required to understand these effects.

Turning to a consideration of item effects in error responses, we will take the *40–60* network as an example, as it is the closest to the original H&S model. Visual errors are distributed throughout the word set. Only four of the words, BED, PIG, RAT, and HIP, produce no visual errors for any of the lesions. For the rest of the words there is a wide range of rates, with the highest being for COT and PORE, both having about four times the average rate. In fact, there is a significant correlation (0.49, $P < 0.005$) between the observed visual error rates and the expected rates given the distribution of visual similarity throughout the word set. Thus, the distribution of visual errors across words is relatively unbiased with respect to visual similarity.

Semantic errors are somewhat less uniformly distributed. Nine of the words produce no semantic errors, whereas DOG produces almost twice as many as the word with the next highest rate, GEM. Outdoor objects have a uniformly low rate of semantic errors, whereas the rates for body parts are relatively high and distributed throughout the category. The 7 words with the highest rates account for 56% of the semantic errors, with the remaining errors spread across all but 9 of the 33 remaining words. The correlation of the distribution of semantic errors with that expected from the semantic similarity of the word set is marginally significant (0.30, $P < 0.06$).

In contrast, the network shows a strong bias to produce mixed visual-and-semantic errors for particular pairs of words. Almost half (18) of the words do not produce any mixed errors. Of the remaining words, the top 3 (PAN, HIP, and LIP) account for 45% of the errors; the top 6, over 65%. There is no correlation (0.09 ns) between the distribution of mixed errors across words and the distribution of visual-and-semantic similarity.

Overall, the variation of the rates of various types of errors across words demonstrates that the effects in error patterns produced under damage do not arise from idiosyncratic characteristics of a few words. A possible exception is the mixed visual-and-semantic errors—the one theoretically important topic where the original H&S findings did not generalise consistently. However, the considerable degree of variability of error types across categories raises a concern about the use of these categories in defining semantic similarity. In the next section we address this issue directly.

Definitions of Visual and Semantic Similarity

Following H&S, we have considered a pair of words to be visually similar if they overlap in at least one letter, and semantically similar if they come from the same category. These definitions are intended to approximate the criteria used in categorising the reading responses of patients. However, they are at best only coarse approximations. In particular, our definition of visual similarity is considerably more lax than that used for patients, where typically a stimulus and response must share at least 50% of their letters to be considered a visual error (Morton & Patterson, 1980).

In order to ensure that our results are not biased by the particular definitions of similarity we used, we reclassified the errors produced by the *40–60* network using criteria for visual and semantic similarity based on the actual proximity values of each stimulus-response pair. For ease of comparison, the values of these criteria were defined so that the incidence of error types among all word pairs occurring by chance approximated that for the original definitions. Specifically, a pair of words was considered visually similar if the proximity of their orthographic representations was greater than 0.55, and semantically similar if the proximity of their semantic representations was greater than 0.47. Although these criteria result in only a 0.5% decrease in the incidence of visual similarity and a 1.3% increase in the incidence of semantic similarity, they significantly change the distributions of these similarities over word pairs. This is because proximity is based on shared features, so that letters can resemble other letters without being identical, and words can be semantically related without being in the same category. As a result, there is only a 0.64 correlation between the assignment of visual similarity using letter overlap and using the proximity criterion. The correlation for semantic similarity is only 0.72. For both, only about three-quarters of the word pairs that are similar using the original definitions remain so using the proximity criteria.

Nonetheless, for lesions to the *40–60* network, the distribution of error types using the proximity-based definitions of visual and semantic similarity is remarkably similar to the distribution obtained with the original definitions (shown in Fig. 12b). When the response criteria are used, the only significant difference is that the proximity-based definitions result in a lower rate of *other* errors for lesions of the direct pathway. Thus, many of the error responses that are considered unrelated to the stimulus when using the original definitions do actually reflect the influences of visual or semantic similarity when measured more accurately. However, it should be noted that *other* errors still occur, as they do in patients. This effect is not apparent when using the output network, although O → I lesions do produce a slightly higher rate of semantic errors with the proximity-based definitions. Overall, the similarity of the pattern of results indicates that the use of the original definitions for visual and semantic similarity, in terms of letter overlap and category membership, does not significantly bias the results.

Visual-then-semantic Errors

In addition to producing error responses that are directly related to the stimulus either visually or semantically, deep dyslexic patients occasionally produce errors in which the relationship between stimulus and response is more complex. For example, Marshall and Newcombe's (1966) patient GR read SYMPATHY as "orchestra." They considered this a visual error, SYMPATHY → "symphony," followed by a semantic error, SYMPHONY → "orchestra," and so termed it a *visual-then-semantic* error. Subsequently, this type of error has been observed in a number of other deep dyslexic patients (see Coltheart, 1980a)—other examples include STREAM → (steam) → "train" by HT (Saffran, Schwartz, & Marin, 1976); FAVOUR → (flavour) → "taste" by DE and COPIOUS → (copies) → "carbon" by PW (Patterson, 1979). Although visual-then-semantic errors are quite rare, the possibility of their occurrence at all is rather perplexing, and certainly theoretically relevant. We know of no attempt to explain them other than Marshall and Newcombe's (1973, p. 186) remark that they are "compound mistakes which are a function of misperception plus semantic substitution." They are generally assumed to arise from the effects of two separate lesions.

Given that visual-then-semantic errors are an acknowledged characteristic of deep dyslexic reading, the question arises as to whether they occur after single lesions to our networks. Because the stimulus and response of a visual-then-semantic error are neither visually nor semantically related, up until now we would classify such errors as *other*. Hence, we analysed the *other* errors produced by the *40–60* network to determine whether some of them are more appropriately classified as visual-then-semantic. A visual-then-semantic error occurs when the stimulus and response are unrelated, but there is a third word, which we will call the *bridge*, that is visually related to the stimulus, semantically related to the response, *and is directly involved in producing the error*. This last point is assumed for patient errors because the likelihood of a response being appropriately related to the stimulus by chance is assumed to be negligible. However, in the simulations the small size of the word set and high chance rate of visual and semantic similarity make it necessary to demonstrate that the relation of the presumed bridge word to the stimulus and response does not arise merely by random selection from the word set.

When using the criteria to generate responses, for each *other* error we identified the potential bridge word as the one whose semantics had the second-best match to those generated by the network under damage (the best matching word is the response). If this word was visually related to the stimulus and semantically related to the response, we considered the error to be visual-then-semantic. Of the 114 *other* errors produced by the *40–60* network, 49 (43.0%) satisfied these criteria. The chance rate of visual-then-semantic errors can be calculated by estimating how often the next-best matching word would meet the criteria even if it had no influence on the error. This rate is just the chance rate that the bridge is visually related to the stimulus times the chance rate that it is semantically related to the response, given that the response is neither visually nor semantically related to the stimulus. The first term is just the overall rate of visual similarity for word pairs other than the stimulus and response (29.9%). The rate that the bridge and response are semantically related by chance is much higher than the overall rate of semantic similarity because the bridge word was selected on the basis of how well its semantics match those generated by the network (which match the response best). We can use as an estimate the rate at which the response and bridge words are semantically related over all *other* errors produced by the network, which is 83.3%. Thus, the chance rate of visual-then-semantic errors is approximately 24.9%, which is only slightly more than half the observed rate.

When using an output network, it is possible for the response generated at the phonological layer to differ from the best matching word at the semantic layer (even with the output network intact). Under these conditions we can apply a more conservative, but also more informative, definition of visual-then-semantic errors. Specifically, for each error in which the stimulus and response are unrelated, we can use the best-matching word at the semantic layer as the potential bridge word. If this word is visually related to the stimulus and semantically related to the response (but not identical or it would be a visual error), the *other* error is considered to be visual-then-semantic. It is clear that the bridge word is playing a role in the error because the phonological response is based solely on the generated pattern of semantic activity, which is most similar to that of the bridge word. Of the 97 *other* errors produced by input lesions to the *40–60* network with the output network generating responses, 12 (12.4%) satisfy the criteria for visual-then-semantic errors (e.g. BOG → [dog] → "rat"). In contrast, only 4 of the *other* errors (4.1%) involve semantic similarity followed by visual/phonological similarity (e.g. COW → (pig) → "pan"). Although the chance rate of this type of error is the same as for visual-then-semantic errors, it is observed much less frequently, both in patients and in the network.

For some of the visual-then-semantic errors (e.g. BOG → [pig: *prox* 0.91, *gap* 0.10] → "ram") the generated semantics match those of the bridge word well enough to satisfy the response criteria (for a *visual* error). Even so, the semantics are sufficiently inaccurate that the (intact) output network produces a semantic error. All but one of the visual-then-semantic errors were caused by damage to the direct pathway, with most arising from O → I lesions. This makes sense given that, under our definition, visual-then-semantic errors consist of a visual confusion in the input network followed by a semantic confusion in the output network. In a sense, we interpret visual-then-semantic errors as visual errors gone awry under semantic influences. Because the damaged input network fails to clean up the visual error completely, the output network is given somewhat corrupted input. Even though it is intact, it may misinterpret this input as a semantically related word.

Effects of Lesion Severity

To this point, all of the data we have presented on the relationship between types of errors have been averaged over a range of lesion severities, typically over those producing correct performance between 15–85%. However, it is possible that the distribution of error types changes with lesion severity. In addition, the extent of this effect may be influenced by the nature of the output system employed. Rather than present detailed data, we simply describe the effects that hold for all of the network architectures.

The most basic effect is that error rates increase with lesion severity. Our main motivation for averaging only over lesions producing a limited range of correct performance in previous analyses is that, otherwise, the results would be dominated by effects from the most severe lesions, which often do not show the typical distribution of error types. In addition, the correct performance of most of the patients we are considering falls within this range.

What is more interesting than the fact that absolute error rates rise with lesion severity is that the distribution of error types changes. Specifically, the rates of visual and *other* errors rise more quickly with increasing lesion severity than the rates of semantic and mixed visual-and-semantic errors. If the same data is reinterpreted in terms of the proportion of each error type, then the proportion of error responses that are unrelated to the stimulus increases steadily as performance gets worse. The proportions of the remaining error types all decrease at about the same rate, both when using the response criteria and the output network. Thus, for the moderate lesions we consider the relative proportions of the various error types do not change drastically with lesion severity, and so our decision to average over lesions producing moderate correct performance appears warranted.

Error Patterns for Individual Lesions

The procedure we have used for lesioning a set of connections involves randomly selecting some proportion of the connections and removing them from the network. In order to ensure that the ensuing effects are not peculiar to the particular connections removed, we carry out 20 instances of each type of lesion and average the results across them. On the other hand, it must be kept in mind that the model is compared with individual patients, each of whom have a particular lesion. In a sense, for a given simulation experiment with 4 locations of 9 severities of lesion, we are creating 720 simulated patients, with a relatively high proportion of them displaying the characteristics of deep dyslexia. However, there are some issues in deep dyslexia, involving the relationship of performance on individual words for the same lesion, that we have been unable to address to this point.

One issue concerns the correct performance on words that are given as responses in errors. Some theories of reading errors in deep dyslexia (e.g. Morton & Patterson, 1980) assume that a word produces an error when its lexical entry is missing from some lexicon, with a closely matching word whose lexical entry is present being given as the response. If we also assume that words are read correctly when their entries are present in the lexicon, such a theory predicts that words given as responses in errors should always be read correctly.

In fact, patients usually, but not always, adhere to this pattern. For example, DE read SWEAR as "curse" but then gave the response "I don't know" to CURSE as stimulus (K. Patterson, personal communication). GR gave no response to SHORT or GOOD, but produced the errors LITTLE → "short" and BRIGHT → "good," as well as the errors BLUE → "green" and GREEN → "peas" (Barry & Richardson, 1988). In fact, at another time GR read correctly only 54% of words he had previously given as responses in semantic errors—just slightly better than his original correct performance of 45% (Marshall & Newcombe, 1966).

If we examine the pattern of correct and incorrect performance for individual lesions of the *40–60* network when using the response criteria, we find that only 64.1% of the words given as the response in an error are read correctly; 31.2% of error responses produce an omission and 4.6% lead to another error. The high rate of omissions may simply be due to our stringent criteria for overt responses. However, the fact that 4.6% of error responses produce errors when presented as stimuli clearly violates the prediction of a theory that explains errors in terms of missing lexical entries. In the damaged network, the attractor for a word is not either present or absent, but rather it can effectively operate to produce a response given some inputs but not others.

It is possible for an even more perplexing relationship to hold among the words producing errors in a patient. It has been observed that a pair of words may produce each other as error responses. For example, GR produced THUNDER → "storm" and STORM → "thunder" (Marshall & Newcombe, 1966), while DE produced ANSWER → "ask" and ASKED → "answer" (K. Patterson, personal communication). It is hard to imagine how a mechanism that maps letter strings to pronunciations via meaning might possibly produce such behaviour under damage.

Such response reversals occur in our simulations, but they are very rare. None are found in the corpus of errors produced by the *40–60* network. However, both the *10–15d* and *40–80i* networks produce a few of them when using the response criteria. For example, a O → I(0.1) lesion to the *10–15d* network resulted in the visual errors MAT → "mud" and MUD → "mat;" a O → I(0.7) lesion produced the visual errors MUG → "nut" and NUT → "mug." Similarly in the *40–80i* network, a O → I(0.3) produced the *other* errors MUG → "hock" and HOCK → "mug;" a O → I(0.7) lesion produced the mixed visual-and-semantic errors HIP → "lip" and LIP → "hip."

How might a network produce such response reversals? Recalling Fig. 10, we can interpret damage to the direct pathway as corrupting the initial pattern of semantic activity derived from orthography. One explanation for the existence of response reversals is that the attractors for words are sensitive to different aspects of this pattern. For example, suppose that the attractor for HIP depends on some particular set of initial semantic features to distinguish it from LIP, but the attractor for LIP depends on a *different* set to distinguish it from HIP (this cannot be represented in a two-dimensional rendition of semantic feature space like that in Fig. 10). If both of these sets of features are lost due to a particular lesion, the errors HIP → "lip" and LIP → "hip" are both possible. In essence, an explanation for response reversals must allow a more complicated interaction between orthographic and semantic information than is typically provided in theories based on discrete lexical entries for words.

Summary

An examination of the effects of lesions on five alternative architectures for mapping orthography to semantics has served both to demonstrate the generality of the basic H&S results as well as to clarify the influences of aspects of network architecture on the detailed pattern of errors. Extending networks to generate phonological output on the basis of semantics leads to qualitatively similar effects under damage as does applying criteria to semantics. A consideration of more specific effects at the level of individual lesions, error types, and words reinforced the correspondence of network and patient behaviour.

Perhaps the most general principle to emerge from these experiments is the importance of the nature of the attractors developed by the network. Although network architecture can have a strong influence on this process, ultimately it is the learning procedure that derives the actual connection weights that implement the attractors. Thus, it is important that we evaluate whether the nature of the attractors, and hence the behaviour they exhibit under damage, are the result of specific characteristics of the back-propagation learning procedure, or whether the results would generalise to other types of attractor networks. The next section addresses this issue by attempting to replicate and extend the results obtained thus far using a deterministic Boltzmann Machine.

THE RELEVANCE OF TRAINING PROCEDURE

Learning plays a central role in connectionist research. The knowledge needed to perform a task must be encoded in terms of weights on connections between units in a network. For tasks that involve fairly simple constraints between inputs and outputs, it is sometimes possible to derive analytically a set of weights that is guaranteed to cause the network to settle into good solutions (Hopfield, 1982; Hopfield & Tank, 1985). However, for tasks involving more complex relationships between inputs and outputs, such as mapping orthography to phonology via semantics, correct behaviour requires such highly complex interactions among units that it is no longer feasible to hand-specify the weights between them. In this case, it is necessary to rely on a learning procedure that takes these interactions into account in deriving an appropriate set of weights.

Although the error on a task is the result of the combined effects of all the weights, the crux of most learning procedures is a simplification that calculates how each weight in the network should be changed to reduce the error *assuming the rest of the weights remain fixed*. A natural way to change the weight is in proportion to its influence on the error—that is, in proportion to the partial derivative of the errror with respect to the weight. Although the weight changes are calculated as if other weights will not change, if they are small enough their collective effect is guaranteed to reduce (very slightly) the overall error.

In understanding this procedure, it helps to think of a high-dimensional space with a dimension for each weight. This may be easiest to imagine for a network with only two weights. Each point in this space—a plane in two dimensions—defines a set of weights that produces some amount of error if used by the network. If we represent this error along an additional dimension corresponding to height, then the error values of all possible weight sets form an *error surface* in weight space (see Fig. 17). A good set of weights has low error and corresponds to the bottom of a valley in this surface. At any stage in learning, the network can be thought of as being at the point on the error surface above the point for the current set of weights, with a height given by the error for those weights. Possible weight changes consist of movements in different directions along the surface. Changing each weight in proportion to its error derivative amounts to moving in the direction of steepest descent. Often, learning can be accelerated by using the error derivatives in more complex ways in determining how far and in what direction to move in weight space, although the issues regarding the application of these techniques can be separated from those concerning the calculation of the error derivatives themselves.

The most widespread procedure for computing error derivatives in connectionist networks is back-propagation (Bryson & Ho, 1969; le Cun, 1985; Parker, Note 6; Rumelhart et al., 1986a; 1986b; Werbos, Note 11). The power and generality of back-propagation has dramatically extended the applicability of connectionist networks to problems in a wide variety of domains. However, this power also raises concerns about its appropriate-

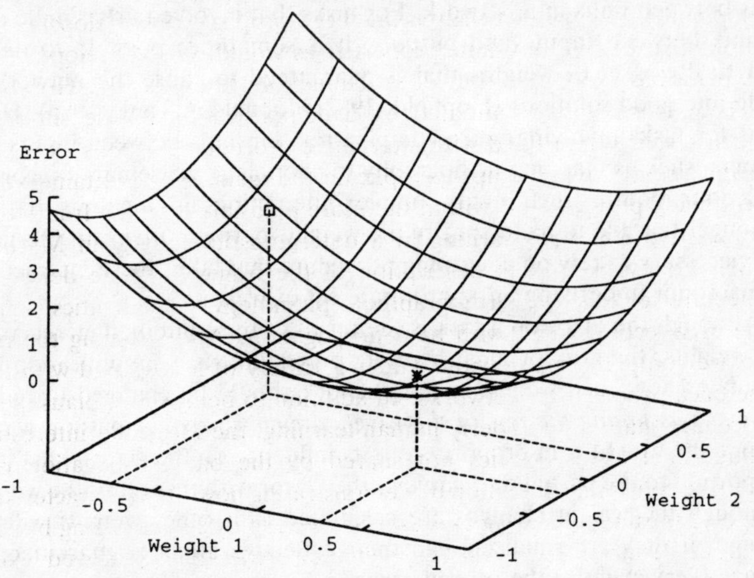

FIG. 17 A hypothetical error surface for a network with two weights. The current error is plotted as a small box above the point corresponding to the current values of the weights (Weight 1 = −0.7, Weight 2 = 0.3). The error for the optimal set of weights (Weight 1 = 0.3, Weight 2 = −0.2) is also plotted (as an asterisk). Gradient descent learning involves modifying the current weights such that the point corresponding to their errors moves downhill along this surface, eventually arriving at the optimal point.

ness for the purposes of modelling in cognitive psychology and neuropsychology. In particular, the procedure uses information in ways that seem neurophysiologically implausible—a straightforward implementation of the procedure would require error signals to travel backward through synapses and axons (Crick, 1989; Grossberg, 1987). As such, it seems unlikely that back-propagation is what underlies human learning, and thus its use in modelling the *results* of human learning is somewhat suspect.

Proponents of the use of back-propagation in cognitive modelling have replied to this argument in two ways. The first is to demonstrate how the procedure might be implemented in a neurophysiologically plausible way (e.g. Parker, Note 6). The more common reply, and the one adopted by H&S, is to argue that back-propagation is only one of a number of procedures for performing gradient descent learning in connectionist networks. As such, it is viewed merely as a programming technique for developing networks that perform a task, and is not intended to reflect any aspect of human learning per se (although see, e.g., Bates & Elman, 1993; Elman, 1993; Karmiloff-Smith, 1992; McClelland & Jenkins, 1990; Plunkett & Sinha, 1991; Seidenberg & McClelland, 1989, for alternative views on the relevance of connectionist modelling to issues in cognitive development). The implicit claim is that back-propagation develops representations that exhibit the same properties as would those developed by a more plausible procedure, but does it much more efficiently. However, this claim is rarely substantiated by a demonstration of the similarity between systems developed with alternative procedures.[9]

In this section, we attempt to replicate the main results obtained thus far with back-propagation, within the more plausible learning framework of contrastive Hebbian learning in a deterministic Boltzmann Machine (DBM). Following a brief description of the framework, we define an architecture for mapping orthography to phonology via semantics similar to the architectures used with back-propagation. After training the network, we compare its behaviour under a variety of lesions and with that of the back-propagation networks. In addition to being more plausible as a procedure that might underly human learning, the DBM has interesting computational characteristics not shared by the back-propagation networks. We conclude the section by demonstrating how these characteristics are useful for understanding two aspects of deep dyslexic reading behaviour: greater confidence in visual vs. semantic errors, and preserved lexical decision with impaired naming.

[9]Terry Sejnowski (personal communication) has successfully re-implemented NETtalk (Sejnowski & Rosenberg, 1987), a feed-forward back-propagation network that maps orthography to phonology, as a stochastic Boltzmann Machine. However, he made no direct comparisons of the representations that the two procedures developed.

Deterministic Boltzmann Machines

Deterministic Boltzmann Machines (Hinton, 1989; Peterson & Anderson, 1987) were originally developed as approximations to stochastic Boltzmann Machines (Ackley et al., 1985; Hinton & Sejnowski, 1983). Details on the nature of processing and learning in these networks are presented in the Appendix—here we only summarise their characteristics.

In a DBM, the states of units change slowly over time, and all connections are bidirectional, so that settling is much more gradual and interactive than in the back-propagation networks. In addition, during settling the summed inputs to units are divided by a global *temperature* parameter that starts high and is gradually reduced to 1.0—a process known as *simulated annealing*. At the end of settling, the unit states minimise a global *energy* measure, which represents the degree to which the constraints encoded by the weights are violated.

The training procedure, known as *contrastive Hebbian learning*, involves running the network twice for each input. In the *negative* phase—roughly corresponding to the forward pass in back-propagation—the input units are clamped, and the hidden and output units gradually settle into a stable pattern of activity that represents the network's interpretation of the input. In the *positive* phase—corresponding to the backward pass—both the input and output units are clamped correctly, and only the hidden units update their states. Learning involves changing each weight in proportion to the difference in the product of unit states for the positive and negative phases. This form of learning is somewhat more biologically plausible than back-propagation primarily because information about the correct states of output units is used in the same way as information about the input—that is, by propagating weighted unit activities, rather than passing error derivatives backward across connections.

Both back-propagation and contrastive Hebbian learning can be characterised as performing gradient descent in weight space in terms of an explicit measure of how well the network is performing the task. This has led most researchers to assume that the nature of the representations developed by the two procedures in most tasks would be qualitatively equivalent. However, the ways in which they compute weight derivatives based on unit states are quite different. These differences raise the issue as to whether the lesion results we have obtained with back-propagation arise only in networks trained with that powerful, rather implausible procedure. In order to investigate this issue, we define a version of the task of reading via meaning, and describe a DBM architecture for accomplishing it. After training the network with contrastive Hebbian learning, we systematically lesion it and compare its impaired performance with that of damaged back-propagation networks.

The Task

In order to help the DBM learn the structure between the input and output patterns (i.e. to reproduce the co-occurrences of unit states), we will use a more symmetric version of the task of reading via meaning than was used with the back-propagation networks. Specifically, the network will be trained to map between orthography and phonology via semantics *in either direction*. This requirement can be broken down into three subtasks: (1) generate semantics and phonology from orthography, (2) generate orthography and phonology from semantics, and (3) generate semantics and orthography from phonology. Although only the first subtask is strictly required for reading via meaning, training on the other subtasks ensures that the network learns to model orthographic structure and its relationship to semantics in the same way as for phonological structure. Our use of a training procedure that involves learning to produce semantics from phonology in addition to producing phonology from semantics is in no way intended to imply a theoretical claim that input and output phonology are identical—it is solely a way of helping the network to learn the appropriate relationships between semantic and phonological representations. This is important if we want to use the energy measure to compare the "goodness" of each kind of representation. Also, learning the task in both directions should result in stronger and more robust attractors, in a similar way as for the back-propagation networks with feedback connections (*80fb* and *40–40fb*). In order to make generating orthography as closely analogous as possible to generating phonology, we use the original H&S representations for letters, involving a position-specific grapheme unit for each possible letter in a word.

The Network Architecture

Figure 18 depicts the architecture of a DBM for mapping among orthography, semantics, and phonology. The network has 40 intermediate units bidirectionally connected with the 28 grapheme units and 68 sememe units, and another 40 intermediate units bidirectionally connected with the sememe units and 33 phoneme units. Each of these sets of connections has full connectivity density. In addition, there is full connectivity within each of the grapheme, sememe, and phoneme layers, except that units are not connected with themselves. In total, the network has 11,273 bidirectional connections. This is about twice the number of connections in one of the back-propagation networks. This extra capacity is justified because contrastive Hebbian learning is not as efficient as back-propagation in using a small number of weights to solve a task.

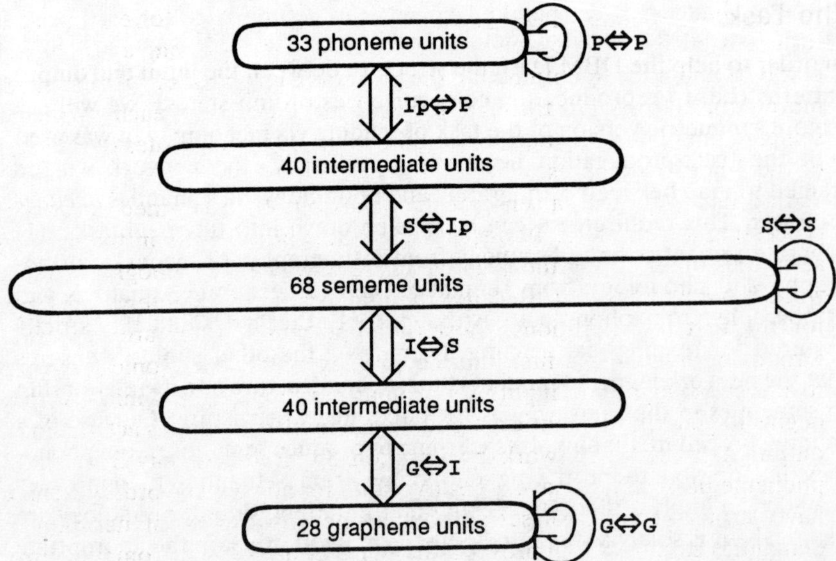

FIG. 18 The DBM architecture for mapping among orthography, semantics, and phonology.

The Training Procedure

The procedure used to train the DBM is exactly as described earlier and in the Appendix, with a slight elaboration. In order to train the network to perform each of the three subtasks mentioned previously, each presentation of a word involved three negative phases. In the first of these, the grapheme units are clamped to the letters of the word. The remaining units, including the sememe and phoneme units, then update their states (while the temperature is concurrently annealed) until no unit state changes by more than 0.01. In the second negative phase, the semantics of the word are clamped correctly, and the network settles into patterns of activity over the grapheme and phoneme units. In the third, the phonemes of the word are clamped, and the network generates semantic and orthographic representations. The pairwise products of unit states in each of these negative phases are subtracted from the pending weight changes. The positive phase involves clamping the grapheme, sememe, and phoneme units appropriately, and computing states for the 2 layers of intermediate units.[10] In order to balance the 3 negative phases, the products of unit states in the positive phase are multiplied by 3 before being added into the pending

[10]No settling is required in the positive phase because all of the connections of both sets of intermediate units are from units that are clamped, so the summed input to each intermediate unit is constant. In this case, the final states that these units would ultimately achieve if settling were used can be computed directly using no cascading nor temperature in their update functions (i.e. $\lambda = 0$ and $T = 1$ in Equation 1 in the Appendix).

weight changes. These pending changes are accumulated for each word in turn, at which point the weights are actually changed (using a weight step $\epsilon = 0.01$ and no momentum) and the procedure is repeated.[11] After slightly more than 2100 sweeps through the word set, the state of each grapheme, sememe, and phoneme unit was within 0.2 of its correct states during each of the 3 negative phases.

In order to provide a sense of the behaviour of the trained network in processing a word, Fig. 19 displays the states of the units in the network at various times during the negative phase in which the orthography of the word RAT is presented. Because the temperature parameter is very high for the first few iterations, most (noninput) unit states are near zero. Gradually, units in the first intermediate layer start to become active due to direct orthographic input. By around iteration 30, this initial activity begins to generate semantic activity, which in turn generates activity in the output half of the network by iteration 35. Because only 3 of the 33 phoneme units should have a positive state for any given word, these units have strong negative biases, producing negative states at iteration 40. Semantics continue to improve, although they are still far from the correct semantics for RAT, as shown by comparison with the states for the last iteration. Close inspection reveals that the erroneous semantic features are due to contamination with the features for CAT. However, even before the semantic pattern settles completely it begins to activate thc appropriate phonemes—first the vowel around iteration 50, and then the consonants. Between iterations 60 and 75, the phoneme units clearly settle into the correct pronunciation. Interestingly, some semantic features are still undecided or incorrect at this state (e.g. the 2 leftmost features, relating to size). The correct phonology feeds back to semantics to provide additional clean-up, and by iteration 100 all of the semantic features are in their correct states. In this way, the DBM behaves quite differently from networks that map from orthography to phonology via semantics in a strictly feed-forward manner (i.e. all the back-propagation networks without feedback connections). Having learned to map between semantics and phonology in both directions, it takes advantage of their interaction to settle into the correct representations for each. The settling behaviour of the DBM when presented with other words is qualitatively similar, although it should be pointed out that, in general, phonology comes in much later than semantics (see Plaut, Note 8, for details). This is also true of RAT in that *most* of the correct semantic features are active prior to the correct phonemes.

In comparing the training and operation of the DBM with that of the back-propagation networks, it is important to keep in mind that processing

[11]Although the current simulations involve *batch* learning, in which all 40 words are presented before changing the weights, *online* learning, in which the weights are updated after every word presentation, would have been equally effective.

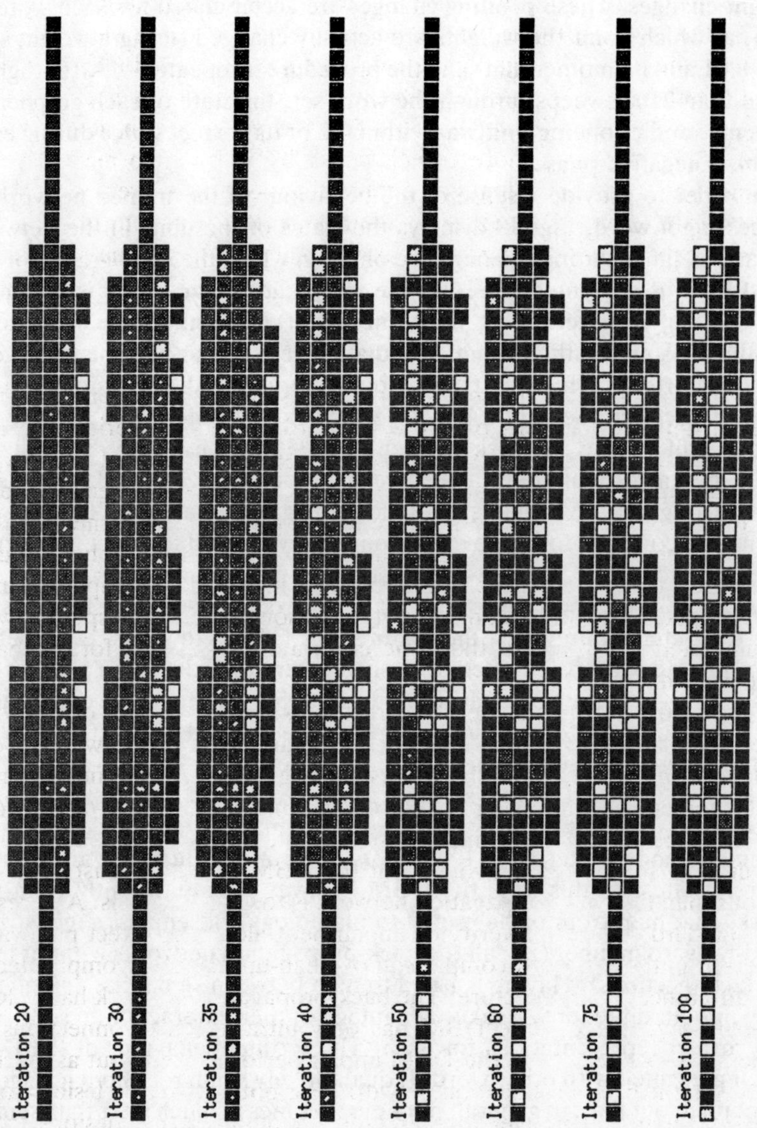

FIG. 19 The states of the DBM at selected iterations in processing the word RAT. Each row of the display for an iteration represents a separate layer of units, with grapheme units at the bottom, semene units in the long middle row, and phoneme units at the top. The second and fourth rows from the bottom are the input and output intermediate units, respectively. The state of each unit is represented by the size of a black (for negative) or white (for positive) blob. A grey square indicates that the unit has a state near zero. Thus, the bottom (orthographic) row for each iteration has three white squares, corresponding to the three graphemes of RAT that are clamped on throughout settling.

a word in the DBM requires about 40 times more computation.[12] On the other hand, the DBM has the significant advantage that it was trained all at once—the back-propagation networks had to be trained incrementally, using a rather ad hoc procedure in the case of the output networks (see the section on "Generating Phonological Responses"). In addition, the DBM is performing a more complex task by learning to map between orthography and phonology in either direction. However, our major interest is to compare the effects of damage on the behaviour of these two types of network in reading via meaning rather than the time required to learn the task per se.

The Effects of Lesions

After training, each of the sets of connections in the DBM were subjected to 20 instances of lesions over the standard range of severity. We also subjected the semantic units to lesions of the same range of severity, in which the appropriate proportion of semantic units are selected at random and removed from the network. Since we are primarily concerned with the task of generating semantics and phonology from orthography, we only considered behaviour in the negative phase in which the grapheme units are clamped. For each lesion, correct, omission, and error responses were accumulated according to the same criteria as those used for the back-propagation networks.

Figure 20 presents the overall correct rates of performance of the DBM after lesions throughout the network. Compare these results with the correct performance data for the corresponding lesions to the full semantic route implementation using back-propagation (based on *40–60* network; see Fig. 15). Considering input lesions first, I ↔ S lesions are equally debilitating in the two networks, but the DBM is more robust to G ↔ I lesions than the back-propagation network is to O → I lesions. As a result, the standard order of severity of impairment along the direct pathway is reversed in the DBM. A comparison of clean-up lesions is complicated by the differences in architecture: The back-propagation network has a clean-up pathway, whereas the DBM has only intra-sememe connections. In general, S ↔ S lesions in the DBM impair performance about as much as C → S in the back-propagation network. For both networks, lesions to the semantic units themselves are far more debilitating than lesions to the connections among them, particularly in the DBM.

[12]We can approximate the computational demands of presenting a word during learning by the number of connections × the number of phases × the number of iterations per phase. The DBM has about twice the number of connections and requires 4 phases, compared with 2 for a back-propagation network (the forward and backward passes). In addition, the DBM requires about 10 times more iterations to settle (about 150 vs. 14 for one of the back-propagation networks).

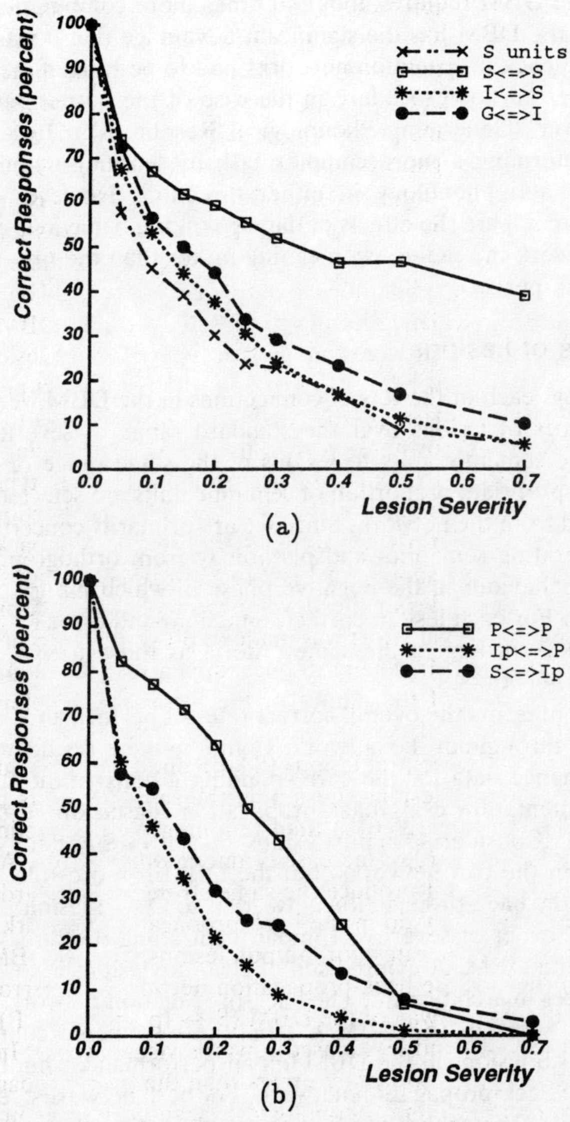

FIG. 20 Overall correct performance of the DBM (a) after input and central lesions, and (b) after output lesions.

As for output lesions, the DBM is somewhat less robust than the back-propagation network to S ↔ Ip lesions, but, in general, direct pathway lesions affect the two networks similarly. Phonological clean-up lesions in the two networks result in similar behaviour as well, producing a sharp decline in correct performance with increasing lesion severity.

An interesting characteristic of the DBM is that it tends to settle into unit states that are very close to ±1, even under damage. This results in very clean phonological output when it responds. Considering the phonological output criterion, the *worst* phoneme has a probability above 0.8 for almost all correct and omission responses, whereas very few are above this level for the back-propagation network. In addition, only 9.2% of omissions fail because of the criterion of a minimum slot response probability of 0.6 for responses. The large majority (90.8%) of omissions fail the requirement that exactly one phoneme be active—no phoneme is active in 87.2% of these.Thus, the phonological output criterion could be eliminated entirely without substantially altering the results with the DBM.

Figure 21 presents the distribution of error types for each lesion location of the DBM, averaged over severities that resulted in correct performance between 15–85%. Comparing with results for input lesions to the back-propagation network (shown in Fig. 16), the DBM is producing about 4–8 times higher error rates. In fact, the distribution of error types is quite similar for the two networks. Both show a very high proportion of visual errors for lesions to input pathways. Furthermore, like the back-propagation network, the DBM shows very low rates of blend responses. This is interesting because, unlike in the development of the back-propagation output network, no special effort was made to prevent blends in the design or training of the DBM. Their absence appears to be a natural and felicitous consequence of the nature of the attractors developed by the DBM.

The error pattern for central lesions (S ↔ S and S units) is quite similar to the pattern for input lesions. Lesioning the semantic units produces a higher overall error rate (25.6%) than lesioning the connections among them (19.6%), but the largest increase is among *other* errors. Also, in the DBM these lesions do not produce the same strong bias towards semantic similarity in errors as they do in the back-propagation network.

The pattern of error rates for output lesions to the DBM is quite different from that for the back-propagation network. The error rates for lesions to the direct pathway of the DBM (S ↔ Ip and Ip ↔ P) are lower than for input lesions, and less biased towards visual errors. In addition, the DBM produces far fewer *other* errors than the back-propagation network. Perhaps more striking, phonological clean-up lesions in the DBM (P ↔ P) still produce significant error rates, fairly evenly distributed across type, whereas the analogous lesions in the back-propagation network (P → Cp and Cp → P) produce virtually no error responses. With phonological clean-up damage, the DBM can use the bidirectional interactions with the intermediate units as a residual source of clean-up. This redundancy of clean-up is similar to that of the hybrid *40–40fb* network.

All lesion locations in the DBM show a mixture of error types, and their ratios with the *other* error rates are higher than for randomly chosen error

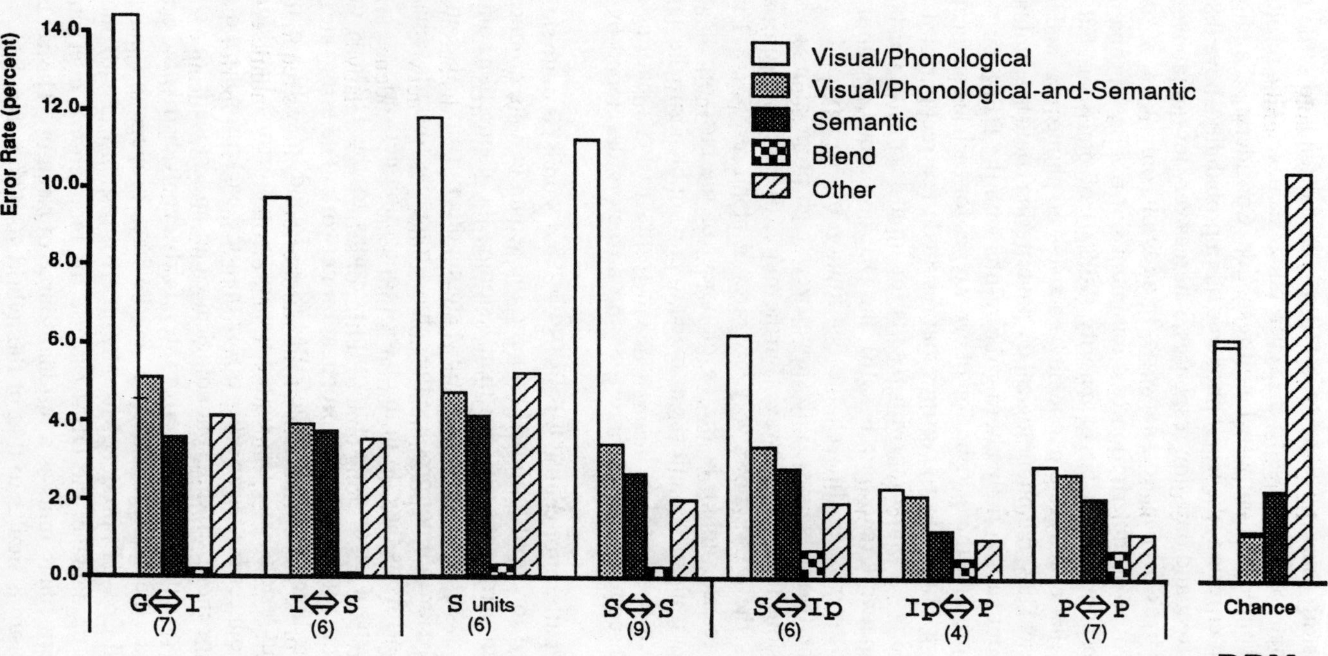

FIG. 21 Error rates produced by lesions to each main set of connections, as well as to the semantic units, in the DBM.

responses. In addition, the rates of mixed visual-and-semantic errors are higher for all lesion locations than expected from the independent rates of visual errors and semantic errors (although only slightly so for central lesions). Thus, the DBM replicates the main H&S results.

The similarity of the results produced by input lesions to the DBM with those produced by the back-propagation network lends credence to the notion that the *strength* of the attractors for words is a much more important factor in determining the pattern of results than is the procedure by which those attractors are developed. However, the DBM develops strong attractors naturally, without the need for incremental training with noisy input. Furthermore, the interactive nature of processing in the DBM makes a large difference for lesions at the phonological level. Unlike the back-propagation output network, the DBM can fall back on bidirectional interactions with semantics (via the intermediate units) to provide clean-up that can partially compensate for lesions to intra-phoneme connections.

In addition to these computational advantages of the DBM, there are some aspects of the reading behaviour of deep dyslexic patients that are much more effectively addressed using a network that settles gradually and has a well-defined measure of the goodness of representations. Two examples of this are the differences that some patients show in the relative confidence they have in some types of error responses, and the relative preservation of the ability to distinguish words from nonwords.

Confidence in Visual vs. Semantic Errors

Patterson (1978) found that deep dyslexic patients DE and PW were more confident that their visual error responses were correct compared with their semantic error responses. It is difficult to interpret these results because it is hard to know how to operationalise how "confident" the network is in a response. One possible interpretation is that a lack of confidence arises when the network takes a long time to settle, or settles into relatively poor representations.

Figure 22 presents distributions of the number of iterations required to settle for correct responses, omissions, visual errors, and semantic errors produced by lesions to the DBM that resulted in correct performance between 15–85%. Not surprisingly, word presentations producing correct responses tend to settle most quickly. What is surprising is that the network takes longer on average to settle into an error response than an omission. However, remember that over 90% of omissions arise because no phoneme is active in some slot. Apparently the network is quick to turn off all the phoneme units in a slot if none of them receive sufficient support from the intermediate units as a result of damage. Accumulating enough support to

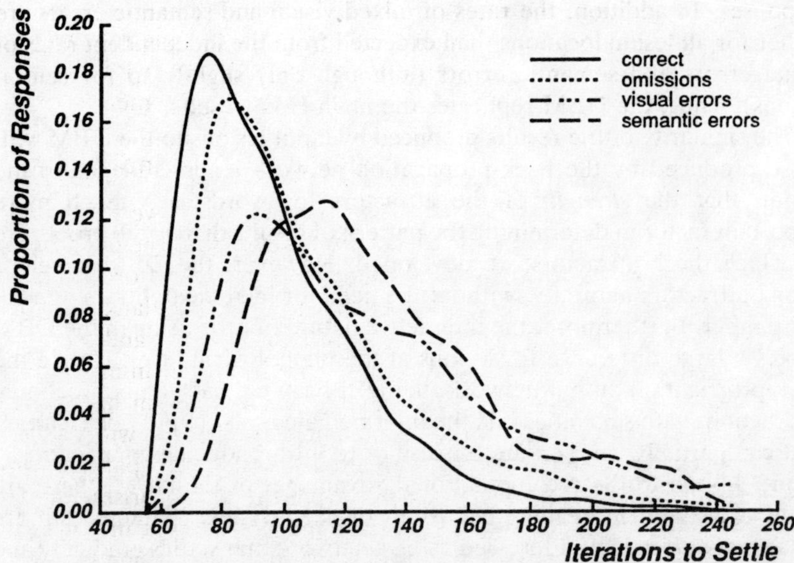

FIG. 22. Distributions of the number of iterations to settle for correct responses, omissions, visual errors, and semantic errors produced by the DBM under damage.

activate a phoneme unit fully in each slot (and inhibit all others) often requires many more iterations (see Fig. 19). The two error types also show the most variability in settling time. Although there is a high degree of overlap between the two distributions, on average visual errors settle more quickly (mean 127.2 iterations) than do semantic errors (mean 139.4 iterations, $F[1, 4458] = 56.8$, $P < 0.001$). Thus, increased settling time for semantic errors might account for patients' reduced confidence that these error responses are correct.

Another possible contribution to the confidence that patients have in their responses is the degree to which the system settles into "good" representations, defined to be those with low energy. We compared visual and semantic errors in terms of their energy in different parts of the network. Considering the energy in the sets of connections between semantics and phonology ($S \leftrightarrow Ip$ and $Ip \leftrightarrow P$), visual errors have lower energy than semantic errors in the DBM (means −214.2 visual vs. −211.6 semantic, $F[1, 3456] = 25.0$, $P < 0.001$). This was true after both input and output lesions. In contrast, for the sets of connections between orthography and semantics, there was no difference between the energy for visual vs. semantic errors ($F[1, 2647] = 1.4$ ns). Thus, differences in energy can account for the increased confidence that some deep dyslexic patients have in visual compared with semantic errors only under the assumption that their judgement is based on the energy between semantics and phonology.

Lexical Decision

Even when they are unable to read words, most deep dyslexic patients can often distinguish them from orthographically legal nonwords. Coltheart (1980a) describes 9 of the 11 cases of deep dyslexia for whom there was data as being "surprisingly good" at lexical decision. For example, Patterson (1979) found that both DE and PW were nearly perfect at distinguishing function words from nonwords that differed in a single letter (e.g. WITH, WETH), whereas explicit correct reading performance on the words was only 38% for DE and 8% for PW. In a more difficult test involving 150 abstract words, again paired with nonwords differing by a single letter (e.g. ORIGINATE, ORIGILATE), DE produced a d' score of 1.74; d' was 2.48 for PW. By comparison, d' was 3.30 for normal age-matched controls. DE read only 19 of the 150 words correctly (12.7%), whereas PW read only 31 (20.7%). Thus, PW shows almost normal lexical decision performance with words he has difficulty reading; DE's performance is significantly impaired but still much better than chance ($d' = 0$).

Hinton and Shallice (Note 4) attempted to model preserved lexical decision under conditions of poor explicit reading performance in the following way. They constructed two sets of "nonword" stimuli with equivalent orthographic structure to the words (see Table 7). The nonwords in the *close* set were created by changing a single letter of one of the words; those in the *distant* set differed from every word by at least two letters. The two sets are matched in the frequency with which particular letters occur at particular positions, but not with respect to the word set. It is important to note that these stimuli are "nonwords" in the sense that they are unfamiliar to the network—it has not learned to associate them with any semantics. The fact that many of them are, in fact, English words (e.g. DONE) is irrelevant to the network's behaviour.

H&S modelled the task of lexical decision by changing the criteria used to generate responses. Specifically, a stimulus was accepted as a word if the proximity of the generated semantics to the nearest familiar semantics exceeded 0.7, ignoring the gap between this and other matches. The rationale for using a reduced proximity criterion and no gap criterion was

TABLE 7
The "Nonwords" Used in the Lexical Decision Simulation

Close				*Distant*			
BUD	GEG	LIM	PIP	BERK	GAG	LUR	PET
BUT	GIM	MED	POCK	BIT	GAP	MOB	PICK
CAR	HACK	MUT	RAB	CICE	HUB	MOM	REN
DEN	HARK	NAT	ROR	DAP	HUR	NOD	RUNK
DONE	LIB	NUG	TOP	DIT	LAD	NOM	TAG

that the semantic match required to indicate that the stimulus is a word needn't be as precise as the match required to specify a particular word for explicit naming. However, when this procedure was applied to the responses generated by the network after damage, there was little difference between words and nonwords. For example, for a lesion of G → I(0.4), which produces 18% explicit correct performance, 67.3% of words were accepted, whereas 55.5% of close nonwords and 64.0% of distant nonwords were incorrectly accepted as words ($d' = 0.31$ and 0.09, respectively). For I → S(0.2) lesions (21.5% correct performance), 57% of words, 39% of close nonwords, and 45% of distant nonwords were accepted as words ($d' = 0.46$ and 0.30, respectively). Thus, H&S failed to demonstrate preserved lexical decision performance in their network when explicit correct performance is poor.

In the context of modelling the nonsemantic route from orthography to phonology, Seidenberg and McClelland (1989) argue that, under some circumstances, normal subjects can perform lexical decision solely on the basis of orthographic or phonological *familiarity*. In their model, orthographic familiarity is defined as the degree to which a letter string (word or nonword) can be re-created from the internal representation it generates, measured in terms of an orthographic error score. Phonological familiarity as a basis for lexical decision is more problematic as it depends on the ability of the network to generate the correct pronunciations of both words and nonwords, which at least for nonwords is less than satisfactory (Besner, Twilley, McCann, & Seergobin, 1990). Nonetheless, Seidenberg and McClelland demonstrate that words tend to have lower orthographic error scores than do orthographically regular nonwords, and hence their *undamaged* model is capable of distinguishing most words from nonwords on the basis of orthographic familiarity (but see Fera & Besner, 1992).

These results suggest that some measure of orthographic familiarity in the DBM network might provide a basis for lexical decision. The DBM network was given connections among grapheme units and trained to generate orthography from semantics so that it would learn the orthographic structure among words in the same way that it learned semantic and phonological structure. However, if the network is to be required to actually *recreate* orthography, we cannot present input by clamping the grapheme units into their correct states as in previous simulations.[13] Rather, we must provide the grapheme units with external input and require them to update their states in the same way as other units in the network. This is the same *soft clamping* technique that was used to train the phonological clean-up pathway of the back-propagation output net-

---

[13]Seidenberg and McClelland (1989) avoid this issue by training their network to regenerate orthography over a group of orthographic units *separate* from the ones used to present input.

work. Specifically, we presented a letter string to the network by providing each grapheme unit with fixed external input sufficient to generate a state of 0.9 if its correct state was 1, or −0.9 if its correct state was −1. The initial states of grapheme units were set to 0.0 and updated over iterations just like the rest of the units in the network. The external input to grapheme units does not uniquely determine their final states because they also receive input from each other and from semantics via the intermediate units throughout the course of settling.

We used as a measure of familiarity of a letter string the proximity between the correct states of the grapheme units and their final states after settling when presented with the letter string as external input. We will refer to this measure as *orthographic/semantic familiarity* because it reflects the consistency of a letter string with both of these types of knowledge. The undamaged network produces an orthographic/semantic familiarity greater than 0.995 (maximum 1.0) for 35 of the words—it fails on CAN, MAT, DOG, HAM, and HOCK.[14] By contrast, only 3 of the "nonwords," all in the *close* set, are considered this familiar: DONE, MED, and PIP. This performance yields a $d' = 2.59$ if this measure and criterion were adopted in a lexical decision task.

If the network is damaged, the support that words receive from semantics is somewhat degraded and so we would expect the differences between words and nonwords to be reduced. However, the network remains able to distinguish fairly reliably nonwords from words it cannot read. Averaging across all lesion locations and severities producing correct performance between 15–85%, and including only word trials producing errors or omissions, an orthographic/semantic familiarity criterion of 0.995 yields a $d' = 2.08$ overall (*close*: 1.66, *distant*: 3.02). Lexical decision is much better for words producing omissions ($d' = 2.49$) than for those producing errors ($d' = 1.31$). Also, performance improves as lesions are located further from orthography (d' for input lesions: 1.36, central lesions: 2.12, output lesions: 2.31). Thus, like most deep dyslexic patients, the damaged network is able to distinguish words from nonwords even when it cannot read the words.

Summary

The lesion experiments in this section attempt to serve three major purposes. The first is to demonstrate the generality of the H&S results across networks developed with very different learning procedures. The second is to defend the use of back-propagation in cognitive modelling against

[14]These misses reflect the fact that the network was not trained with soft clamping—during training the grapheme units are clamped to their correct states through settling. Training the network with soft clamping would have eliminated these misses without substantially affecting the other results presented in this section.

criticisms based on its biological implausibility by providing evidence that the representations it develops have qualitatively similar properties to those developed with a more plausible learning framework. The third is to illustrate how certain aspects of this alternative framework are particularly useful in understanding some additional characteristics of deep dyslexia—specifically, greater confidence in visual errors, and preserved lexical decision with impaired naming.

The primary focus of the simulations presented thus far has been on demonstrating and understanding the degree to which the replication of deep dyslexic reading behaviour in lesioned attractor networks depends on various aspects of their design. However, in many ways the empirical limitations of the original H&S model are more severe than its computational ones. Only the most basic aspects of the syndrome were modelled: the co-occurrence of semantic, visual, and mixed visual-and-semantic errors. Our simulations have extended the range of empirical phenomena that have been addressed to include additional error types, confidence ratings, and lexical decision. However, there are fundamental characteristics of the patients' reading behaviour, such as effects of word imageability/concreteness and part-of-speech, that remain unaccounted for. The next section presents simulations that attempt to overcome these limitations and extend the empirical adequacy of attractor networks for modelling deep dyslexia.

EXTENDING THE TASK DOMAIN: EFFECTS OF CONCRETENESS

The final aspect of the H&S model that we investigate is the definition of the task of reading via meaning. Defining a task for a network involves choosing a set of input–output pairs to be presented to the network, as well as specifying how these are represented as patterns of activity over groups of units. Formulating a reasonable task definition for the purposes of modelling human behaviour involves a trade-off between being as faithful as possible to what is known about the nature of representations from empirical work, while remaining within the often severe constraints imposed by the available computational resources.

First and foremost, the task that the network performs must adequately approximate the task faced by subjects, or the network's behaviour, however interesting in its own right, will have little relevance to understanding human behaviour. However, exactly what constitutes "adequate" is very much a matter of debate. In essence, the decisions that are made in creating a simplified version of the task for the network constitute empirical claims about what aspects of the information available to subjects is crucial for understanding their behaviour. Although our empirical understanding of the nature of how different types of information are represented provides useful constraints, it remains insufficiently detailed to specify the precise representations of each input–output pair as patterns of activity over groups of units. This is where computational considerations of what types of representation networks find easy or difficult to use come into play.

The main computational limitations in specifying a task stem from the fact that the time to train a network increases with the size of the network and the number of examples it is trained on. Thus, there is strong pressure to use as few units as possible to represent the input and output, and to keep the size of the training set within reasonable limits. For tasks with considerable statistical structure among examples, such as mapping orthography to phonology, it may be necessary to use a large number of training cases in order to guarantee good performance on novel inputs. For tasks involving unrelated associations, such as mapping orthography to semantics, it may be sufficient to use a small number of examples. However, a drawback of using a small training set is that it becomes difficult to include all of the types of variation among examples that are empirically relevant. The fact that the H&S model was trained on only 40 words is a serious limitation, not so much because the nature of the mapping from orthography to semantics would be fundamentally different if more words were involved, but because only the most general semantic distinction, category membership, could be investigated. The influences of many other variables known to affect patients' reading behaviour were not examined.

In particular, a distinction among words known to have a significant effect on reading in deep dyslexia is their imageability or concreteness. This issue could not be addressed using the original H&S word set because it contains only concrete nouns. The purpose of this section is to demonstrate that the approach taken by H&S can be extended to account for additional detailed characteristics of deep dyslexic reading behaviour, relating to the effects of the concreteness of stimuli and responses, and interactions with visual influences in errors.[15]

Effects of Concreteness in Deep Dyslexia

The effect of the concreteness of the stimulus on deep dyslexic reading has been investigated in a number of ways. The most basic is its effect on the probability that a word will be read correctly. Coltheart et al. (1987) claim that all patients who make semantic errors find concrete words easier to read than abstract ones. In many patients a very large difference is observed: 73% vs. 14% for KF (Shallice & Warrington, 1975), 67% vs. 13% for PW and 70% vs. 10% for DE (Patterson & Marcel, 1977).

[15]A condensed description of the major results of this section can be found in Plaut and Shallice (1991).

A more subtle effect is the way that the concreteness of a word can affect the probability of the occurrence of visual errors. Shallice and Warrington (1975) noted in their patient KF that the responses tended to be more concrete than the stimuli when visual errors were made. This has since also been observed in patients BL (Nolan & Caramazza, 1982) and GR (Barry & Richardson, 1988); patient PS (Shallice & Coughlan, 1980) showed a strong trend ($P < 0.06$) in the same direction. The same effect is also apparent in the corpus of errors made by PW and DE (see Coltheart, Patterson, & Marshall, 1980, Appendix 2). The relative concreteness of the stimuli on which different types of responses occur has been investigated in three patients. In two, PD (Coltheart, 1980b) and FM (Gordon et al., Note 3), visual errors occurred on less concrete words than did semantic errors, whereas in GR (Barry & Richardson, 1988) there was no significant difference. Finally, in two patients, visual errors occurred significantly more often for stimuli less than a certain level of concreteness by comparison with more concrete stimuli (KF [Shallice & Warrington, 1980] $C < 6$ vs. $C > 6$; PS [Shallice & Coughlan, 1980] $C < 4.6$ vs. $C > 4.6$). Thus, a semantic variable—concreteness—clearly influences the nature of *visual* errors.

There is a single known exception to the advantage for concrete words shown by deep dyslexic patients: Patient CAV with *concrete word dyslexia* (Warrington, 1981). CAV failed to read concrete words like MILK and TREE but succeeded at highly abstract words such as APPLAUSE, EVIDENCE, and INFERIOR. Overall, abstract words were more likely to be read correctly than concrete words (55% vs. 36%). In complementary fashion, 63% of his visual error responses were more abstract than the stimulus. However, the incidence of visual errors was approximately equal for words above and below the median in concreteness. Although CAV made no more semantic errors than might be expected by chance (see Ellis & Marshall, 1978), he appeared to be relying at least in part on the semantic route because his performance improved when given a word's semantic category. CAV is clearly a very unusual patient, but any account of the relation between visual errors and concreteness can hardly ignore him.

A Semantic Representation for Concrete and Abstract Words

The type of semantic feature representation used by H&S is quite similar to that frequently employed in psychological theorising on semantic memory (e.g. Smith, Shoben, & Rips, 1974; Smith & Medin, 1981). More complex representations, such as frames (Minsky, 1975), can be implemented using this approach if units can represent a conjunction of a role and a property of its filler (Derthick, 1990; Hinton, 1981). More critically for the present purpose, there is a natural extension to the problem of the effects of imageability/concreteness. Jones (1985) has argued that words vary greatly in the ease with which predicates about them can be generated, and that this measure reflects a psychologically important property of semantic representation. For example, more predicates can be generated for basic-level words than for subordinate or superordinate words (Rosch, Mervis, Gray, Johnson, & Boyes-Braem, 1976). Jones showed that there is a very high correlation (0.88) between a measure of ease-of-predication and imageability, and that the relative difficulty of parts-of-speech in deep dyslexia maps perfectly onto their ordered mean ease-of-predication scores. He argued that the effects of both imageability and part-of-speech in deep dyslexia can be accounted for by assuming that the semantic route is sensitive to ease-of-predication. Within the present framework, the natural way to realise this distinction is by representing the semantics of concrete and abstract words in terms of differing numbers of features.

A similar position is taken by Saffran (1980, p. 400): "While the core meaning of a reference term is relatively fixed (a rose *is* a rose), the meaning of an abstract word depends to a large extent on the linguistic context in which it is embedded (e.g. the *phase* of the moon, the *phase* of development, and so on). An isolated abstract word may not generate enough semantic information to specify an oral response." A similar contrast appears to hold between nouns and verbs—another category deep dyslexic patients find difficult. Indeed, Gentner (1981) shows that verbs are broader in meaning, are more mutable under paraphrase, and vary more in retranslation through some other language. Presupposing that verbs and abstract nouns contrast with concrete nouns in a similar fashion, this would correspond to their having fewer features that are consistently accessed. If a connectionist learning procedure were applied in a network for generating phonological responses from such representations, it would come to rely on features that are consistently present. Therefore, on this approach, an appropriate first approximation to how the contrast between abstract and concrete words would be realised in a connectionist network is to use semantic representations that differ considerably in their number of features.

To examine the effect of concreteness on visual errors, a set of 20 abstract and 20 concrete words were chosen such that each pair of words

TABLE 8
Twenty Concrete-abstract Word Pairs Used in the Simulation

TART	TACT	GRIN	GAIN	FLAN	PLAN	REED	NEED
TENT	RENT	LOCK	LACK	HIND	HINT	LOON	LOAN
FACE	FACT	ROPE	ROLE	WAVE	WAGE	CASE	EASE
DEER	DEED	HARE	HIRE	FLEA	PLEA	FLAG	FLAW
COAT	COST	LASS	LOSS	STAR	STAY	POST	PAST

differed by a single letter (see Table 8). We represented the semantics of each of these words in terms of 98 semantic features, listed in Table 9. The first 67 of these are based on the H&S semantic features for concrete words (e.g. *main-shape-3d*, *found-woods*, *living*) with minor changes being made to accommodate the different range of meanings in this word set. The remaining 31 features (e.g. *has-duration*, *relates-location*, *quality-difficulty*) are required to make distinctions among abstract words, but occasionally apply to concrete words as well. The ordering of the features and, in particular, the separation of concrete and abstract features, is irrelevant to the simulation. Figure 23 displays the assignment of semantic features to words. Concrete and abstract words differ systematically in their

TABLE 9
Semantic Features for the Concrete and Abstract Words

1 max-size-less-foot	35 found-in-transport	68 positive
2 max-size-foot-to-two-yards	36 found-in-factories	69 negative
3 max-size-greater-two-yards	37 surface-of-body	70 no-magnitude
4 main-shape-1D	38 above-waist	71 small
5 main-shape-2D	39 natural	72 large
6 main-shape-3D	40 mammal	73 measurement
7 cross-section-rectangular	41 bird	74 superordinate
8 cross-section-circular	42 wild	75 true
9 cross-section-other	43 does-fly	76 fiction
10 has-legs	44 does-swim	77 information
11 has-arms	45 does-run	78 action
12 has-neck-or-collar	46 living	79 state
13 white	47 carnivore	80 has-duration
14 brown	48 plant	81 unchanging
15 colour-other-strong	49 made-of-metal	82 involves-change
16 varied-colours	50 made-of-liquid	83 temporary
17 dark	51 made-of-other-nonliving	84 time-before
18 hard	52 got-from-plants	85 future-potential
19 soft	53 got-from-animals	86 relates-event
20 sweet	54 pleasant	87 relates-location
21 moves	55 unpleasant	88 relates-money
22 indoors	56 dangerous	89 relates-possession
23 in-kitchen	57 man-made	90 relates-work
24 on-ground	58 container	91 relates-power
25 on-surface	59 for-eating-drinking	92 relates-reciprocation
26 otherwise-supported	60 for-wearing	93 relates-request
27 outdoors-in-city	61 for-other	94 relates-interpersonal
28 in-country	62 for-lunch-dinner	95 quality-difficulty
29 found-woods	63 particularly-assoc-child	96 quality-organised
30 found-near-sea	64 particularly-assoc-adult	97 quality-bravery
31 found-near-streams	65 used-for-games-or-recreation	98 quality-sensitivity
32 found-mountains	66 human	
33 found-on-farms	67 female	
34 found-in-public-buildings		

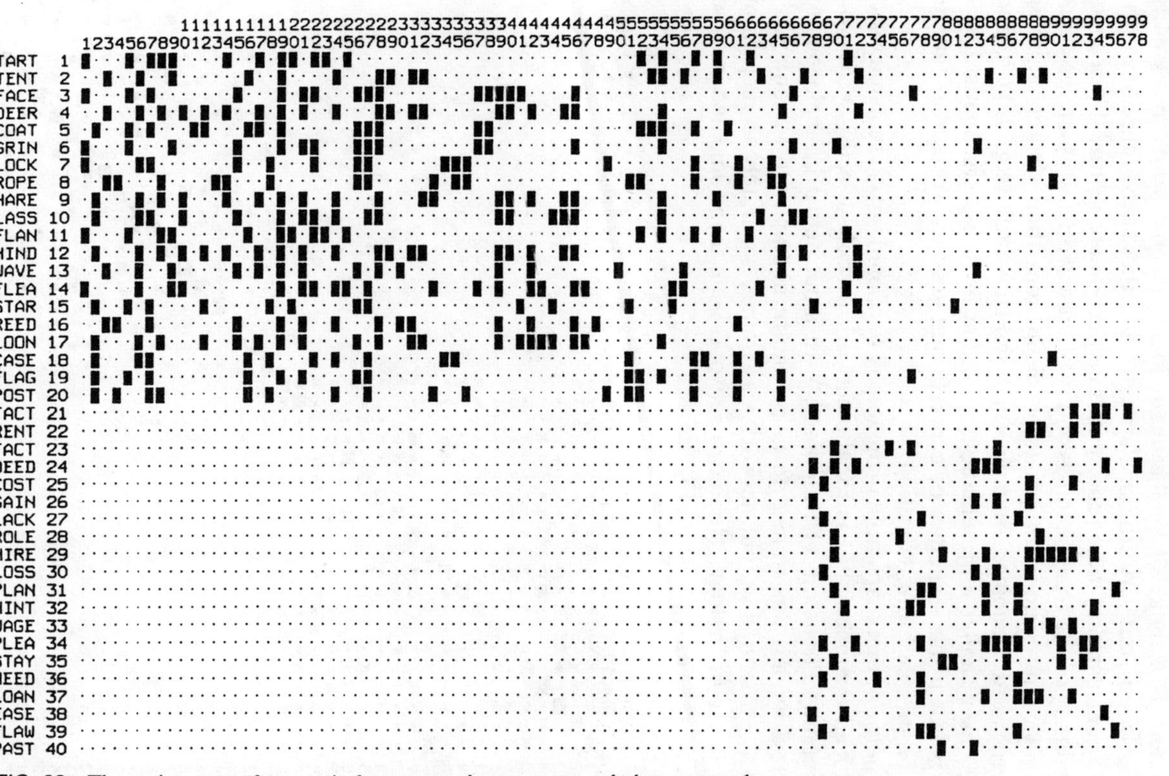

FIG. 23 The assignment of semantic features to the concrete and abstract words.

semantic representations: Concrete words have an average of 18.2 features whereas abstract words have an average of only 4.7 features. The similarity matrix among semantic representations, shown in Fig. 24, clearly illustrates that there is a range of similarities among concrete words and among abstract words, but very little similarity between these two groups of words. We do not claim that these representations adequately capture the richness and subtlety of the true meanings of any of these words. Rather, we claim that they capture important qualitative distinctions about the relationships *between* word meanings—namely, that similar words (e.g. LACK and LOSS) have similar representations, and that there is a systematic difference between the semantics of concrete and abstract words that reflects their relative ease-of-predication.

A network that maps from orthography to phonology via semantics was developed incrementally, as for the network described in the section on "Generating Phonological Responses." An input network, analogous to the H&S model, was trained to map from orthography to semantics. A similarly structured output network was trained separately to map from semantics to phonology. These two networks were then combined into the complete network, shown in Fig. 25.

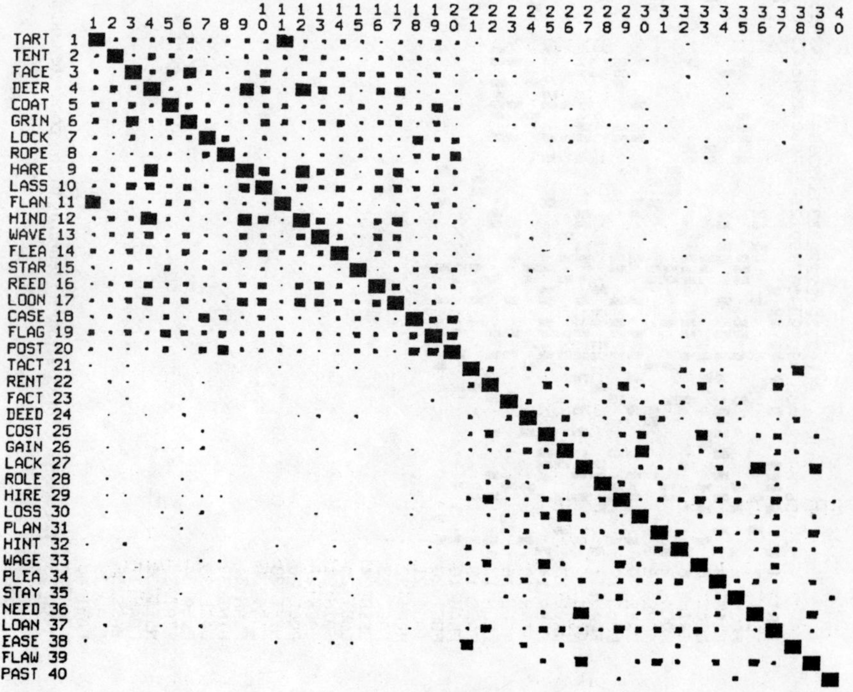

FIG. 24 The similarity matrix for the semantic representations of words.

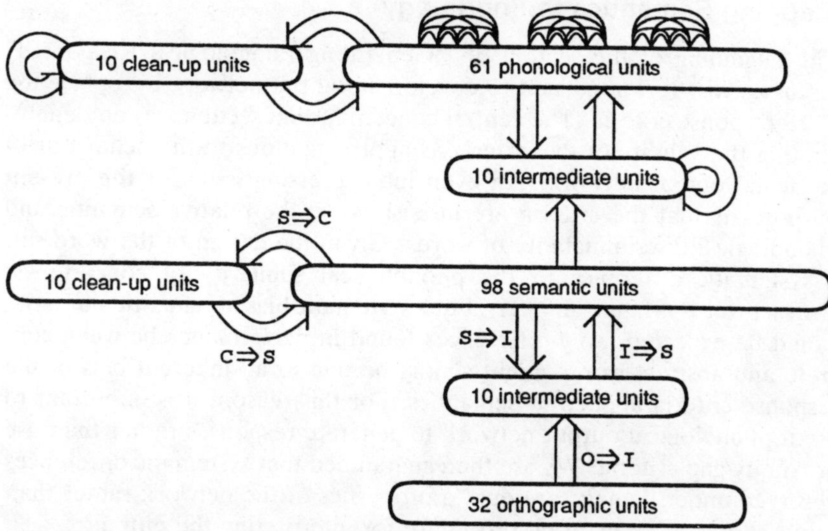

FIG. 25 The network for mapping orthography to phonology via semantics. The additional recurrent connections at the intermediate and clean-up layers in the output network were intended to facilitate the development of strong phonological attractors.

Mapping Orthography to Semantics

The task of the input network is to generate the semantics of each word from its orthography. Orthography is represented using the same 8-feature distributed code used previously (see Table 3). The architecture of the input network, shown in the bottom half of Fig. 25, is broadly similar to the H&S network except that it has (1) full rather than partial (25%) connectivity density, (2) fewer intermediate units (10 vs. 40) and clean-up units (10 vs. 60), (3) no interconnections among semantic units, and (4) a feedback pathway from the semantic units to the intermediate units. In this sense it is something of a hybrid of the *10–15d* and *40–40fb* networks.[16] The general motivation for these changes was to encourage the network to develop stronger semantic attractors while keeping the number of connections reasonable.

The input network was trained with back-propagation to activate the appropriate semantic units for a word when presented with the word's orthography corrupted by independent gaussian noise with mean 0.0 and standard deviation 0.1. After 4700 sweeps through the training set, the state of each semantic unit was accurate to within 0.1 over the last 3 of 8 iterations for each word.

---

[16]A second input network, with the same architecture as the *40–40fb* network, produced qualitatively similar results as the network described here.

Mapping Semantics to Phonology

The beginning of the section on "Generating Phonological Responses" discusses why it is important to develop an output network to replace the H&S response criteria. The central concern in that section was on demonstrating the validity of the criteria as approximations to the behaviour of an actual output network. An even more pressing issue for the present purposes is that the criteria are insensitive to the relative semantic and phonological discriminability of words. Given the design of the word set, a systematic difference in the phonological similarity of concrete vs. abstract words is highly unlikely, but a systematic bias in semantic similarity would be expected. Any differences found in performance between concrete and abstract words might simply be due to an inherent bias of the response criteria applied to semantics. For this reason, it is important to use a phonological output network to generate responses rather than use proximity/gap criteria. We are then guaranteed that systematic differences observed under damage are due to properties of the network rather than to properties of an external procedure for interpreting the output.

The word set requires a somewhat more complicated phonological representation than the one used for the H&S word set. Phonology is represented in terms of seven sets of position-specific, mutually exclusive phoneme units. These groups consist of three slots for phonemes from the initial (onset) consonant cluster, one slot for the vowel (nucleus), and three slots for phonemes from the final (coda) consonant cluster. The allowable phonemes for each slot, and the resulting phonological representation for each word, are given in Table 10. Each of the six consonant slots includes a unit for the *null* phoneme in order to represent explicitly the absence of any phoneme at that slot in the pronunciation of a word. As a result, the representation of every word has exactly one active unit in each slot. A total of 61 phoneme units are required to represent the pronunciations of all 40 words. As suggested earlier, there is no significant difference in the average pairwise proximity among the phonological representations of concrete vs. abstract words (mean pairwise proximity: concrete 0.44, abstract 0.42; $t[378] = 1.41$, $P = 0.16$). Thus, any systematic differences between concrete and abstract words are unlikely to result from phonological differences between the word classes.

The task of the output network is to generate the phonological representation of each word from its semantic representation. The architecture of this network, shown in the top half of Fig. 25, was designed to facilitate the development of strong phonological attractors. Each major pathway shown has full connectivity density, and phoneme units in the same consonant or vowel cluster are fully interconnected. This connectivity allows units within a slot to develop a winner-take-all strategy while still co-

TABLE 10
Phonological Representations of the Concrete and Abstract Words

(a) Phonemes Allowed in Each Position

Pos.	*Phonemes*
1	s –
2	b ch d dy f g h k m n p sh t v z –
3	l r w y –
4	a ai air ar aw e ee eer ew i ie ire o oa ow u uu
5	l m n s –
6	b d j f g k p sh t v z –
7	s t z –

(b) Assignment of Phonemes to Words

TART	/–t–	ar	–t–/	TACT	/–t–	a	–k t/
TENT	/–t–	e	n t–/	RENT	/––r	e	n t–/
FACE	/–f–	ai	s––/	FACT	/–f–	a	–k t/
DEER	/–d–	eer	–––/	DEED	/–d–	ee	–d–/
COAT	/–k–	oa	–t–/	COST	/–k–	o	s t–/
GRIN	/–g r	i	n––/	GAIN	/–g–	ai	n––/
LOCK	/––l	o	–k–/	LACK	/––l	a	–k–/
ROPE	/––r	oa	–p–/	ROLE	/––r	oa	l––/
HARE	/–h–	air	–––/	HIRE	/–h–	ire	–––/
LASS	/––l	a	s––/	LOSS	/––l	o	s––/
FLAN	/–f l	a	n––/	PLAN	/–p l	a	n––/
HIND	/–h–	ie	n d–/	HINT	/–h–	i	n t–/
WAVE	/––w	ai	–v–/	WAGE	/––w	ai	–j–/
FLEA	/–f l	ee	–––/	PLEA	/–p l	ee	–––/
STAR	/s t–	ar	–––/	STAY	/s t–	ai	–––/
REED	/––r	ee	–d–/	NEED	/–n–	ee	–d–/
LOON	/––l	ew	n––/	LOAN	/––l	oa	n––/
CASE	/–k–	ai	s––/	EASE	/–––	ee	z––/
FLAG	/–f l	a	–g–/	FLAW	/–f l	aw	–––/
POST	/–p–	oa	s t–/	PAST	/–p–	a	s t–/

The letter(s) used to represent phonemes are not from a standard phonemic alphabet but rather are intended to have more intuitive pronunciations. A "–" stands for the "null" phoneme.

operating with units in other slots within the same cluster. Co-ordination and competition between clusters can only be accomplished via the clean-up units.

As with the output network for the H&S word set, the current output network was trained in a way that maximises the strength of the attractors it develops, without regard for how well this approximates human speech development. Specifically, the direct pathway from semantics to phonology was trained to produce the correct phonemes of each word during the last 2 of 5 iterations when presented with its semantics corrupted by gaussian noise with standard deviation 0.1. After about 3000 sweeps through the training set, the activity of each phoneme unit was accurate to within 0.2 of its correct value for each word. At this point, intra-phoneme connections and the clean-up pathway were added and the amount of input noise was increased to 0.2. In this way the clean-up pathway learned to compensate for the limitations of the direct pathway when pressed by severely corrupted input.[17] The network was trained to produce the correct phonemes over the last 3 of 8 iterations to within 0.1 of their correct values. The amount of noise prevented the network from achieving this criterion consistently, and after 18,000 training sweeps performance had ceased to improve. However, the network easily satisfied the criterion for every word given uncorrupted input.

The output network was then combined with the input network to produce a network that maps from orthography to phonology via semantics. In order to ensure that the output network would operate appropriately with its input generated by the input network, the complete network was given additional training at generating the correct phonology of each word over the last 3 of 14 iterations when given the uncorrupted orthography of the word. The weights of the input network were not allowed to change during training to ensure that it continued to generate the correct semantics of each word. This final training required less than 100 sweeps through the words.

The Effects of Lesions

After training, the complete network successfully derives the semantics and phonology of each word when presented with its orthography. Each of the five main sets of connections in the input network was subjected to lesions of the standard range of severity. Fifty instances of each location and severity of lesion were carried out, and correct, omission, and error responses were accumulated using a phonological output criterion of 0.6. Table 11 lists the rates of correct performance for concrete and abstract words for each lesion location as a function of lesion severity. In the following analyses, we include data only from lesions producing overall correct performance between 15–85% (listed in italic in the table).

Overall, concrete words are read correctly more often than abstract words (mean difference in correct performance: 6.4%; $F[1, 1549] = 6.28$, $P < 0.001$). However, it is clear from the table that the pattern of results

[17]This procedure is slightly different from the one used to train the phonological output networks for the original H&S stimuli, in which the direct and clean-up pathways were trained separately and then combined (see the section on "Generating Phonological Responses").

TABLE 11
Correct Performance for Concrete and Abstract Words for Each Lesion Location as a Function of Lesion Severity

Lesion Location	*Word Type*	*Lesion Severity* 0.05	0.10	0.15	0.20	0.25	0.30	0.40	0.50	0.70
O→I	concrete	*88.6*	*75.0*	*67.1*	*52.7*	*44.2*	*38.3*	*23.0*	16.7	7.4
	abstract	*69.0*	*50.8*	*40.0*	*25.4*	*21.3*	*16.1*	*10.4*	4.4	1.5
	difference	*19.6*	*24.2*	*27.1*	*27.3*	*22.9*	*22.2*	*12.6*	12.3	5.9
I→S	concrete	*75.1*	*54.8*	*38.2*	*28.2*	19.9	14.1	6.3	4.2	0.9
	abstract	*53.9*	*26.6*	*16.4*	*10.0*	6.1	3.0	1.2	0.8	0.0
	difference	*21.2*	*28.2*	*21.8*	*18.2*	13.8	11.1	5.1	3.4	0.9
S→I	concrete	97.9	94.2	92.3	89.3	*85.9*	*81.1*	*76.7*	*74.4*	*67.7*
	abstract	96.2	93.0	90.9	87.8	*83.7*	*83.6*	*79.8*	*72.8*	*67.0*
	difference	1.7	1.2	1.4	1.5	*2.2*	*−2.5*	*−3.1*	*1.6*	*0.7*
S→C	concrete	94.6	91.2	*83.6*	*78.9*	*71.4*	*65.8*	*57.2*	*43.5*	*28.4*
	abstract	93.5	87.0	*84.1*	*78.8*	*71.2*	*69.2*	*61.8*	*56.4*	*42.7*
	difference	1.1	4.2	*−0.5*	*0.1*	*0.2*	*−3.4*	*−4.6*	*−12.9*	*−14.3*
C→S	concrete	88.7	*79.4*	*67.2*	*59.4*	*45.0*	*42.3*	*30.8*	*18.8*	*12.2*
	abstract	83.1	*74.0*	*65.0*	*54.6*	*48.6*	*42.3*	*33.3*	*27.2*	*21.6*
	difference	5.6	*5.4*	*2.2*	*4.8*	*−3.6*	*0.0*	*−2.5*	*−8.4*	*−9.4*

Data for lesions resulting in overall performance between 15–85% correct are listed in italic.

depends critically on lesion location. For lesions to the direct pathway (O → I and I → S), the advantage for concrete over abstract words is far more dramatic (mean difference: 22.3%; $F[1, 548] = 27.4$, $P < 0.001$). Although this difference is not quite as large as is found with most deep dyslexic patients, it is nonetheless quite substantial.

By contrast, lesions to the feedback connections (S → I) produce no significant differences in relative correct performance of concrete and abstract words ($F[1, 249] < 1$). This is also true of moderate lesions to the clean-up pathway (S → C and C → S; $F[1, 549] < 1$ for lesions of severity less than 0.5). However, severe clean-up lesions result in the reverse advantage—abstract words are responded to more accurately than concrete words ($F[1, 49] > 22$, $P < 0.001$ for each of S → C[0.5, 0.7] and C → S[0.5, 0.7]). This type of lesion and pattern of performance are consistent with what is known about the concrete word dyslexic patient, CAV (Warrington, 1981). His reading disorder was quite severe initially, and he also showed an advantage for abstract words in picture-word matching with auditory presentation, suggesting modality-independent damage at the level of the semantic system.

As mentioned earlier, the error responses of deep dyslexic patients tend to be more concrete than the stimuli which produce them. For the damaged network, we tested this by counting how often a stimulus and response were of the opposite type. Overall, abstract words are over twice as likely to produce a concrete response than vice versa (33.4% vs. 15.6% of total errors, $F[1, 2598] = 53.9$, $P < 0.001$). Post hoc analyses for each lesion location and severity showed a similar pattern as for correct performance: A tendency for responses to be more concrete for all lesions within the direct pathway, but the opposite tendency for severe lesions within the semantic clean-up pathway.

Error responses were categorised in terms of their visual and semantic similarity to the stimulus. Words were considered visually similar if they overlapped in two or more letters—which corresponds to the standard neuropsychological criterion—and semantically similar if their semantic representations overlapped by at least 84% for concrete words and 95% for abstract words. The definition of semantic similarity is more complicated because of the systematic differences between concrete and abstract semantics and because the semantic representations are not organised into categories as in the H&S simulations. Note that two typical unrelated words have roughly 67% semantic overlap if both are concrete and 91% if both are abstract. Thus, the values of the semantic relatedness criteria for concrete and abstract words are each approximately halfway between the corresponding expected value for unrelated word pairs of the same type and 100%.

Figure 26 shows the rates of each error type produced by each lesion location, for concrete and abstract words separately. Also included in the figure is the distributions of each error type for "chance" error responses chosen randomly from the word set in response to concrete or abstract stimuli. Notice that the criteria for visual and semantic relatedness are quite stringent—almost 85% of all possible stimulus-response pairs are unrelated. One consequence of this is that only 4 of the 190 pairs of abstract words are both visually and semantically related, and none of the concrete pairs are. Thus, by definition, concrete words cannot produce mixed visual-and-semantic errors. Nonetheless, when errors to concrete and abstract words are taken together, the ratios of the rates of each error type with that of *other* errors is at least 4 times the chance value for every lesion location. In fact, this also holds for each word type separately, except for visual errors to abstract words produced by clean-up lesions, where the ratios are only about twice the chance value, and for $S \rightarrow C$ lesions, which produced no semantic errors to abstract words. Also, the rates of mixed visual-and-semantic errors among the abstract words for all lesion locations are at least 3 times the rates expected from the independent rates of visual and semantic errors. Thus, the network replicates, on a different word set,

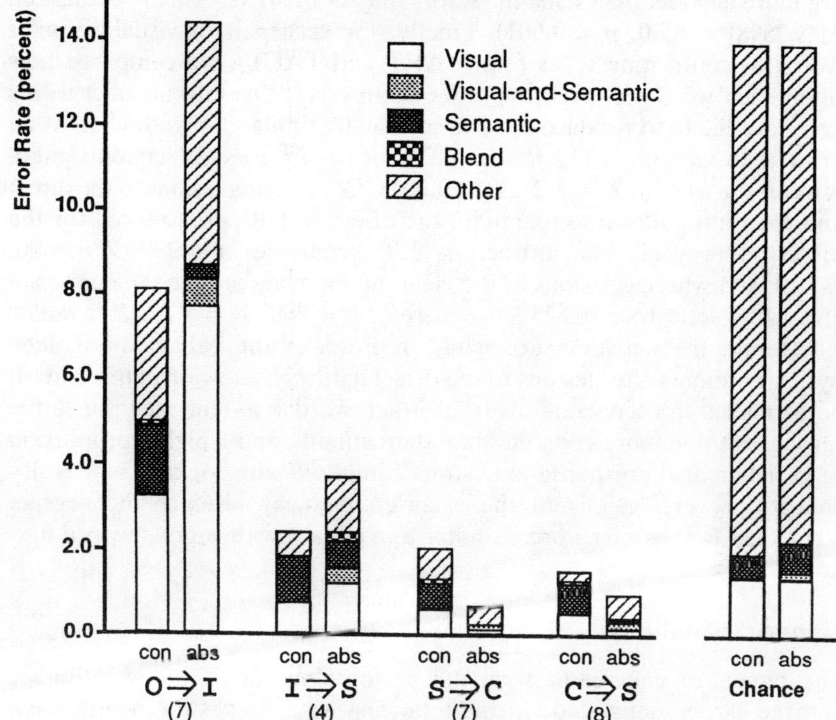

FIG. 26 Overall rates of each error type for concrete (con) and abstract (abs) words for each lesion location (except S → I lesions, which produce virtually no explicit errors).

the H&S finding of mixtures of error types for lesions throughout the network, including purely visual errors for lesions entirely within the semantic clean-up system. In addition, as with the networks trained on the original H&S word set, a number of the *other* errors are actually of the visual-then-semantic type found in deep dyslexia (e.g. PLAN → [flan] → "tart").

A particularly intriguing aspect of the patient data is that abstract words are particularly likely to produce visual errors. The same is true of the network. A comparison of error types for concrete and abstract words revealed that the proportion of errors that are visual is higher for abstract words (41.4% vs. 36.4%, $F[1, 1036] = 3.95$, $P < 0.05$), whereas the proportion of errors that are semantic is higher for concrete words (32.3% vs. 6.4%, $F[1, 1036] = 155.1$, $P < 0.001$). This effect is most clearly shown in Fig. 26 for lesions of the direct pathway. As a measure of the abstractness of the errors produced by a lesion, we used the number of errors to abstract words minus the number of errors to concrete words. Applying this measure to visual and semantic errors separately reveals that visual errors are more abstract than semantic errors (means 0.201 vs. −0.161 per lesion, $F[1, 2598] = 85.0$, $p < 0.001$). Finally, for each pair of visually similar words of contrasting types (e.g. TART and TACT), we compared how often each word produced the other as an error. Overall, abstract words are more likely to produce the paired visually similar concrete word as an error than vice versa (13.1% vs. 6.2% of total errors; Wilcoxon signed-ranks test $n = 520$, $Z = 3.24$, $P < 0.001$). Considering lesions to the direct and clean-up pathways separately, the effect is quite pronounced for the direct pathway (15.6% abstract vs. 3.9% concrete, $n = 220$, $Z = 6.16$, $P < 0.001$) whereas lesions of the clean-up pathway produce the opposite effect (0.0% abstract vs. 23.8% concrete, $n = 300$, $Z = 1.83$, $P < 0.05$).

Overall, the network successfully reproduces the behaviour of deep dyslexic patients after lesions to the direct pathway, showing better correct performance for concrete over abstract words, a tendency for error responses to be more concrete than their stimuli, and a higher proportion of visual errors in response to abstract compared with concrete words. By contrast, severe lesions to the clean-up pathway produce the reverse advantage for abstract words, similar to a patient with concrete word dyslexia.

Network Analysis

The effects of concreteness on the performance of the network under damage can be understood in the following way. As abstract words have fewer semantic features, they are less effective than concrete words at engaging the semantic clean-up mechanism, and must rely more heavily on the direct pathway. Concrete words are read better under lesions to this pathway because of the stronger semantic clean-up they receive. In addition, abstract words are more likely to produce visual errors as the influence of visual similarity is strongest in the direct pathway. Slight or moderate damage to the clean-up pathway impairs what little support abstract words receive from this system, but also impairs concrete words, producing no relative difference. Under severe damage to this pathway, the processing of most concrete words is impaired but many abstract words can be read solely by the direct pathway, producing an advantage of abstract over concrete words in correct performance.

In order to provide more direct evidence for this interpretation, we examined a number of aspects of the operation of the undamaged network. One measure that should be informative is the similarity of concrete and abstract word representations at different times and locations in the network with their final semantic representations. One hypothesis is that, if abstract words rely more heavily on the direct pathway and less on the clean-up pathway, their representations should be more semantically organised than those of concrete words prior to the influence of semantic clean-up. However, this was found not to be the case: Concrete words are consistently more semantically organised than abstract words.

Nonetheless, there is evidence that the clean-up pathway is particularly important in processing concrete words. Figure 27 presents the final clean-up representations of each word, with concrete words on the left and abstract words on the right. The representations for concrete words are far more binary than those for abstract words. When processing a concrete word, most clean-up units receive strong input (positive or negative) from semantics and are driven into states near 0 or 1. In contrast, clean-up units receive relatively weak input from semantics when processing an abstract word, and so tend to remain in states near 0.5. In this sense, the clean-up units play less of a role in generating the correct semantics of abstract words than they do for concrete words.

Summary

The range of empirical phenomena addressed by H&S was quite limited, in part because of limitations of the original model, but also because the restricted definition of the task of reading via meaning they used precluded consideration of many aspects of deep dyslexic reading behaviour. The simulations in this section serve to replicate the original findings of the co-occurrence of error types using a different word set, but more import-

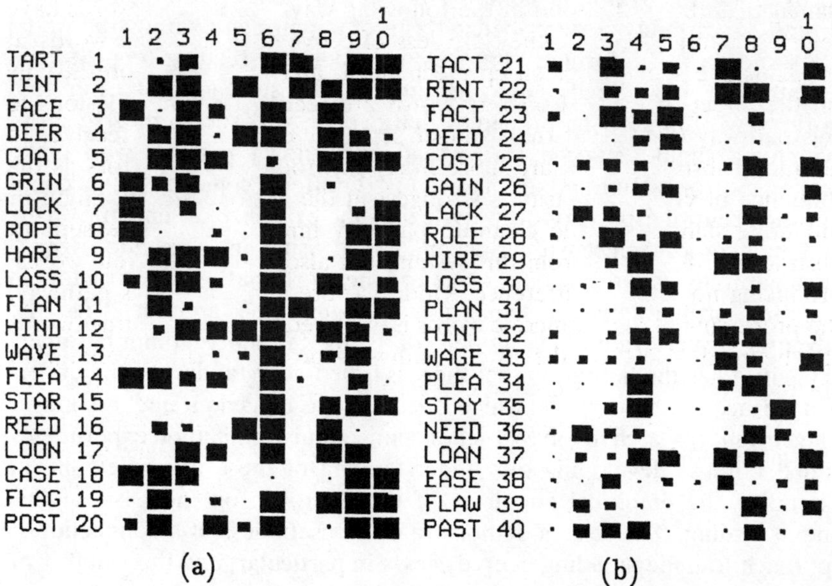

FIG. 27 The final states of the clean-up units for (a) the concrete words and (b) the abstract words.

antly, they extend the empirical adequacy of the approach to include the effects of concreteness in deep dyslexia and its interactions with visual influences in errors. Our explanation for these effects hinges on the claim that far fewer features are activated consistently at the semantic level for abstract words than for concrete words. This difference causes the direct and clean-up pathways of the network to become differentially important in processing each type of word through the course of learning, and is thus reflected in the behaviour of the network under damage. The explanation has some similarities to those previously offered for the interaction between effects of concreteness and visual similarity (e.g. Morton & Patterson, 1980; Shallice & Warrington, 1980) but these were essentially ad hoc verbal extrapolations from cascade notions unrelated to other aspects of the syndrome, without even a principled account of the abstract/concrete difference. The present account is supported by a simulation, is linked to explanations of other aspects of the syndrome, and also offers the possibility of addressing concrete word dyslexia.

GENERAL DISCUSSION

The appeal of connectionist modelling is greatest when the formalism significantly contributes to a natural explanation for empirical phenomena that are counterintuitive when viewed within other formalisms. This book focusses on the symptom complex of deep dyslexia. Although the syndrome can certainly be described in terms of impairments within traditional "box-and-arrow" information-processing models of reading (e.g. Morton & Patterson, 1980; Shallice & Warrington, 1980), such accounts offer little in the way of underlying principles that explain why such a diverse set of symptoms should co-occur in virtually all known patients who make semantic errors. Hinton and Shallice (1991) offer a connectionist account in which central aspects of deep dyslexia—the existence of semantic errors and their co-occurrence with visual and mixed visual-and-semantic errors—arise naturally as a result of damage to a network that builds attractors in mapping orthography to semantics. Although the approach has the advantage over traditional models of being far more computationally explicit, it has the limitation that there is little understanding of the underlying principles of the model which give rise to its behaviour under damage. The current research involves a set of connectionist simulation experiments aimed both at developing our understanding of these principles and at extending the empirical adequacy of the approach on the basis of this understanding. The results demonstrate the usefulness of a connectionist approach to understanding deep dyslexia in particular, and the viability of connectionist neuropsychology in general.

In this final section, we begin by discussing computational issues, focussing on the nature of the principles that underly the ability of networks to reproduce the characteristics of deep dyslexia, and their degree of generality. We then turn to empirical considerations, evaluating the degree to which these computational principles account for the full range of patient behaviour. The relationship between the current approach and other theoretical accounts of deep dyslexia is considered next. We conclude by considering more general issues regarding the impact of connectionist modelling in neuropsychology.

Computational Generality

Most connectionist efforts in modelling acquired dyslexia (e.g. Mozer & Behrmann, 1990; Patterson et al., 1990) have followed the standard approach in cognitive neuropsychology of using a particular model of normal reading to account for disorders of reading as a result of damage. In contrast, H&S never intended their model to be anything but the coarsest approximation to the mechanism by which normal subjects derive the meanings of words. Rather, their network was intended to embody particular computational principles, involving distributed representations and attractors, that were claimed to underly the effects seen in patients. In this way, the H&S model was put forth as representative of a wide class of models, all of which share the same basic principles but differ in other respects, and all of which, it was implicitly claimed, would show the characteristics of deep dyslexia under damage. However, H&S did not demonstrate that models lacking the properties they claimed were central would *not* show the characteristics of deep dyslexia, nor did they investigate the actual nature and scope of the class of models that would. The present research is aimed, in part, at clarifying exactly what aspects of the original model are responsible for its similarity under damage to deep dyslexic patients, and what aspects are less critical. To this end, simulations were carried out that explored the implications of each of the major design decisions that went into the H&S model: The definition of the task including the representation of the orthographic input and semantic output, the specification of network architecture, the use of a particular training procedure, and the means by which the performance of the network is evaluated.

Critical System Properties

The present simulations investigate systems with the following sets of properties:

1. Orthographic and semantic representations are distributed over separate groups of units, such that similar patterns represent similar words in each domain, but similarity is unrelated between domains.
2. Knowledge is encoded in connection weights that are learned by a

procedure for performing gradient descent in some measure of performance on the task of mapping orthography to semantics.

3. Mapping orthography to semantics is accomplished through the operation of attractors (and the lesion does not seriously impair the connections which implement the attractors).

4. The semantic representations of concrete words are much "richer" than those of abstract words (i.e. contain considerably more consistently accessed features).

The purpose of the simulations has been to assess the hypothesis that any system with these four properties will exhibit, when damaged, the following central characteristics of deep dyslexia:

1. Semantic, visual, mixed visual-and-semantic, visual-then-semantic, and *other* (unrelated) errors occur.

2. Concrete words are read better than abstract words.

3. Visual errors (a) tend to have responses that are more concrete than the stimuli, (b) occur more frequently on abstract than concrete words, and (c) have stimuli that are more abstract than do semantic errors.

It should be borne in mind that these characteristics have not been equally thoroughly investigated. Evidence for the generality of the types of system giving rise to the deep dyslexic symptom complex has been obtained only for the error pattern characteristic. Characteristics 2 and 3 have been examined only in one small group of systems, related to the *10–15d* and *40–40fb* back-propagation networks. These latter characteristics are discussed in the next subsection.

As far as Characteristic 1 is concerned, the main empirical results of the simulation experiments are clear: The co-occurrence of semantic, visual, and mixed visual-and-semantic errors after unitary lesions is not due to any idiosyncratic characteristics of the original H&S network. In addition to holding for different lesion locations, as H&S found, it also holds for networks with different architectures, using different output systems, trained with different learning procedures, and performing different versions of the task. Thus, in the section on "The Relevance of Network Architecture," five alternative network architectures were examined in addition to the one H&S used. With minor exceptions of certain lesions to the clean-up pathways giving rise to very low error rates, all networks except one produce the error pattern of Characteristic 1, wherever they are lesioned.

If one considers how the output produced by the system is assessed, the current simulations represent an advance, from a computational point of view, over related work in certain respects. The most important of these is the development of networks that generate explicit phonological responses without the use of a best-match procedure. What is, however, critical for the present purposes is that the various input network architectures have each been implemented with two alternative output systems (although only one is described here; see Plaut, Note 8, for additional details). The networks exhibited qualitatively the same error pattern with both output systems, as well as when response criteria are applied to semantics. The simulations with the DBM network and with the abstract/concrete word set also employed phonological output systems, and each produced a similar pattern of errors.

All the simulations, with the exception of the replication of the H&S network, used a different form of input representation from that used by H&S. The new representation, however, also obeys System Property 1, and did not affect the qualitative error pattern (Characteristic 1). The more general issue of distributed representations is discussed later. As far as the effects of different training procedures are concerned, in the section on "The Relevance of Training Procedure," an algorithm was employed which differs from the iterative back-propagation procedure used by H&S, but which also obeys System Property 2. A qualitatively identical error pattern was still obtained wherever lesions were made. Finally, a completely different version of the task was examined in the section on "Extending the Task Domain," again with no qualitative change in the error pattern.

The fact that the co-occurrence of error types held under virtually all conditions examined does not enable us to isolate necessary as well as sufficient properties that must hold for systems to produce the deep dyslexic error pattern when damaged. Nonetheless, among the simulations that were run, there were some conditions under which the error pattern did not occur. These were of two types. First, very few explicit errors occur for lesions to the phonological clean-up pathway in the back-propagation output networks (see Fig. 16). When no output system was used, this was also true of lesions within the semantic clean-up system in some networks (e.g. the *40–60* network). These are cases in which the pathways responsible for implementing the attractors are themselves damaged. Second, and more directly, explicit errors are almost nonexistent after I $\rightarrow$ S lesions in the *40–80* network when using the response criteria. Here, the lesion is to a pathway in the processing system beyond the region where the attractors are formed. These results provide evidence that supports H&S's claim—for which they presented no evidence—that the existence of attractors is essential to produce the deep dyslexic error pattern.

The importance of attractors, Property 3, can be seen in another way. The robustness of a network to damage of its direct pathway tends to be positively correlated with the rate of explicit error responses. This can be seen from a comparison of O $\rightarrow$ I lesion results across networks in Table

4, and also, although less clearly, in the I → S lesion results. The same pattern also holds across the different output networks that were developed. These effects suggest that the processes responsible for maintaining correct performance after damage are also responsible for the production of errors—namely, the strength of attractors that have been formed.

It would, however, be too strong a claim to make on the basis of the current simulations that Properties 1–4 are *necessary* for a system to exhibit Characteristics 1–3 (Property 4, the relative richness of concrete semantic representations, is discussed later). However, the simulations provide strong evidence that systems obeying these properties exhibit the deep dyslexic error pattern under damage, and that variation in other aspects of their design do not fundamentally alter this pattern of breakdown. It seems plausible, therefore, that humans exhibit deep dyslexia after some types of brain damage because their cognitive systems also obey Properties 1–4.

Potential Limitations on Computational Generality

One effect observed by H&S, which appears to be less general, is that of higher rates of mixed visual-and-semantic errors than predicted by the independent rates of visual errors and semantic errors. When the pressure to build strong attractors was increased by training with noisy input, this effect was observed only in networks in which the intermediate units between orthography and semantics were involved in developing attractors (i.e. the *40–80i*, *80fb*, and *40–40fb* networks). The mixed rate was not higher than predicted in networks in which the attractors operated separately from, and subsequently to, the direct access of semantics from orthography (i.e. the *40–60* and *10–15d* networks). To the degree that patients exhibit a sufficiently high rate of mixed visual-and-semantic errors, the results place constraints on the nature of network architectures that can account for these effects.[18] The non-generality of this effect also emphasises the necessity of exploring a range of models that vary systematically from a particular model that shows some effect. It is difficult to determine which empirical results are robust and which are not on the basis of intuitions alone.

A potential limitation of the original H&S work that has not been addressed in subsequent simulations is the possible effects of using such a small training set. Although we demonstrated that the basic effects hold for two separate word sets—the original set and the abstract/concrete set—

[18]One possible reason for questioning the findings in patients is that a high rate of mixed visual-and-semantic errors might result from a post-lexical editing process that occasionally blocks semantic errors with no phonological or orthographic similarity to the input, as suggested by Levelt et al. (1991) for normal subjects.

both sets contain only 40 words. The question arises as to whether the results are strongly biased by this limitation. In fact, Seidenberg and McClelland (1990) have argued that many of the limitations of their model are due to the fact that it was only trained on about 2900 words. However, there are significant differences between the tasks that the two models perform that provide reasonable justification for the reliability of effects produced in the current networks with only 40 words. Mapping directly from orthography to phonology involves learning statistical relationships among mappings that can then be applied to novel inputs in reasonable ways. Thus, a large number of training cases are required to estimate these statistics reliably, and performance would be expected to improve with a larger training set. In contrast, mapping from orthography to semantics involves *overcoming* statistical regularities, since visual similarity is not predictive of semantic similarity. It is true that a small training set limits the range of similarity that can be expressed *within* orthography or semantics, but it is unlikely to alter the nature of the mapping between them fundamentally. Thus, the small size of the word sets prevented us from investigating the effects of variables such as frequency and syntactic class that are known to influence deep dyslexic reading significantly, and these issues remain open for future research. However, the basic findings of the co-occurrence of error types would still hold if a much larger set of words were used.

Empirical Adequacy

Quantitative Adequacy

The pattern of errors found when the models described here are lesioned fits qualitatively with that observed in deep dyslexia. However, the quantitative fit seems less adequate. If one examines what proportion of all non-correct trials give rise to an explicit error response, then for 7 deep dyslexic patients reviewed by Shallice and Warrington (1980) the value is between 25% and 95% (median 59%). By contrast, for the 19 lesion types shown in Table 4, for only 1 is the value over 30% (O → I lesions in the *10–15d* network), and for only 3 others is it over 10%. Table 4 reports results based on the use of response criteria applied to semantics in lesioned back-propagation networks. The use of a phonological output network leads to higher values (see Figs. 16 and 26), as does the use of the DBM network (see Fig. 21). However, in general, lesions to the networks result in values below, rather than above, 50%.

It would be incorrect, though, to take this quantitative discrepancy between patients and models as strong evidence against the models. For the models, factors that are not central to the theory, such as the way responses are determined, greatly affect absolute error rates. Moreover, many parameters are set for computational convenience, such as the number of intermediate units; or are clearly not realistic, like the number of semantic and visual competitors of a typical word. Variations in such parameters are also likely to affect absolute error rates, although it is the theoretical claim of this book that such variations would not lead to qualitative changes in the error pattern.

One property of the deep dyslexic error pattern is that some patients make far more semantic errors than visual errors, whereas other patients show the opposite tendency. Thus, Patterson's (1978) patient, PW, produced about 4 times as many semantic errors as visual, whereas KF (Shallice & Warrington, 1975) produced 15 times as many visual errors. Can this quantitative difference be explained in terms of a contrast in the effects of lesioning at different places in the same network? The more detailed quantitative aspects of the error pattern in the present simulations confirm H&S's finding that large variations in the ratio of visual errors to semantic errors do occur with different lesion locations in the same network. This ratio differs across lesion sites by a factor between 3 and 10 for each of the back-propagation networks (comparing the O $\rightarrow$ I ratio with the I $\rightarrow$ S ratio, see Table 5). When an output system is added, similar but slightly smaller values are obtained if input lesions are contrasted with output lesions (see Fig. 16 for the extended *40–60* network, and Fig. 21 for the DBM). Thus, although the networks do not produce quite such extreme contrasts as selected patients do, the effects obtained with the networks are generally in line with those shown by patients.

Inspection of Table 5 suggests that errors with a visual component (i.e. visual and mixed visual-and-semantic errors) will always exceed semantic errors, which is not the case in some patients (e.g. PW, Patterson, 1978; GR, Marshall & Newcombe, 1966). However, this effect arises from the particular criteria used to classify all possible errors as visually related (30% by chance) and as semantically related (12% by chance). If the criteria are adjusted so that the chance rates of the two error types are equalised to approximately 10%—somewhat more in line with criteria used empirically—then semantic errors can outnumber visually similar errors. For example, in the *40–60* network, semantic errors are 20% more frequent than visual and mixed visual-and-semantic errors combined after I $\rightarrow$ S lesions, but 30% less frequent after O $\rightarrow$ I lesions.[19] Overall, the quantitative variation in rates of different error types that occur across patients seem broadly compatible with the behaviour of the networks.

[19]With the adjusted criteria, semantic errors can also outnumber visually similar errors in the *10–15d, 40–40fb*, and H&S replication networks, but the rates of mixed visual-and-semantic errors remain high in the *40–80i* and *80fb* networks. This provides further evidence that the relative rates of mixed visual-and-semantic errors are sensitive to architectural details.

Extensions to Further Aspects of Syndrome

The simulations reported in this book have two main goals. The first is to show the computational robustness of the occurrence of the basic deep dyslexia error pattern when models satisfying the four assumptions listed earlier are lesioned. The second goal is to show that other aspects of the deep dyslexia symptom complex arise when individual models of this sort are explored in more detail. This part of the work is more exploratory and less rigorous, as we have investigated the individual models that are *technically* easiest to examine with respect to a particular issue, rather than the full gamut of models used in the work on the basic error pattern. In all cases, though, investigations of other models not reported here produced the same pattern of results. This section, therefore, may be viewed as an exploration of what characteristics other than the basic error pattern would be observed when a network satisfying the four assumptions is lesioned.

Three issues were specifically addressed: the effects of concreteness, how confidence relates to error type, and lexical decision. Information relevant to a fourth issue, visual-then-semantic errors, came to light in the course of the study. A fifth issue, the different subvarieties of deep dyslexia, was indirectly confronted when the problem of generating phonological output was tackled.

Effects of Concreteness. In the simulation described in the section on "Extending the Task Domain," an additional assumption was made, following Jones (1985), Saffran et al. (1980), and Gentner (1981), that, compared with other types of words, concrete nouns have a "richer" semantic representation that is consistently accessed. Specifically, the number of dimensions on which the semantic representation of a word has a specific value independent of the values it has on other dimensions, and across different contexts, is assumed to be greater for concrete nouns than for other words. This corresponds in our model to concrete nouns having more semantic features than do abstract nouns. When this assumption is made, lesions to the direct pathway of the input network lead to an advantage in correct performance for concrete over abstract words. In further experiments not reported in this book, lesions to the output network also resulted in better correct performance on concrete vs. abstract words, although the difference was not as large as for input lesions. It appears that the greater number of active semantic features gives the clean-up circuit more raw material on which to work, allowing stronger attractors to be built. This fits with Funnell and Allport's (1987, p. 396) suggestion that "certain classes of words evoke cognitive representations that are themselves relatively autonomous (strongly auto-associated) and therefore form relatively stable cognitive structures." The magnitude of the effect in the network is not quite as large as that shown in some deep dyslexic patients, but a quantitative difference of this sort is not unexpected given the great difference in scale between the model and the human cognitive system. More surprising than the mere existence of an abstract/concrete effect is the fact that it interacts with the occurrence of visual errors in a similar way to that found in most deep dyslexic patients in whom it has been investigated. After lesions to the direct route in the network, visual errors on average occur on more abstract words than do semantic errors, and the responses of visual errors tend to be more concrete than the stimuli.[20]

Better performance in reading concrete than abstract words is not found in all acquired dyslexic patients. Warrington (1981) reported a patient, CAV, who read abstract words significantly better than concrete words, although the difference (55% vs. 36%) was not as dramatic as the complementary contrast found in certain deep dyslexic patients. The apparent double dissociation of concrete vs. abstract word reading between CAV and deep dyslexic patients is difficult to account for without resorting to the rather extreme position that the semantics for concrete and abstract words are *neuroanatomically* separate (Shallice & Warrington, 1980; Warrington, 1981). The simulation provides an alternative explanation. Severe lesions to the clean-up pathway lead to an abstract word superiority that is, however, smaller than the concrete word advantage obtained from lesions to the direct pathway.

The difference between the two types of explanation is subtle but important. Since in our simulations we allow damage to impair the direct and clean-up pathways independently, we are assuming implicitly that these pathways are neuroanatomically separate. However, it is *not* the case that the direct pathway processes abstract semantics while the clean-up pathway processes concrete semantics. The entire network is involved in generating the semantics of both concrete and abstract words. Rather, the direct and clean-up pathways serve different computational roles in this process, and these roles are differentially important for reading these two classes of words. As in the account given by Shallice and Warrington, the dissociations arise from the selective impairment of a specialised process, but the specialisation is not in terms of the surface distinction (i.e. concrete

[20]The one patient who differed in this respect was GR (Barry & Richardson, 1988). Like the simulation, GR produced visual errors much more frequently on abstract words, but for GR the stimuli producing visual errors and semantic errors were roughly equally concrete. However, GR made semantic errors in matching spoken as well as written words to pictures (Newcombe & Marshall, 1980a). His impairment would therefore seem to involve the semantic system itself, which, when lesioned, would be expected to give rise to a higher number of semantic errors, even for concrete words, as was true of the extended *40–60* network (see Fig. 16).

vs. abstract words) but rather in terms of underlying representational and computational principles (e.g. the influence of differing numbers of semantic features on the development of attractors).

The fact that the model is consistent both with patients showing a concrete word advantage and with patients showing an abstract word advantage may suggest to some readers that the model is underconstrained by the data. There are three possible replies. First, overall, both patients and the model show a concrete word superiority. Second, for both types of superiority, the model predicts that visual error responses will tend to come from the class of words that are read more accurately. As predicted, CAV's visual error responses were more *abstract* than the stimuli (Warrington, 1981). Finally, the model predicts that the complementary patterns would differ on other characteristics, corresponding to the different effects of direct vs. clean-up pathway lesions. CAV also showed an advantage in matching auditorily presented words with pictures, suggesting modality-independent damage at the level of the semantic system. Thus, there are additional aspects of our simulation that counter the challenge that it is underconstrained. However, given the uniqueness of concrete word dyslexia in CAV, its occurrence in the model should be considered suggestive rather than conclusive.[21]

Confidence Judgments. We examined the relative confidence with which visual errors and semantic errors are produced in the DBM network. Two analogues for confidence were developed: The speed of settling, measured in terms of the number of iterations, and the "goodness" of the resulting representation, measured in terms of the energy in different parts of the network. Using both measures, visual errors were produced with more confidence than semantic errors, as has been observed in three deep dyslexic patients by Patterson (1978) and Kapur and Perl (1978), although the differences observed in the network were small.[22]

Lexical Decision. Coltheart (1980a), in his review, rates lexical decision as being "surprisingly good" in nine patients, but most of the evidence is based on personal communication. The published results that are cited pertain only to two of the patients (DE, PW; Patterson, 1979). Lexical decision was not rated "surprisingly good" in three patients; JR (Saffran,

[21]CAV does differ from the predictions of the model in making virtually no semantic errors. However, his nonword reading was not totally eliminated, as on one occasion he read 20% of nonsense syllables (Warrington, 1981). Thus, it remains possible that semantic errors could be edited out by his partially preserved phonological route, in an analogous fashion to the suggestions made by Newcombe and Marshall (1980b) for phonological alexia. However, until a patient is reported who is otherwise similar to CAV but who makes semantic errors, this suggestion remains ad hoc.

[22]A somewhat different pattern of findings on GR (Newcombe & Marshall, 1980a) is not based on an adequate amount of data.

personal communication), PS (Shallice & Coughlan, 1980), and AR (Warrington & Shallice, 1979).[23] Moreover, our attempts to demonstrate preserved lexical decision performance in a lesioned network have also been somewhat indeterminate. In an early investigation, Hinton and Shallice (Note 4) defined a *yes* response in lexical decision in the network by using a lower value of the proximity criterion than required for explicit naming (0.7, down from 0.8) and no gap criterion. This procedure did not result in relatively preserved lexical decision for words that could not be read. However, this effect was obtained in the present investigation when a procedure similar to that employed by Seidenberg and McClelland (1989) was used with the DBM network. According to this procedure, letter strings are given a *yes* response in lexical decision when they can be "recreated" on the basis of orthographic and semantic knowledge. For words that could not be read, this yielded a d' value (2.08) of the same sort of range as that found in DE (1.74; Patterson, 1979). Although these more recent results are promising, it should be kept in mind that aspects of the simulations—in particular, the definition of the task of lexical decision—are too unconstrained for the simulations to constitute a completely adequate characterisation of preserved lexical decision in deep dyslexic patients.

Visual-then-semantic Errors. A phenomenon that was not specifically investigated is the occurrence of visual-then-semantic errors in deep dyslexia (e.g. SYMPATHY → "orchestra," presumably mediated by *symphony*; Marshall & Newcombe, 1966). These are generally thought of as a visual error followed by a semantic error (Coltheart, 1980a), which presumably implies that two different impairments are involved. The present simulations provide a more parsimonious explanation, as the errors can arise when only a single set of connections is lesioned. They were observed unexpectedly using both the original H&S word set and the abstract/concrete word set. The mechanism by which they arise is most clearly seen in the case where the network includes an output system. A lesion to the input system can produce a semantic representation very close to that of a word visually related to the stimulus. However, the attractors in the output system may map this slightly inaccurate semantic activity onto the phonology of a semantic neighbour of this visually related word rather than the phonology of the word itself. It is the *normal* operation of the output system that produces the semantic part of the visual-then-semantic error.

Subvarieties of Deep Dyslexia. The final empirical issue addressed by the present investigation of deep dyslexia is that it can arise in a number of forms. Some patients, such as PS (Shallice & Coughlan, 1980) and KF (Shallice & Warrington, 1980), are much better at comprehending spoken

[23]AR differs from prototypical deep dyslexic patients in a number of ways (see Coltheart, 1980a). Also, his lexical decision was assessed in an unusual fashion.

than written words, suggesting an early locus of impairment, between orthography and semantics. Other patients, such as GR (Newcombe & Marshall, 1980a; 1980b) and FD (Friedman & Perlman, 1982), show similar types of errors across a number of lexical tasks involving variations in the modality of both the stimulus and the response, suggesting an impairment within lexical semantics itself. Still other patients, such as PW (Patterson, 1978; 1979), show relatively intact comprehension of visually presented words, even those they cannot read aloud, suggesting an impairment between semantics and phonology (or within phonology itself). The same divisions can be made on the basis of the relative proportions of visual and semantic errors. As mentioned earlier, some patients make far more visual than semantic errors; the ratio of visual errors to semantic errors was around 2.5 for VS (Saffran & Marin, 1977), 5 for PS, and approached 14 for KF. The two types of errors are approximately equal for other patients (e.g. PD, Kapur & Perl, 1978). Still others make far more semantic errors than visual errors—about 2.5 times more for GR (Barry & Richardson, 1988; Marshall & Newcombe, 1966) and 4 times more for PW. Finally, lexical decision performance, to the limited extent it has been investigated in deep dyslexic patients, varies in the same way as comprehension and error proportion data (Barry & Richardson, 1988; Shallice & Warrington, 1980). Taken together, these distinctions have led researchers to suggest that deep dyslexic patients can be further classified as *input*, *central*, or *output*, based on whether their impairment is located prior to, within, or after semantics (Friedman & Perlman, 1982; Shallice, 1988a; Shallice & Warrington, 1980).

Our simulations show similar variation in comprehension, relative error rates, and lexical decision, as a function of lesion location. Let us consider a misread word to be comprehended correctly when its semantics match those generated by the network better than any other word. Among words that are misread by the extended *40–60* network (both errors and omissions), only 46.1% are comprehended after input lesions (O → I and I → S), whereas 81.2% are comprehended after central lesions (S → C, C → S, and the S units themselves). By contrast, since output lesions to the back-propagation networks leave the semantics they derive unaffected, they would show 100% comprehension of words they could not read. The DBM network shows a similar distinction in comprehension performance, although there is some impairment after output lesions because processing is far more interactive than in the back-propagation networks. Specifically, only 14.6% of incorrectly read words are comprehended after input lesions, and 25.7% after central lesions, but 62.1% are comprehended after output lesions. Furthermore, as described earlier, these networks show changes in the ratio of visual errors to semantic errors as a function of lesion location analogous to those shown across patients (see Table 5 for the back-propagation networks, and Fig. 21 for the DBM network). Finally, lexical decision in the DBM is better after output lesions ($d' = 2.31$) than after input lesions ($d' = 1.80$). Thus, the simulations can account for the variation across the different subtypes of deep dyslexia.

More fundamentally, what has, in the past, been left totally unexplained by the division of deep dyslexic patients into subtypes is their *similarity*: Why should such widely varying impairments give rise to qualitatively equivalent error patterns and word-class effects in oral reading? The current simulations provide a simple explanation. Networks that map among distributed representations of orthographic, semantic, and phonological information using attractors are naturally sensitive to the similarities within these domains, and hence these similarities influence the errors that occur under damage. Indeed, qualitatively equivalent error patterns arise in the simulations from lesions to any stage along the semantic route, from the first set of connections after the orthographic input units to the last set before the phonological output units (see Figs. 16 and 21).

Remaining Empirical Issues

No evidence was obtained relating to certain aspects of the deep dyslexia symptom-complex. Some of these—derivational errors, and part-of-speech effects—can be accounted for by natural extrapolations from the current results. The situation is less clear for others: associative semantic errors, patients who make no visual errors, and the relation to impairments in writing (deep agraphia). We consider each of these in turn.

Derivational Errors. Deep dyslexic patients often make derivational errors, giving a response that is a different inflectional or derivational form of the stimulus (e.g. HITTING → "hit"). Since the word sets and orthographic representations we have used do not involve inflections, we could not have reproduced this type of error directly in our simulations. However, derivational errors can be considered to be one variety of mixed visual-and-semantic error, as they almost always have both a visual and a semantic relation to the stimulus. Therefore, above-chance rates of such errors are to be expected given the rates of mixed errors produced in the simulations. This is not to deny that the representations of inflectional or derivational forms of a word are related in a special way—unlike other visually or semantically related sets of words (Patterson, 1978; 1980)—only to point out that the occurrence of derivational errors in deep dyslexia can be explained without such an assumption (also see Funnell, 1987).

Part-of-speech Effects. In general, deep dyslexic patients read nouns better than adjectives, adjectives better than verbs, and verbs better than function words. Both the H&S word set and the abstract/concrete word set contain only nouns. However, Jones (1985) showed that ordering words in terms of ease-of-predication results in the same overall rank ordering of syntactic classes. In addition, Barry and Richardson (1988) found that part-of-speech had no effect on the reading performance of GR when concreteness, frequency, and "associative difficulty" (closely related to ease-of-predication) were statistically controlled. In the abstract/concrete simulations, we reflected the ease-of-predication of a word in terms of the number of active features in its semantic representation, and found that, after damage, concrete words, with greater ease-of-predication, are read better than abstract words. It would seem appropriate to give different parts-of-speech semantic representations in which the average number of features varied in a similar fashion. By analogy with the effects found with the abstract/concrete word set, one would expect that damage to the main part of the network would result in the same rank order of correct performance, with nouns > adjectives > verbs > function words. Thus, the approach taken in the simulations seems likely to produce the part-of-speech effects found in deep dyslexia (also see Marin, Saffran, & Schwartz, 1976).

Associative Semantic Errors. Coltheart (1980d) argued that two types of semantic errors occur in deep dyslexia: a *shared-feature* type, and an *associative* type. In the present simulations, only the shared-feature type was formally investigated. Comparing Tables 6.1 and 6.2 of Coltheart (1980d, pp. 147–148; also see the error corpora in Coltheart et al., 1980, Appendix 2), this type appears to be the larger group, and over half of those held to be associative by Coltheart appear to have visual (V) or shared-feature (SF) characteristics as well.[24] In some errors, however, the associative aspect completely dominates (e.g. FREE → "enterprise," STAGE → "coach"). Could a network produce such errors?

Notice that words with an associative relationship often follow one another in spoken and written language (see Deese, 1965). In the course of normal fluent reading, the system must move quickly from the representation of one word to the next. Suppose that the system must start from the attractor of the current word, or at least is biased towards it, when beginning to process the next word. For word pairs that frequently follow each other (e.g. WRIST WATCH), the network will learn to lower the energy boundary between the attractor basins for the two words so that the transition can be accomplished more easily.[25] This lower boundary would be more easily corrupted or lost under damage than would the

[24]ANTIQUE → "vase" (SF), NEXT → "exit" (V), PALE → "ale" (V), COMFORT → "blanket" (SF), IDEAL → "milk" (SF), THERMOS → "flask" (SF), INCOME → "tax" (SF), MOTOR → "car" (SF), BRING → "towards" (SF), POSTAGE → "stamps" (SF), WEAR → "clothes" (SF), STY → "pig", BLOWING → "wind" (SF), SHINING → "sun" (SF), CONE → "ice-cream" (SF).

[25]This explanation does not imply that sequences of interpretations are *caused* by temporarily adjusting the energy boundaries between them, but only that an *effect* of learning sequences would be to lower the boundaries between frequent transitions.

boundaries between basins for other word pairs. As a result, presentation of the first word would become more likely to settle into the attractor for the second word, resulting in an associative semantic error. This explanation also predicts that the reverse ordering should also become more likely as an error, which is found in patients (e.g. DIAL → "sun" and CONE → "ice-cream;" Coltheart, 1980d).[26] Of course, these errors would become even more likely if the two words shared any visual or semantic features.

Patients Who Make No Visual Errors. A major contribution of the current connectionist approach to deep dyslexia is the ubiquitous co-occurrence of visual, semantic, and mixed visual-and-semantic errors when an attractor network that maps orthography to semantics is lesioned. Thus, possibly the strongest empirical challenge to the current account is the existence of three patients who make semantic and derivational errors in reading, but no purely visual errors (KE, Hillis et al., 1990; RGB and HW, Caramazza & Hillis, 1990). KE made semantic errors in all other lexical processing tasks as well (e.g. writing to dictation, spoken and written picture–word matching), suggesting damage within the semantic system. In contrast, RGB and HW made semantic errors only in tasks requiring a spoken response, suggesting damage in the output system after semantics. Although a number of the network architectures we examined produced no visual errors with some types of clean-up damage when the response criteria were used (e.g. *40–60* C → S lesions; *80fb* S → I lesions), when an output system was used, all of the networks produced visual/phonological errors for every lesion location other than the phonological clean-up pathway. The primary motivation for developing an output system was to obtain an unbiased procedure for generating explicit responses from semantic activity, rather than to model the human speech production system per se. In fact, there are many ways in which it is clearly inadequate for the latter purpose (cf. Dell, 1986; 1988; Levelt, 1989). However, we have considered the pattern of errors produced by lesioning the output network as helping to explain the existence of an output form of deep dyslexia. Therefore, we can hardly argue that the deficits of RGB and HW, much less KE, are outside the scope of the model.

As far as patient KE is concerned, the initial report on word reading refers to most errors being semantic, but remaining errors include phonologically and/or visually related ones. Such errors only amounted to 1.4% of all non-correct responses in the main experiments reported. However, these experiments involved the presentation of a considerable number of items (e.g. 14) from each of a number of categories (4 or 10),

[26]Both directions of an associative error need not be *equally* likely after damage, because there can be differences in the paths that the network follows in state space, settling from the initial pattern for one word to the final pattern for the other.

with each item presented in a number of different tasks (e.g. 5). Thus, items in a small set of categories were repeatedly presented. It seems likely that KE would learn the categories and use this to limit the number of visual responses, as these would tend not to fall in one of the categories. In addition, a considerable number of mixed errors seem to occur, but this is not analysed in the paper. In the baseline testing situation, in which a word set containing a variety of types of word was used (the Johns Hopkins battery), KE is reported as making some errors "phonologically and/or visually related" to the target. However, there is no direct evidence that KE did learn to edit out putative visual errors.

There appear to be two very different ways in which the absence of visual/phonological errors in RGB and HW can be explained. The first concerns the strategy used by the patient. Deep dyslexic patients at times produce a circumlocutory response—they describe the meaning of the word rather than attempting to read it aloud. However, in general, such responses form only a small part of the patient's output (e.g. GR, DE). In contrast, both RGB and HW produce many responses described as "definitions" of the words they are trying to read (21% and 28% of all non-correct responses, respectively). Caramazza and Hillis (1990) report that, in repetition tasks, RGB produced many circumlocutions, and HW often followed her errors with the comment, "I can't say what you said but that is the idea." Moreover, HW's semantic errors in reading or naming were often followed by a definition, as in her response to a picture of grapes: "wine . . . but that's not what it is, it's what you do with it. . . ." As the patients were clearly frequently trying to communicate that they understood the word, it seems quite plausible that any potential visual/phonological error (that would not be sense-preserving) would be edited out prior to articulation. After all, it is convincingly demonstrated that semantic access from the written word was unimpaired in both patients. Semantic errors, on the other hand, would be more difficult to detect as errors at the semantic level and could, in fact, serve as an approximation to the meaning for communication purposes.

Alternatively, the lack of visual/phonological errors in these patients may be explained by individual differences in the effects of qualitatively equivalent lesions in connectionist networks. The reported simulation results are the sum of a number (typically 20) of random samples of a given lesion type. In a network, qualitatively and quantitatively equivalent lesions, such as instances of $O \rightarrow I(0.3)$, have quantitatively different effects depending on the particular connections removed (also see Patterson et al., 1990). The reported results are means of distributions—the patients who make no visual/phonological errors may correspond to the tail of one of the distributions. In fact, the chance rate of visual errors compared to semantic errors is much higher in the main simulations than it is in analyses of patient data. The simulations are therefore more sensitive to the presence of a low rate of visual errors than are the reported empirical observations (see the section of "Quantitative Adequacy" earlier).

Neither of these solutions to the problem posed to our modelling work by the three patients of Caramazza, Hillis, and colleagues is completely satisfactory. In our account of deep dyslexia, we have accepted that a response produced by a patient can be modelled directly by the output of our network(s), and that the means of the effects of 20 qualitatively and quantitatively equivalent lesions can model the responses produced by a patient with only one lesion. Our two possible accounts of the patients who make no visual errors imply that at least one of these assumptions can at best hold only for the large majority of patients. The theory cannot apply in its strongest form to the results produced by *all* patients who read solely by the semantic route as a result of neurological damage.

Acquired Dysgraphia. The final characteristic of deep dyslexia that Coltheart et al. (1987, p. 145) describe is that "if a patient makes semantic errors in reading isolated words aloud he or she will also . . . have impaired writing and spelling." They argue that this impairment will involve either a global or a deep dysgraphia. However, the converse relation does not hold; there are deep dysgraphic patients who are not deep dyslexic (e.g. Bub & Kertesz, 1982; Howard & Franklin, 1988; Newcombe & Marshall, 1984). The simple presumption, that the processing systems and connections involved in writing are the same as those involved in reading, cannot easily be held; moreover it is not computationally plausible.

According to the present account, deep dyslexia depends on the co-occurrence of at least two major types of damage: the first to the phonological route, and the second (less severe) to the semantic route. One possible explanation of deep or global dysgraphia without deep dyslexia is that, in most people, writing is a less well-learned skill than reading, and so would be more vulnerable to the effects of brain damage. Given this, and the fact that both reading and writing make use of common semantic and phonological systems, damage that is sufficient to produce deep dyslexia would seem likely to impair writing and spelling as well. On this account, though, deep dyslexia without deep or global dysgraphia should eventually be observed. Indeed, relatively recovered pure alexic patients (Coslett & Saffran, 1989) would seem to fit this pattern (also see the patients of Beringer & Stein, 1930, and Faust, 1955, discussed by Marshall & Newcombe, 1980).

Visual vs. Phonological Errors. It has frequently been suggested that some deep dyslexic patients have an impairment in accessing phonological lexical representations from semantics (e.g. Friedman & Perlman, 1982; Patterson, 1978; Shallice & Warrington, 1980). There are three main lines of evidence that lead to this conclusion. First, certain patients (e.g. PW and DE; Patterson, 1978) frequently select the presented word when offered a choice between it and their semantic error, implying that they know the presented word. Second, in auditory–visual matching these patients again usually select the presented word rather than their visual error. Third, certain patients perform as well on visual word–picture matching as on auditory word–picture matching, and perform both at close to normal levels (e.g. VS, Saffran & Marin, 1977; PW, Patterson, 1979), although others are much worse with visual than with auditory presentation of words (e.g. PS, Shallice & Coughlan, 1980; KF, Shallice & Warrington, 1980).

Our simulations present a potential problem for this argument. The output network develops strong phonological attractors in the same way that the input network develops strong semantic attractors. Thus, for the same reason that damage to the input network produces visual and semantic errors, damage to the output network would be expected to produce semantic and *phonological* errors. This prediction conflicts with the inclusion of visual errors per se as a symptom of deep dyslexia.

The word sets used in the current simulations were not designed to differentiate phonological from visual errors. Yet pure phonological errors (e.g. HAWK → "tor") certainly occur when the output pathways are lesioned. Whether phonological errors occur in deep dyslexia has never to our knowledge been empirically investigated, although Goldblum (1985) suggests that the so-called visual errors are actually phonological. However, inspection of the error corpora for a number of patients (Coltheart et al., 1980, Appendix 2) does not support this interpretation. If one takes PW, for example, many errors are more easily explained as visual (e.g. ORATE → "over," CAMPAIGN → "camping") but only one is easier to explain as a phonological error (GRIEF → "greed"). Attempts to simulate the three empirical phenomena that suggest an output lesion might reveal that they are compatible with an input lesion, or more particularly a lesion to the semantic system itself. In any case, the area requires further empirical study and simulations.

Theoretical Issues

The connectionist account of deep dyslexia that we have developed from the position advocated by Hinton and Shallice (1991) is based upon four assumptions, listed in the section on "Critical System Properties," concerning the process of mapping orthography to semantics. The first two of these are standard assumptions within connectionist modelling. Another, concerning the difference between representations of abstract and concrete words, is derived from earlier theorising. Only one, concerning attractors, is at all original to the present approach. In addition to these four assumptions, two more are necessary to account for additional characteristics of deep dyslexia. The first, that the mapping from orthography to semantics is isolated from phonological influences, is standard in accounts of deep dyslexia (see Coltheart et al., 1980). The second, that the pathway from orthography to semantics is also affected by a lesion, is widely but not universally held (see Shallice, 1988a, for discussion).

If one takes the nine characteristics held to apply to deep dyslexia by Coltheart et al. (1987), three are directly explained in a principled fashion on the present account (semantic errors, visual errors, concrete word superiority). Three more (derivational/morphological errors, the part-of-speech effects, and function word substitutions) follow in a straightforward fashion from the simulations, even though they have yet to be implemented. An additional two are an immediate consequence of one standard assumption, that of the absence of phonological processing. Only one, the relation between reading and writing, is at all problematic. In addition, the simulations offer principled accounts of five other phenomena that have been widely investigated empirically: relatively high rates of mixed visual-and-semantic errors, the interaction of semantic factors in the genesis of visual errors, confidence in error types, lexical decision, and, most surprisingly of all, the visual-then-semantic errors. However, as discussed in the preceding section, there are a number of other less central aspects of the disorder which are not yet well accommodated within the approach.

Our account differs from others provided for deep dyslexia—and with few exceptions (e.g. Miceli & Caramazza, 1990; Mozer & Behrmann, 1990), for cognitive neuropsychology as a whole—in providing what we have called a "principled account." By this, we mean that (1) many aspects of the syndrome are explained from a common set of basic assumptions, rather than requiring specific extra assumptions for each aspect; and (2) the explanations are derived from the assumptions computationally rather than intuitively. Consider, as an example, the shared-feature semantic error itself. Various theoretical accounts have been given as to why such errors should occur. Coltheart (1980d), in his review of the phenomenon, considers two theories, but rejects one, the imagery explanation, as being empirically much inferior to the other. The second one, the Marshall and Newcombe (1966) account, takes a position derived from Katz and Fodor (1963) in arguing that the patient lacks the ability to descend a hierarchically organised semantic tree to the appropriate terminal leaf when deriving a phonological form from a semantic representation. Yet, as Coltheart points out, this account would not explain the standard non-synonymous co-ordinate errors (e.g. NIECE → "aunt"). He suggests (Coltheart, 1980d, p. 153): "one needs to suppose that when a determiner is lost, sometimes it leaves some trace: The patient knows that a determiner is lost, so supplies one, without having any way of selecting the correct determiner." Although Coltheart provides some limited empirical arguments in favour of this amended Marshall and Newcombe position, his amendment is not derived from any deeper assumptions and is not used in the explanation of any other phenomenon. It remains, therefore, theoretically ad hoc. The account given by Shallice and Warrington (1980) suffers from similar problems to that of Marshall and Newcombe (1966), and that of Morton and Patterson (1980) introduces specific ad hoc assumptions. By contrast, on the present account, the existence of semantic errors essentially derives from the assumption of attractors, which is also used in explaining many other aspects of the syndrome.

The Right Hemisphere Theory

Two other main classes of theory have been put forward to account for deep dyslexia: the multiple functional impairments position (e.g., Morton & Patterson, 1980; Shallice & Warrington, 1980) and the right hemisphere theory (Coltheart, 1980b; 1983; Saffran et al., 1980; Zaidel & Peters, 1981). The current account adopts the "subtraction" assumptions taken by the multiple functional impairment theories, whereby impaired behaviour is explained by the damaged operation of the same mechanism that subserves normal behaviour. In a sense, our account is a specific version of this class of theory. However, as discussed earlier, multiple functional impairment theories have problems in limiting the number of postulated impairments, and the locus of damage that explains one symptom often differs from that assumed for another. The present version has two advantages in addition to the principled nature of its predictions: It can explain a wide range of symptoms by assuming that the isolated semantic route is subject to only one locus of lesion, and it can also explain why a number of different loci of lesions give rise to qualitatively similar patterns of symptoms.

The right hemisphere theory of deep dyslexia differs from multiple functional impairment theories in that many aspects of the syndrome are derived from a common cause. Here, though, the extrapolation from the basic assumption is an empirical one: The reading behaviour of deep dyslexic patients shares aspects with that of other patients known to be reading with the right hemisphere (and normal subjects under brief left-lateralised presentation). The adequacy of these correspondences is a matter of ongoing debate (see Barry & Richardson, 1988; Baynes, 1990; Coltheart et al., 1987; Glosser & Friedman, 1990; Jones & Martin, 1985; Marshall & Patterson, 1983; 1985; Patterson & Besner, 1984a; 1984b; Patterson et al., 1989; Rabinowicz & Moscovitch, 1984; Shallice, 1988a; Zaidel & Schweiger, 1984). Moreover, a recent PET study (Howard et al., 1992) suggests that deep dyslexic patients may vary in this respect. In two patients, the left hemisphere seemed to have little remaining tissue outside the visual cortex. The third patient's scan, however, showed a much smaller lesion confined to part of the posterior left hemisphere. The lesion in a fourth patient, with deep dysphasia and surface dyslexia, was very similarly located.

For the present approach, the critical point is that a connectionist account can be orthogonal to one based on right hemisphere reading. If the right hemisphere reads by the same principles as the normal mechanism for reading via meaning (although perhaps less effectively), then the connectionist account could still apply. In addition, one would not have to postulate independently that the right hemisphere reading process has a particular set of properties—they could be inferred from the connectionist account. Moreover, the connectionist account could also explain reading patterns similar to deep dyslexia that *are* based on left hemisphere reading (and so can be abolished by a second, left hemisphere stroke; Roeltgen, 1987). In such an account, the total reading system would contain both left hemisphere and right hemisphere units and connections (as well as inter-hemispheric connections), with the left hemisphere ones being more numerous. However, the compatibility of the connectionist and right hemisphere accounts of deep dyslexia depends on the assumption that right hemisphere reading differs from normal reading only quantitatively and not qualitatively. In their review, which is broadly favourable to the right hemisphere theory, Coltheart et al. (1987) leave this issue open.

Attractors vs. Logogens

At a more detailed level, the operation of attractors plays a central role in our account of deep dyslexia. How do attractors relate to other theoretical concepts that have been used in explaining deep dyslexic reading behaviour? The most commonly used concept with some relation to an attractor is that of a *logogen* (Morton, 1969; Morton & Patterson, 1980). We take the defining characteristic of a logogen to be that it is a representation of a word, with an associated activity level, in which all of the information of a particular type relating to the word is packaged together. In the logogen model, words are related to other words via information that is external to the logogens themselves. In this way, logogens operate much like *localist* representations in connectionist networks (Feldman & Ballard, 1982; McClelland & Rumelhart, 1981).

The attractor network that would appear to be closest to the updated logogen model of Morton and Patterson (1980), as far as the process of reading via meaning is concerned, is the *40–80i* network, in which attractors are built at the level of the intermediate units between orthographic and semantic representations. However, a major difference between the logogen model and this attractor network should be noted. The similarity metric of the relation between logogens is purely visual/orthographic. If the activation level of a second logogen is near to that of the one that reaches threshold then this implies only that the two represent stimuli that are visually similar. In contrast, the similarity metric for attractors is both visual and semantic. Thus, damage to attractors can produce both visual and semantic influence in errors, whereas damage to logogens can result only in visual confusions.

However, a system in which semantics can feed back to influence the input logogens might also show semantic errors after damage. In fact, on the output side, Dell (1986; 1988) uses an interactive system with localist lexical units to model semantic and phonological influences in speech production errors. One might imagine that an analogous system on the input side would, under damage, replicate our findings of co-occurrences of visual, mixed visual-and-semantic, and semantic errors under damage. To test this possibility, we developed a DBM model that maps orthography to semantics via 40 intermediate units trained to be localist lexical representations (i.e. each unit responds to exactly one word and is inactive for all others). After lesions, the network produces explicit error rates that are higher than in most of our simulations, but the increase is almost exclusively limited to *other* errors. Although the rates of visual errors are well above chance, the rates of semantic errors are only slightly above chance, even for lesions within semantics itself (S $\leftrightarrow$ S lesions). Furthermore, the semantic errors are particularly idiosyncratic: Over 20% of all semantic errors is the particular error CAN $\rightarrow$ "mug." In fact, the responses "mug" and "bone" account for over half of all semantic errors. Clearly this is an unsatisfactory account of the deep dyslexic error pattern, and nothing like that shown by the DBM with distributed intermediate representations. However, our failure at implementing a localist network that reproduces deep dyslexia is only suggestive of the difficulties that others may encounter (cf. Martin, Dell, Saffran, & Schwartz, in press).

A full consideration of the issue of localist vs. distributed representations is far beyond the scope of this book (for discussion, see Feldman, Fanty, & Goddard, 1988; Hinton et al., 1986). Here we raise only one general issue, relating to the degree to which words can operate *independently*. In a localist representation, words can influence other parts of the system in a manner unrelated to the way similar words have influence (e.g. in generating a pronunciation from semantics). This is a strong advantage because the meanings of words are arbitrarily related to their spellings and pronunciations. For this reason, reading for meaning is the paradigmatic domain in which localist representations would appear most appropriate (Hinton et al., 1986). However, capturing the similarity among words involves maintaining the similarity of their incoming and outgoing weights. In contrast, in a distributed representation, words can have effects *only by virtue of their features*, and so other words tend to have similar effects to the degree that they share those features. The use of attractors is a way of compensating for this bias of distributed representations in domains where it is problematic, but the underlying effects of similarity are revealed under damage. Thus, localist and distributed representations are distinguished by what is *natural* for each approach, rather than by what is strictly possible or impossible.

Extensions of the Approach

The connectionist account we have provided for deep dyslexia would seem to be directly generalisable in three ways. The first concerns other types of reading disorders in which processes operating between the orthographic and semantic levels are relevant. Hinton and Shallice (1991) argued that aspects of semantic access dyslexia and pure alexia were explicable in terms of the model. In the context of the current simulations, we have also considered neglect dyslexia (Caplan, 1987; Kinsbourne & Warrington, 1962; Riddoch, 1991; Sieroff, Pollatsek, & Posner, 1988). Howard and Best (Note 5) have recently described two patients of this type. Both patients produce abnormally slow responses to stimuli on the right (contralesional) side after being miscued to the left, and make many more errors on the right parts of words in reading, nearly all of which are visual in nature. Of particular interest is that these patients show marked imageability/concreteness effects, especially for longer words. M.-P. de Partz (personal communication) has found similar effects in another neglect dyslexic patient.

Mozer and Behrmann (1990) have modelled neglect dyslexia in terms of a connectionist network that operates on principles similar to ours. On their model, neglect dyslexia is caused by an attentional deficit that results, on average, in a gradient of activation over low-level visual representations of words. The activity is higher on the ipsilesional side and diminishes monotonically to be lowest contralesionally. Our input network may be thought of as a different implementation of the portions of their model that operate on these low-level representations, with our clean-up pathway corresponding to their Pull-Out net. We therefore considered the effect of presenting the intact abstract/concrete network with monotonically degraded input (activations of 1.0, 0.83, 0.67, 0.5, across feature letter units from left to right, corrupted by normally distributed noise with standard deviation 0.1). Using analogous testing procedures to those used in the abstract/concrete simulations, the ouput was 77% correct for concrete words but only 47% correct for abstract words. In the predominant error form—visual errors—55% of the first and second letters were correct but only 29% of the third and fourth letters. Thus, the simulation shows the same combination of imageability and neglected characteristics as do Howard and Best's patients.[27] Hence, it seems plausible that the model could be utilised as part of the explanation of the patterns of impairment shown by dyslexic patients other than the deep dyslexics with whom this book has been concerned.

The second plausible generalisation of the approach is to other syndromes in which an input/output mapping can be accomplished only via semantics. The two most obvious syndromes for which an analogous explanation could be given are the parallels to deep dyslexia in the auditory domain (deep dysphasia) and in writing (deep dysgraphia).

Deep dysphasia involves the co-occurrence of semantic and phonological errors in repetition, and a concrete word superiority (see, e.g., Howard & Franklin, 1988; Katz & Goodglass, 1990; Martin & Saffran, 1990; Michel & Andreewsky, 1983; Morton, 1980). In some patients (e.g. NC of Martin & Saffran, MK of Howard & Franklin), the parallel with deep dyslexia is very close, as the phonological errors in oral repetition are normally phonologically related words. In other patients (e.g. R of Michel & Andreewsky), responses that are phonologically related to the target are often literal paraphasias. In general, though, this syndrome would fit with an explanation in which repetition must rely on partially impaired semantic mediation, because damage has eliminated the standard, direct route from input phonology to output phonology (see Howard & Franklin, 1988; Katz & Goodglass, 1990; Morton, 1980). Martin et al. (in press) describe a connectionist simulation of deep dysphasia that embodies rather different assumptions from ours about the origins of the patients' difficulties.

If semantic mediation in writing operates by principles analogous to those for reading, then the corresponding pattern of symptoms would be expected to result from lesions. In fact, essentially the same arguments that apply for deep dyslexia also apply for deep dysgraphia (see, e.g., Bub & Kertesz, 1982; Howard & Franklin, 1988; Newcombe & Marshall, 1984). Specifically, phonological mediation in writing is inoperative, and semantic mediation suffers from damage complementary to that in the reading processes simulated in current work.

Third, and more generally, any domain that involves mapping between arbitrarily related domains, analogous to orthography and semantics, would be expected to give rise to error patterns that are analogous to those found in deep dyslexia (except for aspects that are specific to othography

---

[27]The patients produce virtually no semantic errors, whereas the simulation produces some (but very few relative to the lesion simulations). However, it should be noted that the patients may be able to make some use of orthographic-to-phonological process, not available to the network, to edit out semantic errors.

or semantics, such as the effects of concreteness). Along these lines, Plaut and Shallice (1993) account for the semantic and perseverative influences in the visual naming errors of optic aphasic patients by generalising the current approach to the mapping from high-level visual representations of objects to semantics.

The Impact of Connectionist Neuropsychology

Deep dyslexia was first described in a single patient, GR (Marshall & Newcombe, 1966), but it soon began to be conceived as a *symptom-complex* (Marshall & Newcombe, 1973), and then as a *syndrome*—that is, as a collection of behaviours arising from a specific functional impairment (Coltheart, 1980a; Marshall & Newcombe, 1980). Almost immediately this position was criticised. Morton and Patterson (1980) rejected the concept of a syndrome. Shallice and Warrington (1980) argued that the pattern of symptoms could have a number of different origins (also see Coltheart & Funnell, 1987). Caramazza (1984) and Schwartz (1984) argued against the general methodology of assuming that frequently observed combinations of symptoms represented the effects of a single underlying impairment. One of us (Shallice, 1988a), although willing to accept syndromes based on dissociations, rejected errors in particular as a fruitful basis on which to generalise across patients. Even Coltheart et al. (1987), in their later review, seem rather pessimistic about characterising deep dyslexia as a syndrome, unless the right hemisphere theory were correct.

The present investigation has both positive and negative theoretical implications for the validity of the concept of a syndrome, in deep dyslexia and more generally (also see Shallice & Plaut, 1992). On the positive side, the work was motivated by the possibility that deep dyslexia is indeed a coherent functional entity. However, there is a critical difference in the nature of the functional entity as envisaged in the current research, and the formulation that has been accepted, either implicitly or explicitly, both by critics (e.g. Caramazza, 1984; 1986) and by defenders (e.g. Coltheart, 1980a; Shallice, 1988a) of the syndrome concept. According to the standard formulation, if a symptom-complex is to be of theoretical interest, it must arise from the same functional lesion site for all patients who exhibit it. If it can be demonstrated that some aspects of the symptom-complex do not always co-occur across patients, then this is considered evidence that the symptom-complex can arise from more than one locus of damage. The symptom-complex becomes a "psychologically weak syndrome" and hence of little or no theoretical interest (see Caramazza, 1984; Coltheart, 1980a, for relevant discussion).

Although this logic seems appropriate for theoretical analyses in terms of conventional "box-and-arrow" systems, the present research shows that it is not appropriate for at least some connectionist systems. Part of the overall symptom pattern may occur as a result of lesions in many parts of a complex system, for reasons that derive directly from the nature of the computation that the whole system is carrying out. An example is given in the present simulations by the qualitative similarity of error patterns whenever lesions are made between orthographic input and phonological output. At the same time, other aspects of the symptom-complex may differ between lesion sites. Thus, lesions to the clean-up network do not show the concrete word superiority effects shown by lesions to the direct pathway, even though they produce the same qualitative pattern of visual and semantic similarity in errors. This means that, even when patients differ in some respects, the aspects of their behaviour that are similar may still have a common functional origin. Thus, considering these patients together may be a valuable guide to understanding the impaired system. In this way, even the existence of so-called "weak syndromes" can be theoretically productive.

There is also a negative side to the general methodological implications of the current simulations. Hinton and Shallice (1991) showed that a "strong dissociation" (Shallice, 1988a) between the processing of different semantic categories can occur when particular lesions are made to the clean-up pathway. The category foods was selectively preserved in a striking manner. However, when lesions were made to a second network that was essentially the same except for the use of a different random starting point for the learning procedure, the dissociation did not occur. The present simulations show similarly dramatic effects when the same set of connections are lesioned, but again, minor changes in architecture lead to different category effects: Animals were performed over 20 times better than body parts for the *10–15d* network, and over 3 times better than outdoor objects in the *40–40fb* network. It would appear that the strong dissociations obtained may reflect idiosyncrasies in the learning experience of particular networks.

Almost two decades ago, Marin et al. (1976) responded to criticisms of the relevance of neuropsychological findings for understanding normal cognition by pointing to high-energy physics, where studying the effects of random damage has produced substantial theoretical results. The results obtained in this paper, together with analyses of equivalent depth that are beginning to be made of other syndromes as well, suggest that the analogy may be closer than Marin and colleagues intended. If our simulations are valid, in principle even if not in detail, then neuropsychological evidence, such as deep dyslexia syndrome, will provide strong support for a particular organisation of the cognitive system that would probably prove difficult to obtain by the use of experiments on normal subjects. On the other hand, without detailed simulations, appropriate interpretations of many aspects of the syndrome would be virtually impossible. In this case, cognitive neuropsychology will benefit most extensively from an interplay between empirical and computational approaches in future work.

ACKNOWLEDGEMENTS

Most of the work reported here was carried out while the authors were visiting scientists in the Departments of Psychology and Computer Science at the University of Toronto. The work could not have been carried out without the generous support and guidance of Geoff Hinton. We would like to thank Gus Craik for his help with many aspects of our visits to Toronto. We also wish to thank Marlene Behrmann, Max Coltheart, Argye Hillis, and two anonymous reviewers for their detailed suggestion on an earlier version. All of the simulations were run on a Silicon Graphics Iris-4D/240S using an extended version of the Xerion simulator developed by Tony Plate. This research was supported by grant 87-2-36 from the Alfred Sloan Foundation. Much of the work was carried out while Tim Shallice was a member of the Medical Research Council's Applied Psychology Unit.

REFERENCES

Ackley, D.H.,, Hinton, G.E., & Sejnowski, T.J. (1985). A learning algorithm for Boltzmann Machines. *Cognitive Science, 9*(2), 147–169.

Allport, D.A. (1987). On knowing the meaning of words we are unable to report: The effects of visual masking. In S. Dornic (Ed.), *Attention and performance VI*. Hillsdale, NJ: Lawrence Erlbaum Associates Inc.

Allport, D.A. (1985). Distributed memory, modular systems and dysphasia. In S.K. Newman & R. Epstein (Eds.), *Current perspectives in dysphasia*. Edinburgh: Churchill Livingstone.

Bapi, R.S., & Levine, D.S. (1990). Networks modeling the involvement of the frontal lobes in learning and performance of flexible movement sequences. In *Proceedings of the 12th Annual Conference of the Cognitive Science Society*. Hillsdale, NJ: Lawrence Erlbaum Associates Inc., 915–922.

Barry, C., & Richardson, J.T.E. (1988). Accounts of oral reading in deep dyslexia. In H.A. Whitaker (Ed.), *Phonological processing and brain mechanisms*. New York: Springer-Verlag.

Bates, E.A., & Elman, J.L. (1993). Connectionism and the study of change. In M.H. Johnson (Ed.), *Brain development and cognition*. Oxford: Blackwell, 623–642.

Baynes, K.A. (1990). Language and reading in the right hemisphere: Highways or byways of the brain? *Journal of Cognitive Neuroscience, 2*(3), 159–179.

Beauvois, M.-F. (1982). Optic aphasia: A process of interaction between vision and language. *Proceedings of the Royal Society of London, Series B, 298*, 35–47.

Beauvois, M.-F., & Derouesné, J. (1979). Phonological alexia: Three dissociations. *Journal of Neurology, Neurosurgery and Psychiatry, 42*, 1115–1124.

Behrmann, M., & Bub, D. (1992). Surface dyslexia and dysgraphia: Dual routes, a single lexicon. *Cognitive Neuropsychology, 9*(3), 209–258.

Behrmann, M., Moscovitch, M., Black, S.E., & Mozer, M.C. (1990). Perceptual and conceptual factors in neglect dyslexia: Two contrasting case studies. *Brain, 113*(4), 1163–1183.

Behrmann, M., Moscovitch, M., & Mozer, M.C. (1991). Directing attention to words and nonwords in normal subjects and in a computational model: Implications for neglect dyslexia. *Cognitive Neuropsychology, 7*, 213–248.

Beringer, K., & Stein, J. (1930). Analyse eines Falles von "Reiner" Alexie. *Zeitschrift für die Gesamte Neurologie und Psychiatrie, 123*, 473–478.

Besner, D., Twilley, L., McCann, R.S., & Seergobin, K. (1990). On the connection between connectionism and data: Are a few words necessary? *Psychological Review, 97*(3), 432–446.

Bisiach, E., & Vallar, G. (1988). Hemineglect in humans. In F. Boller & J. Grafman (Eds.), *Handbook of neuropsychology, Vol. 1*. Amsterdam: Elsevier Science Publishers (North-Holland), 195–222.

Brunn, J.L., & Farah, M.J. (1991). The relation between spatial attention and reading: Evidence from the neglect syndrome. *Cognitive Neuropsychology, 7*, 59–75.

Bryson, A.E., & Ho, Y.C. (1969). *Applied optimal control*. New York: Blaisdell.

Bub, D., Cancelliere, A., & Kertesz, A. (1985). Whole-word and analytic translation of spelling-to-sound in a non-semantic reader. In K.E. Patterson, M. Coltheart, & J.C. Marshall (Eds.), *Surface dyslexia*. Hillsdale, NJ: Lawrence Erlbaum Associates Inc., 15–34.

Bub, D., & Kertesz, A. (1982). Deep agraphia. *Brain and Language, 17*, 146–165.

Burton, M.A., Young, A.W., Bruce, V., Johnston, R.A., & Ellis, A.W. (1991). Understanding covert recognition. *Cognition, 39*(2), 129–166.

Caplan, B. (1987). Assessment of unilateral neglect: A new reading test. *Journal of Clinical and Experimental Neuropsychology, 9*(4), 359–364.

Caramazza, A. (1984). The logic of neuropsychological research and the problem of patient classification in aphasia. *Brain and Language, 21*, 9–20.

Caramazza, A. (1986). On drawing inferences about the structure of normal cognitive systems from the analysis of patterns of impaired performance: The case for single-patient studies. *Brain and Cognition, 5*, 41–66.

Caramazza, A., & Hillis, A.E. (1990). Where do semantic errors come from? *Cortex, 26*, 95–122.

Caramazza, A., & McCloskey, M. (1991). The poverty of methodology. (Commentary on T. Shallice, Précis of From neuropsychology to mental structure.) *Behavioral and Brain Sciences, 14*, 444–445.

Caramazza, A., & Miceli, G. (1990). The structure of graphemic representations. *Cognition, 37*, 243–297.

Cohen, J.D., Romero, R.D., Servan-Schreiber, D., & Farah, M.J. (in press). Disengaging from the disengage function: The relation of macrostructure to microstructure in parietal attentional deficits. *Journal of Cognitive Neuroscience*.

Cohen, J.D., & Servan-Schreiber, D. (1992). Context, cortex, and dopamine: A connectionist approach to behavior and biology in schizophrenia. *Psychological Review, 99*(1), 45–77.

Coltheart, M. (1980a). Deep dyslexia: A review of the syndrome. In M. Coltheart, K.E. Patterson, & J.C. Marshall (Eds.), *Deep dyslexia*. London: Routledge & Kegan Paul, 22–48.

Coltheart, M. (1980b). Deep dyslexia: A right-hemisphere hypothesis. In M. Coltheart, K.E. Patterson, & J.C. Marshall (Eds.), *Deep dyslexia*. London: Routledge & Kegan Paul, 326–380.

Coltheart, M. (1980c). Reading, phonological recoding, and deep dyslexia. In M. Coltheart, K.E. Patterson, & J.C. Marshall (Eds.), *Deep dyslexia*. London: Routledge & Kegan Paul, 197–226.

Coltheart, M. (1980d). The semantic error: Types and theories. In M. Coltheart, K.E. Patterson, & J.C. Marshall (Eds.), *Deep dyslexia*. London: Routledge & Kegan Paul, 146–159.

Coltheart, M. (1983). The right hemisphere and disorders of reading. In A. Young (Ed.), *Functions of the right cerebral hemisphere*. New York: Academic Press.

Coltheart, M. (1985). Cognitive neuropsychology and the study of reading. In M.I. Posner & O.S.M. Marin (Eds.), *Attention and performance XI*. Hillsdale, NJ: Lawrence Erlbaum Associates Inc., 3–37.

Coltheart, M. (Ed.) (1987). *Attention and performance XII: The psychology of reading.* Hillsdale, NJ: Lawrence Erlbaum Associates Inc.

Coltheart, M., & Byng, S. (1989). A treatment for surface dyslexia. In X. Seron & G. Deloche (Eds.), *Cognitive approaches in neuropsychological rehabilitation*. Hillsdale, NJ: Lawrence Erlbaum Associates Inc., 159–174.

Coltheart, M., Curtis, B., Atkins, P., & Haller, M. (1993). Models of reading aloud: Dual-route and parallel-distributed-processing approaches. *Psychological Review, 100*, 589–608.

Coltheart, M., & Funnell, E. (1987). Reading writing: One lexicon or two? In D.A. Allport, D.G. MacKay, W. Printz, & E. Scheerer (Eds.), *Language perception and production: Shared mechanisms in listening, speaking, reading, and writing*. New York: Academic Press.

Coltheart, M., Patterson, K.E., & Marshall, J.C. (1980). *Deep dyslexia*. London: Routledge & Kegan Paul

Coltheart, M., Patterson, K.E., & Marshall, J.C. (1987). Deep dyslexia since 1980. In M. Coltheart, K.E. Patterson, & J.C. Marshall (Eds.), *Deep dyslexia*. London: Routledge & Kegan Paul, 407–451.

Coltheart, M., Sartori, G., & Job, R. (Eds.) (1987). *The cognitive neuropsychology of language*. Hillsdale, NJ: Lawrence Erlbaum Associates Inc.

Coslett, H.B., & Saffran, E.M. (1989). Evidence for preserved reading in "pure alexia." *Brain, 112*, 327–359.

Costello, A.D., & Warrington, E.K. (1987). The dissociation of visual neglect and neglect dyslexia. *Journal of Neurology, Neurosurgery and Psychiatry, 50*, 1110–1116.

Cotman, C.W., & Monaghan, D.T. (1988). Excitatory amino acid neurotransmission: NMDA receptors and Hebb-type synaptic plasticity. *Annual Review of Neuroscience, 11*, 61–80.

Crick, F. (1989). The recent excitement about neural networks. *Nature, 337*, 129–132.

Deese, J. (1965). *The structure of associations in language and thought*. Baltimore: Johns Hopkins Press.

De Haan, E.H.F., Young, A., & Newcombe, F. (1987). Face recognition without awareness. *Cognitive Neuropsychology, 4*, 385–415.

Dehaene, S., & Changeux, J.-P. (1989). A simple model of prefrontal cortex function in delayed-response tasks. *Journal of Cognitive Neuroscience, 1*(3), 244–261.

Dehaene, S., & Changeux, P. (1991). The Wisconsin Card Sorting test: Theoretical analyses and modelling in a neuronal network. *Cerebral Cortex, 1*, 62–79.

Déjerine, J. (1892). Contribution à l'étude anatomoclinique et clinique des differentes variétés de cécité verbale. *Mémoires del la Société de Biologie, 4*, 61–90.

Dell, G.S. (1986). A spreading-activation theory of retrieval in sentence production. *Psychological Review, 93*(3), 283–321.

Dell, G.S. (1988). The retrieval of phonological forms in production: Tests of predictions from a connectionist model. *Journal of Memory and Language, 27*, 124–142.

Denker, J., Schwartz, D. Wittner, B., Sola, S., Howard, R., Jackel, L., & Hopfield, J. (1987). Large automatic learning, rule extraction, and generalisation. *Complex Systems, 1*, 877–922.

Derouesné, J., & Beauvois, M.-F. (1985). The "phonemic" state in the non-lexical reading process: Evidence from a case of phonological alexia. In K.E. Patterson, M. Coltheart, & J.C. Marshall (Eds.), *Surface dyslexia*. Hillsdale, NJ: Lawrence Erlbaum Associates Inc., 399–457.

Derthick, M. (1990). Mundane reasoning by settling on a plausible model. *Artificial Intelligence, 46*, 107–157.

Dudai, Y. (1989). *The neurobiology of memory: Concepts, findings and trends*. Oxford: Oxford University Press.

Ellis, A.W., Flude, B., & Young, A.W. (1987). Neglect dyslexia and the early visual processing of letters in words and nonwords. *Cognitive Neuropsychology, 4*, 439–464.

Ellis, A.W., & Marshall, J.C. (1978). Semantic errors or statistical flukes? A note on Allport's "On knowing the meaning of words we are unable to report." *Quarterly Journal of Experimental Psychology, 30*, 569–575.

Ellis, A.W., & Young, A.W. (1988). *Human cognitive neuropsychology*. Hillsdale, NJ: Lawrence Erlbaum Associates Inc.

Elman, J.L. (1990). Finding structure in time. *Cognitive Science, 14*(2), 179–211.

Elman, J.L. (1993). Learning and development in neural networks: The importance of starting small. *Cognition, 48*, 71–79.

Farah, M.J. (1990). *Visual agnosia: Disorders of object recognition and what they tell us about normal vision*. Cambridge, Mass.: MIT Press.

Farah, M.J. (1994). Neuropsychological inference with an interactive brain: A critique of the locality assumption. *Behavioral and Brain Sciences, 17*, 43–104.

Farah, M.J., & McClelland, J.L. (1991). A computational model of semantic memory impairment: Modality-specificity and emergent category-specificity. *Journal of Experimental Psychology: General, 120*(4), 339–357.

Farah, M.J., O'Reilly, R.C., & Vecera, S.P. (1993). Dissociated overt and covert recognition as an emergent property of lesioned attractor networks. *Psychological Review, 100*, 571–588.

Faust, C. (1955). *Die zerebralen herdstörungen bei hinterhauptsverletzungen und hir beurteilung*. Stuttgart: Thieme.

Feldman, J.A., & Ballard, D.H. (1982). Connectionist models and their properties. *Cognitive Science, 6*, 205–254.

Feldman, J.A., Fanty, M.A., & Goddard, N.H. (1988). Computing with structured neural networks. *IEEE Computer, 21*(3), 91–103.

Fera, P., & Besner, D. (1992). The process of lexical decision: More words about a parallel distributed processing model. *Journal of Experimental Psychology: Learning, Memory and Cognition, 18*(4), 749–764.

Fodor, J.A. (1983). *The modularity of mind*. Cambridge, Mass.: MIT Press.

Friedland, R.P., & Weinstein, E.A. (1977). Hemi-inattention and hemisphere specialisation: Introduction and historical review. In E.A. Weinstein & R.P. Friedland (Eds.), *Advances in neurology 18: Hemi-inattention and hemisphere specialisation*. New York: Raven Press.

Friedman, R.B., & Perlman, M.B. (1982). On the underlying causes of semantic paralexias in a patient with deep dyslexia. *Neuropsychologia, 20*, 559–568.

Funnell, E. (1983). Phonological processing in reading: New evidence from acquired dyslexia. *British Journal of Psychology, 74*, 159–180.

Funnell, E. (1987). Morphological errors in acquired dyslexia: A case of mistaken identity. *Quarterly Journal of Experimental Psychology, 39A*, 497–539.

Funnell, E., & Allport, A. (1987). Non-linguistic cognition and word meanings: Neuropsychological exploration of common mechanisms. In A. Allport, D. MacKay, E. Scheerer, & W. Prinz (Eds.), *Language perception and production*. London: Academic Press, 367–400.

Gentner, D. (1981). Some interesting differences between verbs and nouns. *Cognition and Brain Theory, 4*(2), 161–178.

Glosser, G., & Friedman, R.B. (1990). The continuum of deep/phonological alexia. *Cortex, 26*, 343–359.

Glushko, R.J. (1979). The organisation and activation of orthographic knowledge in reading aloud. *Journal of Experimental Psychology: Human Perception and Performance, 5*(4), 674–691.

Goldblum, M.C. (1985). Word comprehension in surface dyslexia. In K.E. Patterson, M. Coltheart, & J.C. Marshall (Eds.), *Surface dyslexia*. Hillsdale, NJ: Lawrence Erlbaum Associates Inc., 175–205.

Graham, K.S., Hodges, J.R., & Patterson, K.E. (1994). The relation between comprehension and oral reading in progressive fluent aphasia. *Neuropsychologia, 32*, 299–316.

Gregory, R.L. (1961). The brain as an engineering problem. In W.H. Thorpe & O.L. Zangwill (Eds.), *Current problems in animal behaviour*. Cambridge: Cambridge University Press.

Grossberg, S. (1987). From interactive activation to adaptive resonance. *Cognitive Science, 11*, 23–63.

Hertz, J., Krogh, A., & Palmer, R.G. (1991). *Introduction to the theory of neural computation*. Reading, Mass.: Addison-Wesley.

Hillis, A.E., Rapp, B., Romani, C., & Caramazza, A. (1990). Selective impairments of semantics in lexical processing. *Cognitive Neuropsychology, 7*, 191–243.

Hinton, G.E. (1981). Implementing semantic networks in parallel hardware. In G.E. Hinton & J.A. Anderson (Eds.), *Parallel models of associative memory*. Hillsdale, NJ: Lawrence Erlbaum Associates Inc., 161–188.

Hinton, G.E. (1989a). Connectionist learning procedures. *Artificial Intelligence, 40*, 185–234.

Hinton, G.E. (1989b). Deterministic Boltzmann learning performs steepest descent in weight-space. *Neural Computation, 1*(1), 143–150.

Hinton, G.E., & Anderson, J.A. (Eds.) (1981). *Parallel models of associative memory*. Hillsdale, NJ: Lawrence Erlbaum Associates Inc.

Hinton, G.E., McClelland, J.L., & Rumelhart, D.E. (1986). Distributed representations. In D.E. Rumelhart, J.L. McClelland, & the PDP Research Group (Eds.), *Parallel distributed processing: Explorations in the microstructure of cognition. Vol. 1: Foundations*. Cambridge, Mass.: MIT Press, 77–109.

Hinton, G.E., & Plaut, D.C. (1987). Using fast weights to deblur old memories. In *Proceedings of the 9th Annual Conference of the Cognitive Science Society*. Hillsdale, NJ: Lawrence Erlbaum Associates Inc., 177–186.

Hinton, G.E., & Sejnowski, T.J. (1983). Analysing co-operative computation. In *Proceedings of the 5th Annual Conference of the Cognitive Science Society*. Hillsdale, NJ: Lawrence Erlbaum Associates Inc.

Hinton, G.E., & Sejnowski, T.J. (1986). Learning and relearning in Boltzmann Machines. In D.E. Rumelhart, J.L. McClelland, & the PDP Research Group (Eds.), *Parallel distributed processing: Explorations in the microstructure of cognition. Vol. 1: Foundations*. Cambridge, Mass.: MIT Press, 282–317.

Hinton, G.E., & Shallice, T. (1991). Lesioning an attractor network: Investigations of acquired dyslexia. *Psychological Review, 98*(1), 74–95.

Hopfield, J.J. (1982). Neural networks and physical systems with emergent collective computational abilities. *Proceedings of the National Academy of Science, USA, 79*, 2554–2558.

Hopfield, J.J. (1984). Neurons with graded responses have collective computational properties like those of two-state neurons. *Proceedings of the National Academy of Science, USA, 81*, 3088–3092.

Hopfield, J.J., & Tank, D.W. (1985). Neural computation of decisions in optimisation problems. *Biological Cybernetics, 52*, 141–152.

Howard, D., & Franklin, S. (1988). *Missing the meaning?* Cambridge, Mass.: MIT Press.

Howard, D., Patterson, K.E., Wise, R., Brown, W.P., Friston, K., Weiller, C., & Frakowaik, R.S.J. (1992). The cortical localisation of the lexicons: Positron Emission Tomography evidence. *Brain, 115*, 1769–1782.

Humphreys, G.W., Freeman, T., & Müller, H.J. (1992). Lesioning a connectionist model of visual search: Selective effects on distractor grouping. *Canadian Journal of Psychology, 46*, 417–460.

Humphreys, G.W., & Riddoch, M.J. (1987). *To see but not to see: A case-study of visual agnosia*. Hillsdale, NJ: Lawrence Erlbaum Associates Inc.

Jared, D., McRae, K., & Seidenberg, M.S. (1990). The basis of consitency effects in word naming. *Journal of Memory and Language, 29*, 687–715.

Jones, G.V. (1985). Deep dyslexia, imageability, and ease of predication. *Brain and Language, 24*, 1–19.

Jones, G.V., & Martin, M. (1985). Deep dyslexia and the right-hemisphere hypothesis for semantic paralexia: A reply to Marshall and Patterson. *Neuropsychologia, 23*, 658–688.

Jordan, M.I. (1985). Attractor dynamics and parallelism in a connectionist sequential machine. In *Proceedings of the 8th Annual Conference of the Cognitive Science Society*. Hillsdale, NJ: Lawrence Erlbaum Associates Inc., 531–546.

Kapur, N., & Perl, N.T. (1978). Recognition reading in paralexia. *Cortex, 14*, 439–443.

Karmiloff-Smith, A. (1992). *Beyond modularity: A developmental perspective on cognitive science*. Cambridge, Mass.: MIT Press.

Karnath, O.H. (1988). Deficits of attention in acute and recovered hemi-neglect. *Neuropsychologia, 26*(1), 27–43.

Katz, J.J., & Fodor, J.A. (1963). The structure of a semantic theory. *Language, 39*, 170–210.

Katz, R.B., & Goodglass, H. (1990). Deep dysphasia: Analysis of a rare form of repetition disorder. *Brain and Language, 39*, 153–185.

Kinsbourne, M., & Warrington, E.K. (1962). A variety of reading disability associated with right-hemisphere lesions. *Journal of Neurology, Neurosurgery, and Psychiatry, 25*, 339–344.

Kirkpatrick, S., Gelatt, C.D., & Vecchi, M.P. (1983). Optimisation by simulated annealing. *Science, 220*, 671–680.

Kolen, J.F., & Pollack, J.B. (1991). Back propagation is sensitive to initial conditions. In R.P. Lippmann, J.E. Moody, & D.S. Touretzky (Eds.), *Advances in neural information processing systems 3*. San Mateo: Morgan Kaufmann, 860–867.

Kosslyn, S.M. (1987). Seeing and imagining in the cerebral hemispheres: A computational approach. *Psychological Review, 94*(2), 148–175.

Kosslyn, S.M., Flynn, R.A., Amsterdam, J.B., & Wang, G. (1990). Components of high-level vision: A cognitive neuroscience analysis and accounts of neurological syndromes. *Cognition, 34*(3), 203–277.

Kremin, H. (1982). Alexia: Theory and research. In R.N. Malatesha & P.G. Aaron (Eds.), *Reading disorders: Varieties and treatments*. New York: Academic Press.

Kuçera, H., & Francis, W.N. (1967). *Computational analysis of present-day American English*. Providence, RI: Brown University Press.

Lachter, J., & Bever, T. (1988). The relation between linguistic structure and theories of language learning: A constructive critique of some connectionist learning models. *Cognition, 28*, 195–247.

le Cun, Y. (1985). Une procedure d'apprentissage pour reséau à seuil asymmétrique (a learning scheme for asymmetric threshold network). In *Cognitiva 85: A la frontière de l'intelligence artificielle des sciences de la connaissance des neurosciences (Paris 1985)*. Paris: CESTA, 599–604.

Levelt, W.J.M. (1989). *Speaking: From intention to articulation*. Cambridge, Mass.: MIT Press.

Levelt, W.J.M., Schriefers, H., Vorberg, D., Meyer, A.S., Pechmann, T., & Havinga, J. (1991). The time course of lexical access in speech production: A study of picture naming. *Psychological Review, 98*(1), 122–142.

Levine, D.S. (1986). A neural network theory of frontal lobe function. In *Proceedings of the 8th Annual Conference of the Cognitive Science Society*. Hillsdale, NJ: Lawrence Erlbaum Associates Inc., 716–727.

Levine, D.S., & Prueitt, P.S. (1989). Modelling some effects of frontal lobe damage—Novelty and perseveration. *Neural Networks, 2*, 103–116.

Lhermitte, F., & Beauvois, M.-F. (1973). A visual-speech disconnexion syndrome: Report of a case with optic aphasia, agnosic alexia and colour agnosia. *Brain, 96*, 695–714.

Marin, O.S.M., Saffran, E.M., & Schwartz, D.F. (1976). Dissociations of language in aphasia: Implications for normal functions. *Annals of the New York Academy of Sciences, 280*, 868–884.

Marr, D. (1976). Early processing of visual information. *Proceedings of the Royal Society of London, Series B, 275*, 483–524.

Marr, D. (1982). *Vision*. San Francisco: W.H. Freeman.

Marshall, J.C., & Newcombe, F. (1966). Syntactic and semantic errors in paralexia. *Neuropsychologia, 4*, 169–176.

Marshall, J.C., & Newcombe, F. (1973). Patterns of paralexia: A psycholinguistic approach. *Journal of Psycholinguistic Research, 2*, 175–199.

Marshall, J.C., & Newcombe, F. (1980). The conceptual status of deep dyslexia: An historical perspective. In M. Coltheart, K.E. Patterson, & J.C. Marshall (Eds.), *Deep dyslexia*. London: Routledge & Kegan Paul, 1–21.

Marshall, J.C., & Patterson, K.E. (1983). Semantic paralexias and the wrong hemisphere: A note on Landis, Regard, Graves, and Goodglass (1983). *Neuropsychologia, 21*, 425–427.

Marshall, J.C., & Patterson, K.E. (1985). Left is still left for semantic paralexias: A reply to Jones and Martin. *Neuropsychologia, 23*, 689–690.

Martin, N., Dell, G.S., Saffran, E.M., & Schwartz, M.F. (in press). Origins of paraphasias in deep dyslexia: Testing the consequences of a decay impairment to an interactive spreading activation model of lexical retrieval. *Brain and Language*.

Martin, N., & Saffran, E.M. (1990). Repetition and verbal STM in transcortical sensory aphasia: A case study. *Brain and Language, 39*, 254–288.

McCann, R.S., & Besner, D. (1987). Reading pseudohomophones: Implications for models of pronunciation and the locus of the word-frequency effects in word naming. *Journal of Experimental Psychology: Human Perception and Performance, 13*, 14–24.

McCarthy, R., & Warrington, E.K. (1986). Phonological reading: Phenomena and paradoxes. *Cortex, 22*, 359–380.

McCarthy, R., & Warrington, E.K. (1990). *Cognitive neuropsychology*. New York: Academic Press.

McClelland, J.L. (1979). On the time relations of mental processes: An examination of systems of processes in cascade. *Psychological Review, 86*, 287–330.

McClelland, J.L. (1988). Connectionist models and psychological evidence. *Journal of Memory and Language, 27*, 107–123.

McClelland, J.L., & Jenkins, E. (1990). Nature, nurture, and connections: Implications of connectionist models for cognitive development. In K. Van Lehn (Ed.), *Architectures for intelligence*. Hillsdale, NJ: Lawrence Erlbaum Associates Inc., 41–73.

McClelland, J.L., & Rumelhart, D.E. (1986). Amnesia and distributed memory. In J.L. McClelland, D.E. Rumelhart, & the PDP research group (Eds.), *Parallel distributed processing: Explorations in the microstructure of cognition. Vol. 2: Psychological and biological models*. Cambridge, Mass.: MIT Press, 503–528.

McClelland, J.L., & Rumelhart, D.E. (1981). An interactive activation model of context effects in letter perception: Part 1. An account of basic findings. Psychological Review, 88(5), 375–407.

McClelland, J.L., Rumelhart, D.E., & the PDP Research Group (1986). *Parallel distributed processing: Explorations in the microstructure of cognition. Vol. 2: Psychological and biological models*. Cambridge, Mass.: MIT Press.

McCloskey, M. (1991). Networks and theories: The place of connectionism in cognitive science. *Psychological Science, 2*(6), 387–395.

McCloskey, M., Badecker, W., Goodman-Shulman, R.A., & Aliminosa, D. (1994). The structure of graphemic representations in spelling: Evidence from a case of acquired dysgraphia. *Cognitive Neuropsychology, 11*, 341–392.

McCloskey, M., & Caramazza, A. (1991). On crude data and impoverished theory. (Commentary on T. Shallice, Précis of From neuropsychology to mental structure.) *Behavioral and Brain Sciences, 14*, 453–454.

Miceli, G., & Caramazza, A. (1990). The structure of orthographic representations in spelling. *Cognition, 37*, 243–297.

Michel, F., & Andreewsky, E. (1983). Deep dysphasia: An analogue of deep dyslexia in the auditory modality. *Brain and Language, 18*, 212–223.

Miller, D., & Ellis, A.W. (1987). Speech and writing errors in neologistic jargon aphasia: A lexical activation hypothesis. In M. Coltheart, G. Sartori, & R. Job (Eds.), *The cognitive neuropsychology of language*. Hillsdale, NJ: Lawrence Erlbaum Associates Inc., 253–271.

Milner, B. (1963). Effects of different brain lesions on card-sorting. *Annual Review of Neuroscience, 9*, 90–100.

Milner, B. (1966). Amnesia following operation on the temporal lobes. In C.M.W. Whitty & O.L. Zangwill (Eds.), *Amnesia*. London: Butterworth.

Minsky, M. (1975). A framework for representing knowledge. In P.H. Winston (Ed.), *The psychology of computer vision*. New York: McGraw-Hill, 211–277.

Minsky, M., & Papert, S. (1969). *Perceptrons: An introduction to computational geometry*. Cambridge, Mass.: MIT Press.

Morton, J. (1969). The interaction of information in word recognition. *Psychological Review, 76*, 165–178.

Morton, J. (1980). Two auditory parallels to deep dyslexia. In M. Coltheart, K.E. Patterson, & J.C. Marshall (Eds.), *Deep dyslexia*. London: Routledge & Kegan Paul, 189–196.

Morton, J., & Patterson, K. (1980). A new attempt at an interpretation, or, an attempt at a new interpretation. In M. Coltheart, K.E. Patterson, & J.C. Marshall (Eds.), *Deep dyslexia*. London: Routledge & Kegan Paul, 91–118.

Mozer, M.C. (1983). Letter migration in word perception. *Journal of Experimental Psychology: Human Perception and Performance, 9*, 531–546.

Mozer, M.C. (1990). *The perception of multiple objects: A connectionist approach*. Cambridge, Mass.: MIT Press.

Mozer, M.C., & Behrmann, M. (1990). On the interaction of selective attention and lexical knowledge: A connectionist account of neglect dyslexia. *Journal of Cognitive Neuroscience, 2*(2), 96–123.

Mozer, M.C., & Behrmann, M. (1993). Reading with attentional impairments: A brain-damaged model of neglect and attentional dyslexia. In N. Sharkey & R. Reilly (Eds.), *Connectionist approaches to natural language processing*. Hillsdale, NJ: Lawrence Erlbaum Associates Inc.

Newcombe, F., & Marshall, J.C. (1980a). Response monitoring and response blocking in deep dyslexia. In M. Coltheart, K.E. Patterson, & J.C. Marshall (Eds.), *Deep dyslexia*. London: Routledge & Kegan Paul, 160–175.

Newcombe, F., & Marshall, J.C. (1980b). Transcoding and lexical stabilisation in deep dyslexia. In M. Coltheart, K.E. Patterson, & J.C. Marshall (Eds.), *Deep dyslexia*. London: Routledge & Kegan Paul, 176–188.

Newcombe, F., & Marshall, J.C. (1984). Task- and modality-specific aphasias. In F.C. Rose (Ed.), *Advances in neurology, Vol. 42: Progress in aphasiology*. New York: Raven Press.

Nolan, K.A., & Caramazza, A. (1982). Modality-independent impairments in word processing in a deep dyslexic patient. *Brain and Language, 16*, 237–264.

Nowlan, S.J. (1988). Gain variation in recurrent error propagation networks. *Complex Systems, 2*, 305–320.

Patterson, K., & Hodges, J.R. (1992). Deterioration of word meaning: Implications for reading. *Neuropsychologia, 30*(12), 1025–1040.

Patterson, K.E. (1978). Phonemic dyslexia: Errors of meaning and the meaning of errors. *Quarterly Journal of Experimental Psychology, 30*, 587–608.

Patterson, K.E. (1979). What is right with "deep" dyslexics? *Brain and Language, 8*, 111–129.

Patterson, K.E. (1980). Derivational errors. In M. Coltheart, K.E. Patterson, & J.C. Marshall (Eds.), *Deep dyslexia*. London: Routledge & Kegan Paul, 286–306.

Patterson, K.E. (1982). The relation between reading and psychological coding: Further neuropsychological observations. In A.W. Ellis (Ed.), *Normality and pathology in cognitive functions*. New York: Academic Press.

Patterson, K.E. (1990). Alexia and neural nets. *Japanese Journal of Neuropsychology, 6*, 90–99.

Patterson, K.E., & Besner, D. (1984a). Is the right hemisphere literate? *Cognitive Neuropsychology, 3*, 341–367.

Patterson, K.E., & Besner, D. (1984b). Reading from the left: A reply to Rabinowicz and Moscovitch and to Zaidel and Schweiger. *Cognitive Neuropsychology, 1*, 365–380.

Patterson, K.E., Coltheart, M., & Marshall, J.C. (Eds.) (1985). *Surface dyslexia*. Hillsdale, NJ: Lawrence Erlbaum Associates Inc.

Patterson, K.E., & Marcel, A.J. (1977). Aphasia, dyslexia, and the phonological coding of written words. *Quarterly Journal of Experimental Psychology, 29*, 307–318.

Patterson, K.E., & Marcel, A.J. (1992). Phonological ALEXIA or PHONOLOGICAL alexia? In J. Alegria, D. Holender, J. Junca de Morais, & M. Radeau (Eds.), *Analytic approaches to human cognition*. New York: Elsevier, 259–274.

Patterson, K.E., Seidenberg, M.S., & McClelland, J.L. (1990). Connections and disconnections: Acquired dyslexia in a computational model of reading processes. In R.G.M. Morris (Ed.), *Parallel distributed processing: Implications for psychology and neuroscience*. London: Oxford University Press.

Patterson, K.E., Vargha-Khadem, F., & Polkey, C.E. (1989). Reading with one hemisphere. *Brain, 112*, 39–63.

Pearlmutter, B.A. (1989). Learning state space trajectories in recurrent neural networks. *Neural Computation, 1*(2), 263–269.

Peterson, C., & Anderson, J.R. (1987). A mean field theory learning algorithm for neural nets. *Complex Systems, 1*, 995–1019.

Petersen, S.E., Fox, P.T., Posner, M.I., Mintun, M., & Raichle, M.E. (1988). Positron emission tomographic studies of the cortical anatomy of single-word processing. *Nature, 331*, 585–589.

Pinker, S., & Prince, A. (1988). On language and connectionism: Analysis of a parallel distributed processing model of language acquisition. *Cognition, 28*, 73–193.

Plaut, D.C. (1992). Relearning after damage in connectionist networks: Implications for patient rehabilitation. In *Proceedings of the 14th Annual Conference of the Cognitive Science Society*. Hillsdale, NJ: Lawrence Erlbaum Associates Inc., 372–377.

Plaut, D.C. (in press). Relearning after damage in connectionist networks: Toward a theory of rehabilitation. *Brain and Language*.

Plaut, D.C., Behrmann, M., Patterson, K.E., & McClelland, J.L. (1993). Impaired oral reading in surface dyslexia: Detailed comparison of a patient and a connectionist network. (Abstract.) In *Proceedings of the 34th Annual Meeting of the Psychonomic Society*. Washington, DC.

Plaut, D.C., & Hinton, G.E. (1987). Learning sets of filters using back propagation. *Computer Speech and Language, 2*, 35–61.

Plaut, D.C., & McClelland, J.L. (1993). Generalisation with componential attractors: Word and nonword reading in an attractor network. In *Proceedings of the 15th Annual Conference of the Cognitive Science Society*. Hillsdale, NJ: Lawrence Erlbaum Associates Inc., 824–829.

Plaut, D.C., & Shallice, T. (1991). Effects of abstractness in a connectionist model of deep dyslexia. In *Proceedings of the 13th Annual Conference of the Cognitive Science Society*. Hillsdale, NJ: Lawrence Erlbaum Associates Inc., 73–78.

Plaut, D.C., & Shallice, T. (1993). Perseverative and semantic influences on visual object naming errors in optic aphasia: A connectionist account. *Journal of Cognitive Neuroscience, 5*(1), 89–117.

Plunkett, K., & Sinha, C. (1991). Connectionism and developmental theory. *Psykologisk Skriftserie Aarhus, 16*(1).

Posner, M.I., Walker, J.A., Friedrich, F.J., & Rafal, R.D. (1984). Effects of parietal injury on covert orienting of visual attention. *Journal of Neuroscience, 4*, 1863–1864.

Quinlan, P. (1991). *Connectionism and psychology: A psychological perspective on new connectionist research*. Chicago: University of Chicago Press.

Rabinowicz, B., & Moscovitch, M. (1984). Right-hemisphere literacy: A critique of some recent approaches. *Cognitive Neuropsychology, 1*, 343–350.

Riddoch, M.J. (1991). *Cognitive neuropsychology: Neglect and the peripheral dyslexias*. Hillsdale, NJ: Lawrence Erlbaum Associates Inc.

Riddoch, M.J., & Humphreys, G.W. (1983). The effect of cueing on unilateral neglect. *Neuropsychologia, 21*, 589–599.

Riddoch, M.J., & Humphreys, G.W. (1987). Visual object processing in optic aphasia: A case of semantic access agnosia. *Cognitive Neuropsychology, 4*(2), 131–185.

Riddoch, M.J., Humphreys, G.W., Cleton, P., & Fery, P. (1990). Levels of coding in neglect dyslexia. *Cognitive Neuropsychology, 7*, 479–518.

Roberts, S., & Sternberg, S. (1992). The meaning of additive reaction-time effects: Tests of three alternatives. In D.E. Meyer & S. Kornblum (Eds.), *Attention and performance XIV*. Cambridge, Mass.: MIT Press, 611–653.

Roeltgen, D.P. (1987). Loss of deep dyslexic reading ability from a second left hemisphere lesion. *Archives of Neurology, 44*, 346–348.

Rosch, E., Mervis, C., Gray, W., Johnson, D., & Boyes-Braem, P. (1976). Basic objects in natural categories. *Cognitive Psychology, 8*, 382–439.

Rumelhart, D.E., Hinton, G.E., & Williams, R.J. (1986a). Learning internal representations by error propagation. In D.E. Rumelhart, J.L. McClelland, & the PDP Research Group (Eds.), *Parallel distributed processing: Explorations in the microstructure of cognition. Vol. 1: Foundations*. Cambridge, Mass.: MIT Press.

Rumelhart, D.E., Hinton, G.E., & Williams, R.J. (1986b). Learning representations by back-propagation errors. *Nature, 323*(9), 533–536.

Rumelhart, D.E., & McClelland, J.L. (1986). On learning the past tenses of English verbs. In J.L. McClelland, D.E. Rumelhart, & the PDP research group (Eds.), *Parallel distributed processing: Explorations in the microstructure of cognition. Vol. 2: Psychological and biological models*. Cambridge, Mass.: MIT Press, 216–271.

Rumelhart, D.E., McClelland, J.L., & the PDP research group (Eds.) (1986b). *Parallel distributed processing: Explorations in the microstructure of cognition. Vol. 1: Foundations*. Cambridge, Mass.: MIT Press.

Saffran, E.M., Bogyo, L.C., Schwartz, M.F., & Marin, O.S.M. (1980). Does deep dyslexia reflect right-hemisphere reading? In M. Coltheart, K.E. Patterson, & J.C. Marshall (Eds.), *Deep dyslexia*. London: Routledge & Kegan Paul, 381–406.

Saffran, E.M., & Marin, O.S.M. (1977). Reading without phonology. *Quarterly Journal of Experimental Psychology, 29*, 515–525.

Saffran, E.M., & Schwartz, M.F., & Marin, O.S.M. (1976). Semantic mechanisms in paralexia. *Brain and Language, 3*, 255–265.

Sartori, G., Masterson, J., & Job, R. (1987). Direct-route reading and the locus of lexical decision. In M. Coltheart, G. Sartori, & R. Job (Eds.), *The cognitive neuropsychology of language*. Hillsdale, NJ: Lawrence Erlbaum Associates Inc., 59–77.

Schwartz, M.F. (1984). What the classical aphasia categories don't do for us and why. *Brain and Language, 21*, 3–8.

Schwartz, M.F., Marin, O.S.M., & Saffran, E.M. (1979). Dissociations of language function in dementia: A case study. *Brain and Language, 7*, 277–306.

Schwartz, M.F., Saffran, E.M., & Marin, O.S.M. (1980). Fractioning the reading process in dementia: Evidence for word-specific print-to-sound associations. In M. Coltheart, K.E. Patterson, & J.C. Marshall (Eds.), *Deep dyslexia*. London: Routledge & Kegan Paul, 259–269.

Seidenberg, M.S. (1985). The time course of phonological code activation in two writing systems. *Cognition, 19*, 1–10.

Seidenberg, M. (1988). Cognitive neuropsychology and language: The state of the art. *Cognitive Neuropsychology, 5*(4), 403–426.

Seidenberg, M.S. (1993). Connectionist models and cognitive theory. *Psychological Science, 4*(4), 228–235.

Seidenberg, M., & McClelland, J.L. (1989). A distributed, developmental model of word recognition and naming. *Psychological Review, 96*, 523–568.

Seidenberg, M.S., & McClelland, J.L. (1990). More words but still no lexicon: Reply to Besner et al. (1990). *Psychological Review, 97*(3), 477–452.

Seidenberg, M.S., Waters, G.S., Barnes, M.A., & Tanenhaus, M.K. (1984). When does irregular spelling or pronunciation influence word recognition? *Journal of Verbal Learning and Verbal Behaviour, 23*, 383–404.

Sejnowski, T.J., Koch, C., & Churchland, P.S. (1989). Computational neuroscience. *Science, 241*, 1299–1306.

Sejnowski, T.J., & Rosenberg, C.R. (1987). Parallel networks that learn to pronounce English text. *Complex Systems, 1*, 145–168.

Shallice, T. (1987). Impairments of semantic processing: Multiple dissociations. In M. Coltheart, G. Sartori, & R. Job (Eds.), *The cognitive neuropsychology of language*, Hillsdale, NJ: Lawrence Erlbaum Associates Inc., 111–128.

Shallice, T. (1988a). *From neuropsychology to mental structure*. Cambridge: Cambridge University Press.

Shallice, T. (1988b). Specialisation within the semantic system. *Cognitive Neuropsychology, 5*, 133–142.

Shallice, T. (1991). Précis of From neuropsychology to mental structure. *Behavioural and Brain Sciences, 14*, 429–469.

Shallice, T., & Coughlan, A.K. (1980). Modality-specific word comprehension deficits in deep dyslexia. *Journal of Neurology, Neurosurgery, and Psychiatry, 43*, 866–872.

Shallice, T., & McCarthy, R. (1985). Phonological reading: From patterns of impairment to possible procedures. In K.E. Patterson, M. Coltheart, & J.C. Marshall (Eds.), *Surface dyslexia*. Hillsdale, NJ: Lawrence Erlbaum Associates Inc., 361–398.

Shallice, T., & McGill, J. (1978). The origins of mixed errors. In J. Requin (Ed.), *Attention and performance VII*. Hillsdale, NJ: Lawrence Erlbaum Associates Inc., 193–208.

Shallice, T., & Plaut, D.C. (1992). From connectionism to neuropsychological syndromes. In J. Alegria, D. Holender, J. Junca de Morais, & M. Radeau (Eds.), *Analytic approaches to human cognition*. New York: Elsevier, 239–258.

Shallice, T., & Warrington, E.K. (1975). Word recognition in a phonemic dyslexic patient. *Quarterly Journal of Experimental Psychology, 27*, 187–199.

Shallice, T., & Warrington, E.K. (1977). The possible role of selective attention in acquired dyslexia. *Neuropsychologia, 15*, 31–41.

Shallice, T., & Warrington, E.K. (1980). Single and multiple component central dyslexic syndromes. In M. Coltheart, K.E. Patterson, & J.C. Marshall (Eds.), *Deep dyslexia*. London: Routledge & Kegan Paul, 119–145.

Shallice, T., Warrington, E.K., & McCarthy, R. (1983). Reading without semantics. *Quarterly Journal of Experimental Psychology, 35A*, 111–138.

Sieroff, E. Pollatsek, A., & Posner, M.I. (1988). Recognition of visual letter strings following injury to the posterior visual spatial attention system. *Cognitive neuropsychology, 5*(4), 427–449.

Simon, H.A. (1969). *The sciences of the artificial*. Cambridge, Mass.: MIT Press.

Skarda, C.A., & Freeman, W.J. (1987). How brains make chaos in order to make sense of the world. *Behavioral and Brain Sciences, 10*, 161–195.

Small, S.L. (1991). Focal and diffuse lesions of cognitive models. In *Proceedings of the 13th Annual Conference of the Cognitive Science Society*. Hillsdale, NJ: Lawrence Erlbaum Associates Inc., 85–90.

Smith, E.E., & Medin, D.L. (1981). *Categories and concepts*. Cambridge, Mass.: Harvard University Press.

Smith, E.E., Shoben, E.J., & Rips, L.J. (1974). Structure and process in semantic memory: A featural model for semantic decision. *Psychological Review, 81*, 214–241.

Squire, L. (1987). *Memory and brain*. Oxford: Oxford University Press.

Stemberger, J.P. (1985). An interactive activation model of language production. In A.W. Ellis (Ed.), *Progress in the psychology of language, Vol. 1*. Hillsdale, NJ: Lawrence Erlbaum Associates Inc.

Sternberg, S. (1969). The discovery of processing stages: Extensions of Donders' method. *Acta Psychologia, 30*, 276–315.

Taraban, R., & McClelland, J.L. (1987). Conspiracy effects in word recognition. *Journal of Memory and Language, 26*, 608–631.

Van Essen, D.C. (1985). Functional organisation of primate visual cortex. In A. Peters & E.B. Jones (Eds.), *Cerebral cortex, Vol. 3*. New York: Plenum Press, 259–329.

Van Orden, G.C., Pennington, B.F., & Stone, G.O. (1990). Word identification in reading and the promise of subsymbolic psycholinguistics. *Psychological Review, 97*(4), 488–522.

Warrington, E.K. (1981). Concrete word dyslexia. *British Journal of Psychology, 72*, 175–196.

Warrington, E.K., & McCarthy, R.A. (1988). The fractionation of retrograde amnesia. *Brain and Cognition, 7*, 184–200.

Warrington, E.K., & Shallice, T. (1979). Semantic access dyslexia. *Brain, 102*, 43–63.

Warrington, E.K., & Shallice, T. (1984). Category-specific semantic impairments. *Brain, 107*, 829–853.

Waters, G.S., & Seidenberg, M.S. (1985). Spelling-sound effects in reading: Time course and decision criteria. *Memory and Cognition, 13*, 557–572.

Wickelgren, W.A. (1969). Context-sensitive coding, associative memory, and serial order in (speech) behaviour. *Psychological Review, 76*, 1–15.

Williams, R.J., & Peng, J. (1990). An efficient gradient-based algorithm for on-line training of recurrent network trajectories. *Neural Computation, 2*(4), 490–501.

Zaidel, E., & Peters, A.M. (1981). Phonological encoding and ideographic reading by the disconnected right hemisphere: Two case studies. *Brain and Language, 14*, 205–234.

Zaidel, E., & Schweiger, A. (1984). On wrong hypotheses about the right hemisphere: Commentary on K. Patterson & D. Besner, "Is the right hemisphere literate?" *Cognitive Neuropsychology, 1*, 351–364.

REFERENCE NOTES

1. Galland, C.C., & Hinton, G.E. (1989). Deterministic Boltzmann learning in networks with asymmetric connectivity. *Technical Report CRG-TR-89-6*. Toronto: University of Toronto: Department of Computer Science.
2. Galland, C.C., & Hinton, G.E. (1990). Experiments on discovering high-order features with mean field modules. *Technical Report CRG-TR-90-3*. Toronto: University of Toronto, Department of Computer Science.
3. Gordon, B., Goodman-Schulman, R., & Caramazza, A. (1987). Separating the stages of reading errors. *Technical Report 28*. Baltimore, Maryland: Johns Hopkins University, Cognitive Neuropsychology Laboratory.
4. Hinton, G.E., & Shallice, T. (1989). Lesioning a connectionist network: Investigations of acquired dyslexia. *Technical Report CRG-TR-89-3*. Toronto: University of Toronto, Department of Computer Science.
5. Howard, D., & Best, W. (1991, July). *Visual dyslexia?* Paper presented at the Experimental Psychology Society meeting, Brighton, UK.
6. Parker, D.B. (1985). Learning-logic. *Technical Report TR-47*. Cambridge, Mass.: Massachusetts Institute of Technology, Centre for Computational Research in Economics and Management Science.
7. Peterson, C., & Hartman, E. (1988). Explorations of the mean field theory learning algorithm. *Technical Report ACA-ST/HI-065-88*. Austin Texas: Microelectronics & Computer Technology Corporation.
8. Plaut, D.C. (1991). Connectionist neuropsychology: The breakdown and recovery of behaviour in lesioned attractor networks. *Technical Report CMU-CS-91-185*. PhD thesis, School of Computer Science, Carnegie Mellon University, Pittsburgh.
9. Plaut, D.C., & Shallice, T. (1991). Deep dyslexia: A case study of connectionist neuropsychology. *Technical Report CRG-TR-91-3*. Toronto: University of Toronto, Department of Computer Science.
10. Plaut, D.C., McClelland, J.L., Seidenberg, M.S., & Patterson, K.E. (1994). *Understanding normal and impaired word reading: Computational principles in quasi-regular domains*. (Technical Report PDP-CNS-94-5). Pittsburgh, PA: Carnegie Mellon University, Department of Psychology.
11. Werbos, P.J. (1974). *Beyond regression: New tools for prediction and analysis in the behavioral sciences*. PhD thesis, Harvard University, Cambridge, Mass.

APPENDIX: DETERMINISTIC BOLTZMANN MACHINES

Deterministic Boltzmann Machines (Peterson & Anderson, 1987; Hinton, 1989b) were originally derived as mean-field approximations to stochastic Boltzmann Machines (Ackley et al., 1985; Hinton & Sejnowski, 1983). However, in order to simplify the presentation we will describe only the deterministic version. The units in a DBM are closely related to those in a standard back-propagation network. The output, or state $s_i^{(t)}$ of each unit i at time t is a nonlinear function of its summed input.

$$s_i^{(t)} = \lambda s_i^{(t-1)} + (1 - \lambda) \tanh \left(\frac{1}{T} \sum_j s_j^{(t-1)} w_{ij} \right) \tag{1}$$

Unit states change gradually over time, so that the new state is a weighted average (with proportion $\lambda = 0.6$ for our simulations) of the old state and the contribution from the new input. The hyperbolic tangent function "tanh" is the symmetric version of the sigmoid function, ranging from -1 to 1 instead of 0 to 1, and T is a parameter called *temperature* that adjusts the sharpness of the sigmoid (see Fig. 28). Also, each connection is bi-directional and each weight is symmetric, so that $w_{ij} = w_{ji}$.

Energy Minimisation

As in a back-propagation network, input is presented to the DBM by clamping the states of some designated input units. If the other units in the network update their states synchronously and repeatedly according to Equation 1, it can be shown (Hopfield, 1984) that the network will eventually settle into a set of states corresponding to a minimum of the *free energy* function,

$$F = -\sum_{i<j} s_i s_j w_{ij} + T \sum_i (s'_i \log s'_i + (1 - s'_i) \log(1 - s'_i)) \quad (2)$$

where $s'_i = (s_i + 1)/2$. The first term corresponds to the *energy* of the network, and measures the extent to which the states of units satisfy the constraints imposed by the weights. If two units have a positive weight between them and both have positive states (satisfying the constraint), the contribution of the weight to the energy will be positive, thus reducing the total energy. If the units have states of opposite sign (violating the con-

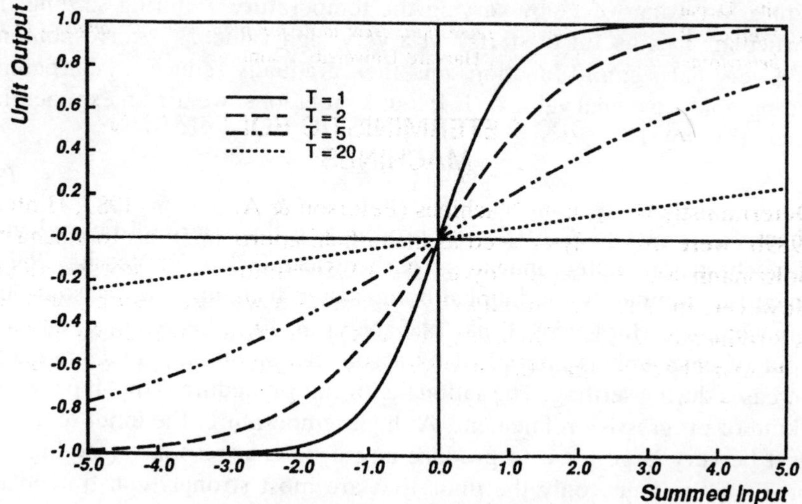

FIG. 28 The input–output function of units in a DBM for four different temperatures.

straint of the weight), their contribution will be negative and will increase the energy. The second term corresponds to the negative of the *entropy* of the network (weighted by temperature), and measures the degree to which unit states are at their extremes. At $T = 1$, the term for a unit has a minimum values of $\log(0.5) = -0.693$ when the unit is least extreme (has a state of 0) and approaches 0 as the unit's state approaches ± 1. Minimising the free energy F amounts to finding nonextreme unit states that satisfy the weight constraints.

It may help to think of a *state space* that is analogous to weight space, but has a dimension for the state of each unit in the network, and an extra dimension for free energy. For a given set of weights, each possible pattern of activity over the units can be represented as a point in state space, whose height along the extra dimension corresponds to its free energy. The entire set of these points forms an *energy surface* in state space, with hills and valleys, analogous to the error surface in weight space (see Fig. 17). The initial unit states define a starting point on this surface. As each unit updates its state according to Equation 1, the pattern of activity of the network as a whole can be thought of as descending along the free energy surface to find a minimum. This minimum is exactly what we have been calling an attractor, and the free energy valley containing it, its basin of attraction.

Simulated Annealing

The network as defined thus far will always settle into *some* minimum of the free energy function F. It is possible to help it find a *good* minimum, with a low value of F, by varying the temperature T during settling. In particular, it is useful to start T at a very high value T_{init}, corresponding to a very flat sigmoid function, and then gradually reduce it, sharpening the sigmoid, to a final value of 1. In our simulations, we use an exponential decay rate for T,

$$T^{(t)} = 1 + T_{init} d^{t} \tag{3}$$

where $T_{init} = 50$ and $d = 0.9$. This procedure is the deterministic analogue of stochastic simulated annealing (Kirkpatrick, Gelatt, & Vecchi, 1983), which is a commonly used global optimisation technique. It is also called *gain variation* (Hopfield & Tank, 1985; Nowlan, 1988) because the summed input of each unit is multiplied by a gain factor of $1/T^{(t)}$ that gradually increases during settling. The rationale for this procedure is that it provides a kind of progressive refinement. At high temperature, the input to a unit must be very large for it to produce any significant response (see Fig. 28 for $T = 20$). Thus, only the units that are most strongly constrained to have positive or negative states initially become active. As the temperature is lowered, units require less input to become active, and becomes sensitive to weaker constraints. Only near the end of annealing do very subtle constraints have influence.

The settling process in a DBM is analogous to the forward pass in back-propagation, in the sense that both compute a set of output states for a given input. However, the existence of a well-defined energy function that characterises this process in a DBM is a major advantage. Although it is possible to compute the value of F for the states and weights in a back-propagation network, there is no direct relationship between this value and the actual operation of the network. In contrast, the value of F for a DBM, either during settling or at a minimum, provides a direct measure of how well the network is satisfying the constraints of the task. Furthermore, it is possible to compute F separately for different sets of connections and units. This makes it possible to locate *where* in the network constraints are being violated when it produces an error under damage.

Another advantage of a DBM over the type of back-propagation network we have used is that the settling process is much more gradual—typically involving 100 or so iterations, compared with 14 for the back-propagation networks. Although this significantly increases the computational demands of simulations, it enables a much finer-grained analysis of the time-course of processing an input (but see Pearlmutter, 1989, for a continuous version of back-propagation through time). For example, we can compare the "goodness" of the semantic and phonological representations (defined in terms of free energy) throughout the course of pronouncing a word. However, the need for long settling times may make the procedure somewhat less biologically plausible, since individual neurons can generate only about 100 spikes in the time required by humans to interpret visual input (Feldman & Ballard, 1982).

Contrastive Hebbian Learning

Initially, the weights in the network are set to small random values (between ± 0.5 in our simulations). When an input is presented, the network will settle into a minimum of F, perhaps even the best possible minimum if simulated annealing is used. However, because the weights are random, the states of the output units at this minimum are very unlikely to correspond to their correct states for this input. Thus, we need a procedure for adjusting the weights in the network to make it more likely that the minimum that the network settles into, given some input, has the appropriate output unit states.

The training procedure for a DBM is remarkably simple and intuitive, although its derivation is beyond the scope of this paper. It is directly analogous to the procedure for stochastic Boltzmann Machines (Ackley et al., 1985). It takes the form of a *negative* phase and a *positive* phase for each input/output pair. The negative phase is just the settling process described earlier: The states of the input units are clamped and the network is annealed to settle into a set of states corresponding to a free energy minimum. The positive phase is run exactly like the negative phase except that, in addition to clamping the input units, the output units are clamped into their correct states. Intuitively, the positive phase amounts to guiding the network to produce the correct response, and the negative phase amounts to letting the network try to produce the correct response on its own.

If the network has learned the task, the states of the output units should be the same in the positive and negative phases. We will use s_i^- to designate the state of unit i at the minimum for the negative phase, and s_i^+ for its state at the minimum for the positive phase. If each weight is changed according to

$$\Delta w_{ij} = \epsilon(s_i^+ s_j^+ - s_i^- s_j^-) \tag{4}$$

then, for small enough ϵ, the network performs steepest descent (in weight space) in an information-theoretic measure of the difference between the output unit states in the positive and negative phases (Hinton, 1989b).[28] The form of this learning rule is simply the product of unit states in the positive phase minus their product in the negative phase. This makes sense if we think of the states in the positive phase as roughly corresponding to correct behaviour, and remember the discussion earlier on how states and weights contribute to the total free energy. If the states of the two units in the positive phase are either both positive or both negative, it is good (i.e. lowers the energy) for the weight to be positive, and it is incremented. We subtract off the product for the incorrect performance in the negative phase. If the product is not as high in this phase as in the positive phase, the net weight change will be positive. This increase in the weight will make it more likely in the future for one unit to be active when the other is active, thus increasing the product of their states, In this way, learning can be thought of as shaping the energy surface, lowering the surface (decreasing the energy) for good combinations of states and raising it for bad ones. These changes make it more likely that the network will settle into a good minimum on the next presentation of the input.

Contrastive Hebbian learning is more biologically plausible than back-

[28]Actually, this is only true if, in the negative phase, the probability of an output vector given an input vector is defined in terms of the free energies of the minima that the network actually settles to in the positive and negative phases, rather than by interpreting the real-valued output vector as representing a probability distribution over possible binary output vectors under a maximum entropy assumption (i.e. that the unit states represent independent probabilities).

propagation for a number of reasons. Although the procedure still requires information about the correct states of output units, this information is used in the same way as information about the input—that is, by propagating weighted unit activities, rather than by passing error derivatives backward across connections. This difference makes its easier for one part of a large DBM to train another part, if the first part can set the states of the output units of the second part appropriately. In addition, there is direct neurophysiological evidence of a Hebbian learning mechanism in at least some parts of the brain (Cotman & Monaghan, 1988; Dudai, 1989). Although the need for symmetric weights is of some concern, connection pathways between brain areas are virtually always reciprocal (Van Essen, 1985), and initially asymmetric weights gradually become symmetric if they are given a slight tendency to decay spontaneously towards zero (Galland & Hinton, Note 1: Hinton, 1989b).

Although contrastive Hebbian learning in a DBM is a relatively new learning paradigm, it has been applied to problems of moderate size with reasonable success (Gallard & Hinton, Note 2; Peterson & Hartman, Note 7). In general, the number of required training presentations is comparable to that for back-propagation, although a DBM can require considerably more computation in processing each sample due to its more gradual settling process.

AUTHOR INDEX

SUBJECT INDEX